The EVERYTHING®
Spanish Practice Book

Dear Reader:

I started learning my first foreign language when I was just a little kid, and ever since then, learning new languages has been a hobby of mine. When you first start to get to know a new language, learning new concepts and vocabulary is fun. But in order to really grasp a language and make it your own, you need lots of practice.

The ideal way of practicing Spanish is by visiting a Spanish-speaking country where you'd be exposed to the language twenty-four hours a day and would be forced to use it. But another, more realistic and cheaper way is to practice with the help of a book and/or audio materials.

I wrote this book, which comes with an audio CD, for people who are already learning Spanish and need some extra practice in order to internalize all the grammar and vocabulary they have memorized. As you work on completing the exercises and listen to the CD, you'll notice that gradually you no longer have to think through the answers—they will come to you naturally. And it is at that point that you'll know you've really made Spanish your own. Good luck!

Julie Gutin

The EVERYTHING® Series

Editorial

Publishing Director	Gary M. Krebs
Associate Managing Editor	Laura M. Daly
Associate Copy Chief	Brett Palana-Shanahan
Acquisitions Editor	Gina Chaimanis
Development Editor	Katie McDonough
Associate Production Editor	Casey Ebert
Language Editors	Susana C. Schultz
	Adriana Cruz Santacroce

Production

Director of Manufacturing	Susan Beale
Associate Director of Production	Michelle Roy Kelly
Cover Design	Paul Beatrice
	Erick DaCosta
	Matt LeBlanc
Design and Layout	Colleen Cunningham
	Holly Curtis
	Sorae Lee
	Daria Perreault
Series Cover Artist	Barry Littmann

Visit the entire Everything® Series at *www.everything.com*

THE
EVERYTHING®
SPANISH PRACTICE
BOOK

Hands-on techniques to improve
your speaking and writing skills

Julie Gutin

Adams Media
Avon, Massachusetts

To my family

An Everything® Series Book.
Everything® and everything.com® are registered trademarks of F+W Publications, Inc.

Published by Adams Media, an F+W Publications Company
57 Littlefield Street, Avon, MA 02322 U.S.A.
www.adamsmedia.com

ISBN: 1-59337-434-8
Printed in the United States of America.

J I H G F E D C B A

Library of Congress Cataloging-in-Publication Data
Gutin, Julie.
The everything Spanish practice book with CD : hands-on techniques
to improve your speaking and writing skills / Julie Gutin.
p.   cm.
ISBN 1-59337-434-8
1. Spanish language—Textbooks for foreign speakers—English. I. Title. II. Series: Everything series.
PQ4129.E5G894 2005
468.2'421--dc22
2005026444

This book is available at quantity discounts for bulk purchases.
For information, please call 1-800-872-5627.

Contents

Acknowledgments

As always, I owe my deepest thanks to my family, who have been supportive of my efforts and encouraging in my explorations. A special thanks to ShihYan, for keeping me sane. And a big thank you to Miguelito—I couldn't have done this without you.

Lots of credit for this book goes to Gina Chaimanis, who turned the idea into a real project and who had the confidence in me to let me make it happen. Thanks to all the other folks at Adams as well—Gary Krebs, Kate McBride, Laura M. Daly, and Katie McDonough. My respect and thanks also go out to the copyeditor of this book, Susana C. Schultz. And, finally, thanks to Peter Martinez for lending his professional voice to the project, and to Dan Cantor of Notable Productions for doing such a great job recording the CD.

Top Ten Reasons to Practice Your Spanish

1. You can take your rusty Spanish to the next level.

2. It'll improve your reading comprehension.

3. You'll never be stumped by verb conjugations again.

4. You'll build up your Spanish vocabulary.

5. You'll learn how to understand spoken Spanish without having to ask people to repeat themselves.

6. Adjective/article/noun agreement will become second nature.

7. You'll once and for all figure out the difference between indicative and subjunctive.

8. You'll become more comfortable with speaking Spanish.

9. You'll discover Spanish literature and will be able to read *Don Quijote* in the original.

10. You'll be able to travel to a Spanish-speaking country without worrying about the language barrier.

Introduction

▶ The process of language acquisition has several steps. The first step is to learn basic grammar and vocabulary. You have already done that, whether at school, from your family or friends who speak Spanish, or by using a book—maybe even *The Everything® Learning Spanish Book* or *The Everything® Spanish Grammar Book*.

You're on the right track, but before you can really gain fluency, you'll need to move on to the next step: practice. And one way of doing that is by using this book—by going through the exercises and practicing until verb endings and the right vocabulary come to you quickly and in the right order. Until you can listen to spoken Spanish and make out the meaning without having to think about it in your head. And until you can even respond in the same language.

The exercises included in this book have been devised primarily to help you practice Spanish grammar: verb conjugations, word agreement, and more. The book is divided into parts, and each part covers a grammatical part of speech, so that you can practice them one at a time. It is not necessary for you to start with Part 1 and go on from there. You can start wherever you prefer, in the section where you think you may need the most practice, and then skip around until you've covered everything.

In addition to the written exercises, some exercises work in conjunction with the audio CD. This extra feature, which distinguishes this book from many other exercise workbooks, is there to help you work on your speaking and listening comprehension. As you complete each audio exercise, try to listen to the track more than once—even if at first you can hardly separate the speech into individual words, eventually you'll be able to catch what is being said. And once you do, see if you can repeat what you are hearing. This will help you improve your Spanish pronunciation, an often-overlooked aspect of learning the Spanish language.

If you are studying Spanish at school or university and are looking for some additional practice, you've come to the right place. This book breaks down each grammatical concept and provides an introduction before you go on to doing the exercises. If you've studied Spanish ages ago and are looking to refresh your memory, you can use this book to do a thorough review. And it's also a good resource for native Spanish speakers who never studied Spanish formally and would like to improve their written Spanish.

Whatever your needs are, as you go through the book and do each exercise, have fun with it. Practicing Spanish doesn't have to be boring. But it is an important step to gaining fluency, to making the Spanish language your own. And don't forget—using this book shouldn't be the only way you practice Spanish—go out for Spanish *tapas* or authentic Mexican food and order from the menu in Spanish. Visit your local Spanish-speaking neighborhood and see if you can strike up a conversation with a local. Pick up a Spanish book for kids at the local library and see how much you can figure out. And for your next vacation, why not book a trip to a country where Spanish is the primary language? Find ways to practice Spanish in your everyday life, and you won't be disappointed with the results. Good luck!

Part 1

Nouns and Articles

This part covers some of the basics of the Spanish language. Use the glossary in the back—or a separate Spanish-English dictionary—to help you with words you don't know. Even if you have a more advanced grasp of the language, this is a good chance to review and maybe pick up a few tidbits of new information.

What Is a Noun?

A noun is a word that names something—a person, place, thing, action (such as "run" in "I went for a run"), or quality (such as "character" in "a woman of good character").

A Few Spanish Nouns			
agua	water	*cosa*	thing
año	year	*hija*	daughter
coche	car	*hijo*	son

Exercise 1: Name a Noun

In each of the following sentences, circle every noun. Hint: Some will have more than one.

1. *Tengo dos billetes.*

2. *Soy de los Estados Unidos.*

3. *A los guatemaltecos les gusta comer la comida guatemalteca.*

4. *El gato come el pescado.*

5. *El río se llama Río Grande.*

6. *Tanta libertad es una tentación.*

7. *La natación es un deporte que exige talento.*

8. *Todos los miembros del equipo han llegado.*

Grammatical Gender

In Spanish, nouns have a gender—either masculine or feminine. Most masculine nouns in Spanish end in –o or –e. However, there are also special endings and exceptions to the rule. Most feminine nouns end in –a.

Nouns that refer to a male, such as *el hombre* (the man) are typically masculine. Words that refer to females, such as *la mujer* (the woman) are usually feminine. However, most nouns with no identifiable gender in English still have a grammatical gender in Spanish, so for example *tomate* (tomato) is masculine and *manzana* (apple) is feminine.

Exercise 2: At Home

TRACK 1

Listen to the track and repeat each masculine noun. Then, listen to the track again and write down what you hear. Check your spelling in the answer key.

1. ....
2. ....
3. ....
4. ....
5. ....
6. ....
7. ....
8. ....
9. ....

10. ....
11. ....
12. ....
13. ....
14. ....
15. ....

Exercise 3: Check the Ending

Identify each underlined noun as either masculine or feminine.

1. *El Señor Escobar tiene una <u>hija</u>.* ....

2. *El <u>perro</u> no ladra mucho.* ....

3. *Acabo de comprar un <u>carro</u> nuevo.* ....

4. *La <u>fiesta</u> fue muy divertida.* ....

5. *Es la <u>hora</u> de celebrar nuestra victoria.* ....

6. *¿Prefieres la <u>falda</u> gris o los pantalones negros?* ....

7. *Vamos a empezar nuestros estudios el próximo <u>año</u>.* ....

8. *Es mejor cocinar con <u>aceite</u> de maíz.* ....

Special Endings

Not all nouns have the endings –e, –o, or –a, which clearly mark them as either masculine or feminine. In such cases, check for any of the following endings:

Masculine	Feminine
*el conduct**or*** (driver)	*la ciu**dad*** (city)
*el coraz**ón*** (heart)	*la esta**ción*** (station)
*el doct**or*** (doctor)	*la liber**tad*** (liberty)
*el idi**oma*** (language)	*la qui**etud*** (quiet)
*el árb**ol*** (tree)	*la espe**cie*** (species)
*el vir**us*** (virus)	*la te**sis*** (thesis)
	*la ve**jez*** (old age)
	*la cica**triz*** (scar)

Note that while nouns ending in –n and –s are masculine, those ending in –ión and –is are feminine.

For many nouns that represent people, a form ending in –o is for males and –a for females. For example: *enfermero* (male nurse), *enfermera* (female nurse). But in some cases, the two words are completely different: *hombre* (man), *mujer* (woman).

Other common ways of differentiating gender are listed here:

el actor (actor)	*la actriz* (actress)
el señor (Mr.)	*la señora* (Mrs.)
el dentista (male dentist)	*la dentista* (female dentist)
el estudiante (male student)	*la estudiante* (female student)

Exercise 4: Feminine Nouns Camouflaged

Circle all the feminine nouns.

serie	*nariz*	*ciudad*	*organización*
papel	*varón*	*tesis*	*vacación*
televisión	*crisis*	*árbol*	*verdad*
cicatriz	*quietud*	*virus*	*luz*
universidad	*niñez*	*amor*	*calambre*
comedor	*interpretación*	*amistad*	*compás*

Exercise 5: It's a Profession

In each sentence, switch the gender of the noun representing a profession. Hint: You'll also have to change the article accompanying the noun—a review of articles will follow in Part 1.

1. *El doctor* .... *cura enfermedades.*

2. *La conductora* .... *conduce el carro.*

3. *El pastor* .... *cuida a sus ovejas.*

4. *La profesora* .... *enseña a los estudiantes.*

5. *El escultor* .... *crea esculturas.*

6. *El enfermero* .... *cuida a los pacientes.*

7. *La pintora* .... *pinta.*

8. *La cocinera* .... *prepara comidas.*

Exceptions to the Rule

Memorizing the noun endings will only get you so far. Some masculine nouns have endings typical of feminine nouns, and vice versa. These are exceptions and you need to keep them in mind.

Some Exceptions to the Rule	
Masculine	**Feminine**
el día (day)	*la carne* (meat)
el mapa (map)	*la radio* (radio)
el avión (airplane)	*la foto* (photo)
el camión (truck)	*la moto* (motorcycle)
el planeta (planet)	*la disco* (disco)
el tranvía (trolley)	*la mano* (hand)

Exercise 6: En Route

Fill in the blanks, using the following words: *día, idioma, leche, mapa, mano, foto, clima, camión*. If necessary, use the glossary in the back to help you translate.

1. *El español es un* ....

2. *Este pequeño pueblo no está en el* ....

3. *¿Cuándo es el* .... *de tu cumpleaños?*

4. *La carta no fue escrita con máquina de escribir, sino a* ....

5. *Para el desayuno, me gustaría un vaso de* ....

6. *Tomé una* .... *del Coliseo la última vez que viajaba por Roma.*

7. *Cuando nos mudamos, transportamos todas las cosas en el*

   ....

8. *Aquí en la región del Mediterráneo, el* ....
   es templado.

Exercise 7: Tricky Endings

In each of the following sentences, label the underlined word as masculine or feminine.

1. *No entiendo el <u>mapa</u>.* ....

2. *Ya tenemos <u>hambre</u>.* ....

3. *¿Qué llevas en la <u>mano</u>?* ....

4. *No he oído esta canción por la <u>radio</u>.* ....

5. *No hay muchas variaciones en el <u>clima</u> de Puerto Rico.* ....

6. *Vivimos en el <u>planeta</u> llamado Tierra.* ....

7. *Es muy fácil llegar allá por <u>tranvía</u>.* ....

8. *Cuando era joven, soñaba con tener mi propia <u>moto</u>.* ....

Singular and Plural

To make a noun plural in Spanish, add an –s (if the noun ends in a vowel) or an –es (if it ends in a consonant). When a word ends in –ón, drop the accent over the "o" as in:

Singular	Plural
la dirección	*las direcciones*
el matón	*los matones*

Also, words ending in "z" become plural by dropping the "z" and adding "ces":

Singular	Plural
la vez	*las veces*

Finally, a very few nouns are the same either way, such as *el paraguas* (the umbrella) in the singular and *los paraguas* (the umbrellas). Also, the days of the week are spelled the same as plural or singular: *el lunes* (Monday) and *los lunes* (Mondays).

Exercise 8: One or More?

If the word is singular, make it plural. If it is plural, make it singular.

1. *fundador* ....

2. *martes* ....

3. *nueces* ....

4. *días* ....

5. *observación* ....

6. *españoles* ....

7. *ingleses* ....

8. *campo* ....

9. *limpiaparabrisas* ....

10. *hija* ....

Indefinite Articles

An indefinite article before a noun indicates a nonspecific example of that noun. In English, a and an are the only indefinite articles used before a singular noun. "A" pen, for instance, refers to any pen in general and not a specific one.

The primary indefinite article in Spanish is used with both singular and plural nouns, and it must match the noun in gender and number.

un	masculine/singular	*un bolígrafo* (a pen)
una	feminine/singular	*una revista* (a magazine)
unos	masculine/plural	*unos libros* (some books)
unas	feminine/plural	*unas revistas* (some magazines)

Exercise 9: The Right Indefinite

Place the correct indefinite article before each noun.

1. .... *gato*

2. .... *falda*

3. .... *billetes*

4. .... *chica*

5. .... *mapa*

6. .... *ciudades*

7. .... *libros*

8. .... *idiomas*

9. .... *doctor*

10. .... *persona*

Exercise 10: Get It Right

Some of these sentences have a mistake. Find the mistake and fix it! Hint: Pay close attention to the indefinite articles.

1. *Quiero el plato con quesos y un cerveza, por favor.*

2. *Busco unas restaurante donde sirven tacos auténticos.*

3. *Mis amigos son unos personas muy inteligentes.*

4. *Ésta no es un actitud muy útil.*

5. *Ella es unas vendedora de postres.*

6. *Necesito unos sellos para mandar un postal.*

7. *La calle Marín está en uno de estos mapas.*

8. *Saquen una papeles y un bolígrafo, por favor.*

Definite Articles

A definite article refers to a specific example of the noun it precedes. "The" is the only definite article in English. In Spanish, the definite article has four forms so it can match the noun in gender and number:

el	masculine/singular	*el bolígrafo* (the pen)
la	feminine/singular	*la revista* (the magazine)
los	masculine/plural	*los bolígrafos* (the pens)
las	feminine/plural	*las revistas* (the magazines)

The only exception to this is when the singular definite article is needed for a feminine noun that begins with an "ah" sound. In this rare case, *el* is used: *el agua* (the water), but *las aguas* (the waters).

Exercise 11: The Right Definite

Place the correct indefinite article before each noun.

1. .... *gato*

2. .... *falda*

3. .... *billetes*

4. .... *chica*

5. .... mapa

6. .... ciudades

7. .... libros

8. .... idiomas

9. .... doctor

10. .... persona

Using Del and Al

Del (of the) and al (to the) are contractions of a preposition and the definite article el:

    del **is** *de + el*   *al* **is** *a + el*

The contractions are there because the final "e" of *de* and the initial "e" of *el* merge; same is true for "a" and "e" in the *al* contraction. Other forms of *de* or *a* plus the definite article remain separate: *de la, de las, de los, a la, a las,* and *a los.*

Exercise 12: To and From

Fill in the blank with one of the following: *del, de la, de las, de los, al, a la, a las, a los.*

1. *Ya no voy* .... *cine.*

2. *El banco está en la calle* .... *Flecha.*

3. *Ama* .... *seres humanos.*

4. *Patricio regresará* .... *viaje mañana.*

5. *El mensajero entrega los paquetes* .... *hora y en el lugar que usted designe.*

6. *El espectáculo empezará* .... *ocho.*

7. *Es la corona* .... *rey.*

8. *Primero, hay que leer la introducción* .... *ensayos.*

9. *Los estudiantes van a elegir* .... *representante de su clase.*

10. *Hoy es la primera presentación* .... *programa.*

Proper Nouns

A proper noun is a noun that names a specific person, place, or thing, such as John, Spain, American Airlines, and Manchester United.

Exercise 13: Merry Old England

TRACK 2

Listen to the audio track, then answer the following questions.

1. *¿Cuál es una ciudad grande?*

....

2. ¿Qué es el Tubo?

....

3. ¿Qué es Big Ben?

....

4. ¿Cómo se llama la reina de Inglaterra?

....

5. ¿Cuál es una de las tiendas más grandes del mundo?

....

6. ¿Dónde está esta tienda grande?

....

7. ¿Dónde se puede probar comida india en Londres?

....

8. ¿Cuál se considera el plato nacional de los británicos?

....

9. ¿Cuál es el deporte más popular en Inglaterra?

....

10. ¿Quién es David Beckham?

....

Exercise 14: Land of the Free

Match each sentence with one of the following proper nouns: *Washington D.C., el Océano Atlántico, George Washington, la Avenida Pennsylvania, el Canadá, las Naciones Unidas, los Estados Unidos, Cracker Jack, la Casa Blanca, Francis Scott Key.*

1. *El país norteamericano donde viven los estadounidenses.*

....

2. *La capital de este país.* ....

3. *El vecino al norte de este país.* ....

4. *El primer presidente de este país.* ....

5. *El hogar del presidente de este país.* ....

6. *La avenida donde está este hogar.* ....

7. *El océano al este de este país.* ....

8. *El autor del himno de este país.* ....

9. *Palomitas de maíz populares en este país, particularmente cuando se asiste a los partidos de béisbol.* ....

10. *Una organización política internacional.* ....

Putting It Together

Now it's time to see what you've learned. Try to complete the following exercises without referring back to the chapter.

Exercise 15: Checking In

Read the conversation between the receptionist and Sr. Ibáñez, and then translate into English.

Q: **El recepcionista:** *Buenos días, señor. ¿Cómo está usted?*
A: **Sr. Ibáñez:** *Bien, gracias. Tengo reserva en este hotel.*

Q: **El recepcionista:** *¿Cuál es su apellido?*
A: **Sr. Ibáñez:** *Ibáñez.*

Q: **El recepcionista:** *¿Cuál es su nombre?*
A: **Sr. Ibáñez:** *Enrique.*

Q: **El recepcionista:** *Muy bien. ¿Cuál es su dirección?*
A: **Sr. Ibáñez:** *Avenida Ochoa número doce, Barcelona, España.*

Q: **El recepcionista:** *¿Cuál es su número de teléfono?*
A: **Sr. Ibáñez:** *Cinco-cinco; cinco-cinco-cinco; uno, dos, tres, cuatro.*

Q: **El recepcionista:** *¿Cuántos días usted planea pasar en nuestro hotel?*
A: **Sr. Ibáñez:** *Cuatro días.*

Q: **El recepcionista:** *Está muy bien. ¡Bienvenido!*
A: **Sr. Ibáñez:** *Gracias.*

Q: Receptionist: ....

A: Sr. Ibáñez: ....

Q: Receptionist: ....

A: Sr. Ibáñez: ....

Q: Receptionist: ....

A: Sr. Ibáñez: ....

Q: Receptionist: ....

A: Sr. Ibáñez: ....

Q: Receptionist: ....

A: Sr. Ibáñez: ....

Q: Receptionist: ....

A: Sr. Ibáñez: ....

Q: Receptionist: ....

A: Sr. Ibáñez: ....

Exercise 16: The Correct Choice

Fill in the correct choice for each of the following sentences.

1. *Hay* .... *(un, una, unos) vaso de vino en la mesa.*

2. *Aquellos chicos son* .... *(el, las, los) hijos de la Señora Martín.*

3. *Carlos es el* .... *(sobrina, sobrino, sobrinos) de Ramón.*

4. *Mi madre está llena* .... *(de, del, la) caridad.*

5. *Cuando hace sol, me gusta ir* .... *(del, de la, a la) playa.*

6. *Las* .... *(intenciones, intención, intenciónes) de ella son buenas.*

7. *Es verdaderamente* .... *(el, una, un) buena idea.*

8. *Nunca vamos* .... *(a la, al, a) cine.*

9. *Es* .... *(una, un, la) tercera vez que pierdes el camino a casa.*

10. *Yo la visité muchas* .... *(vezes, veces, vezos).*

Exercise 17: In (Dis)agreement

Cross out the noun that doesn't match with the article.

1. *las revistas, profesoras, gatos, chicas*

2. *una maldad, interés, criatura, ciencia*

3. *el sentido, tomate, serie, encubridor*

4. *el culminación, fin, cabo, pan*

5. *la mañana, impresión, vejez, aceite*

6. *el mundo, acción, margen, cantante*

7. *un centro, amor, actriz, flor*

8. *unas curas, barbaridades, maridos, pesadumbres*

9. *los cuentos, amaneceres, seres, simpatías*

10. *unos bolsillos, ideas, tranvías, espíritus*

Exercise 18: Dr. Domínguez

TRACK 3

Listen to Señor Domínguez describe himself and his family, then answer the following questions.

1. *¿Cómo se llama el señor?*

....

2. *¿Cuál es su profesión?*

....

3. *¿Dónde trabaja él?*

....

4. *¿Quiénes son sus pacientes?*

....

5. *¿Le gusta su trabajo?*

....

6. *¿De dónde es el doctor?*

....

7. *¿Con quién vive el doctor?*

....

8. *¿Quién es Capitán?*

....

9. *¿Cuál es su dirección?*

....

10. *¿Cuál es su número de teléfono?*

....

Ⓔ *Part 2*

Pronouns

Pronouns replace nouns or noun phrases in a sentence. They're most often used to shorten a sentence—referring to "that big book over there" as "it," for instance—or in a follow-up statement to avoid sounding repetitious. But, as you'll see shortly, there's more to pronouns than meets the eye. Lots of different kinds of words can serve as pronouns in a sentence.

Subject Pronouns

Subject pronouns replace the subject of the sentence. In English, these are "I," "you," "he," "she," "it," "we," and "they." In Spanish, they are:

yo (I)	*nosotros, nosotras* (we)
tú (you, informal)	*vosotros, vosotras* (you, informal used in Spain)
usted (you, formal)	*ustedes* (you)
él, ella, ello (he, she, it)	*ellos, ellas* (they)

In Spanish, the subject pronouns are often optional because verbs are conjugated to complement the subject.

Note that there are four forms of "you," formal (singular and plural) and informal (singular and plural). The informal singular *tú* form is used to address a close friend or family member (though not an elder), and when speaking to children. The formal *usted* (sometimes abbreviated as *Ud.*) is used in all other cases. In the plural, usage varies. In most of Latin America, only *ustedes* is used; *vosotros* is used in Spain as the plural equivalent of *tú* (this form will be included in exercises throughout the book).

Exercise 1: Personal Appearances

Fill in the correct subject pronoun.

1. _____ *(he) es un chico muy guapo.*

2. _____ *(she) es alta y flaca.*

3. _____ *(we) somos morenos.*

4. *Señor Morales,* _____ *(you) es muy elegante.*

5. _____ *(you) eres bajo y joven.*

6. *Charlie y Alberto no son morenos;* .... *(they)*

   son rubios.

7. .... *(I) soy pesado y de altura media.*

8. .... *(we) somos feas.*

Exercise 2: You, You, You

Decide which Spanish version of "you" should be used to address the following people.

1. *el hermano*   ....

2. *los abuelos*   ....

3. *el grupo de gente*   ....

4. *el colaborador del trabajo*   ....

5. *los jóvenes estudiantes*   ....

6. *el policía*   ....

7. *el mejor amigo*   ....

8. *los médicos*   ....

Direct Object Pronouns

Direct object pronouns replace the direct object, the noun or phrase that is the direct receiver of the action of the verb. For example:

Yo quiero un carro. Yo lo quiero.
I want a car. I want it.

Direct Object Pronouns	
singular	**plural**
me (me)	*nos* (us)
te (you, informal)	*os* (you plural, informal in Spain)
lo, la (you, formal)	*los, las* (you plural, formal)
lo, la (him, her, it)	*los, las* (them)

Exercise 3: Make It Direct

Fill in the appropriate direct object pronoun, using the English translation of the sentence as guidance.

1. *Tú* .... *amas.*
   You love me.

2. *Yo tengo los boletos. Yo* .... *tengo.*
   I have the tickets. I have them.

3. *María* .... *ve.*
   Maria sees you (singular, informal).

4. *Ella escribirá las cartas. Ella* .... *escribirá.*
   She will write the letters. She will write them.

5. *José tiene el libro. Él* .... *tiene.*
   Jose has a book. He has it.

6. *María golpeó a José. María* .... *golpeó.*
   Maria hit Jose. Maria hit him.

7. *La profesora* .... *ayudará.*
   The teacher will help you (plural, informal).

8. *Él* .... *lleva al trabajo.*
   He takes us to work.

Exercise 4: In School

TRACK 4

Listen to the sentence and then rewrite it using a direct object pronoun.

1. ....

2. ....

3. ....

4. ....

5. ....

6. ....

7. ....

8. ....

9. ....

10. ....

Indirect Object Pronouns

The indirect object is the word or phrase (usually referring to a person) that receives the action of the verb indirectly. For example:

I buy her flowers.

The direct object, flowers, is what's receiving the action (being bought). "Her" is the indirect receiver of the action—the buying of the flowers results in "her" getting flowers. In English, an indirect object is only present together with a direct object—saying "I buy her" doesn't make much sense—but in Spanish an indirect object may be the only object present.

Naturally, a direct object may be represented by a pronoun. The following are the Spanish indirect object pronouns. Note that in the first and second person, they are identical to direct object pronouns.

Indirect Object Pronouns	
singular	**plural**
me (me)	*nos* (us)
te (you, informal)	*os* (you plural, informal in Spain)
le (you, formal)	*les* (you plural, formal)
le (him, her, it)	*les* (them)

When direct and the indirect objects are both pronouns, the indirect object pronoun *le* or *les* changes to *se* before *lo, la, los,* or *las.* Why the change? Well, saying "*le lo*" out loud would be a bit of a tongue twister. In the following example, *se* is "for her" and *lo* is "it."

Yo se lo compro.
I buy it for her.

Exercise 5: Indirectly Said

Circle the indirect object pronoun in each sentence.

1. *Me contó toda la historia.*

2. *Te lo ruego, déjame en paz.*

3. *Espero que le sea útil.*

4. *Felipe, nos canta una canción.*

5. *Les hablo a los otros estudiantes.*

6. *Le responderé más tarde.*

7. *Cualquier duda que tenga se la podremos solucionar.*

8. *La madre nos prepara el desayuno cada mañana.*

Exercise 6: Give and Take

Fill in the correct indirect object pronoun. The noun being replaced by the pronoun appears in parentheses.

1. *El camarero* .... *da el menú. (los esposos)*
2. *¿Por qué no* .... *das el dulce? (el chico)*
3. .... *los daré la próxima clase. (las estudiantes)*
4. *¿Quién* .... *dio este CD? (tú)*
5. *Voy a dar* .... *una copa de agua. (usted)*
6. *Mi tía* .... *da muchos regalos por su cumpleaños. (mis primos)*
7. *Los empleados del supermercado* .... *darán muestras gratis. (vosotros)*
8. .... *lo daré en un momento. (ustedes)*

Reflexive Pronouns

A reflexive pronoun reflects back upon the subject of the verb—that is, it refers to the same person as the subject. In English, we use words ending in "self"—"myself," "himself," and so on. In Spanish, there's a set of reflexive pronouns that should be used to signal reflexive action. (Whether or not a reflexive pronoun is needed depends on the verb—and that's covered in Part 6.)

Reflexive Pronouns	
singular	**plural**
me (myself)	*nos* (ourselves)
te (yourself, informal)	*os* (yourselves, informal)
se (yourself, formal)	*se* (yourselves, formal)
se (himself, herself, itself)	*se* (themselves)

Here's an example in Spanish:

Yo me herí.
I injured myself.

The subject, *yo,* matches the reflexive pronoun, *me*—both refer to the same person, "I." Reflexive pronouns are very similar to direct and indirect object pronouns, and generally appear in the same place in the sentence— before the verb (with some exceptions, also covered later).

Exercise 7: The Daily Grind

Fill in the correct reflexive pronoun.

1. *Él* .... *despierta tarde.*

2. *Tú* .... *lavas el cabello con el champú especial.*

3. *Ustedes* .... *van a la casa de prisa.*

4. *Vosotros* .... *sentís bien después de descansar.*

5. *Usted* .... *viste de moda.*

6. *El señor Molina* .... *pone el traje para ir a la oficina.*

7. *Elisa y yo* .... *dormimos a las once de la noche.*

8. *Yo* .... *llamo Julia.*

Exercise 8: Reflexive or Not?

Learn to distinguish between reflexive and other pronouns. In the following sentences, label each pronoun as subject, direct object, indirect object, or reflexive.

1. *Él se da cuenta.* ....

2. *Lo bailas muy bien.* ....

3. *Tú te imaginas qué pasará allí.* ....

4. *Ustedes no entienden la situación.* ....

5. *A Alina le gustan las flores.* ....

6. *Se lo prepara para las dos.* ....

7. *Me manda la carta lo más pronto posible.* ....

8. *Es que vosotros estáis listos.* ....

Reciprocal Pronouns

Reciprocal pronouns show a mutual relationship between two subjects; in English, equivalents are "each other" and "one another." They are very similar to the plural reflexive pronouns (using the same words: *nos, os,* and *se*).

Out of context, *nos miramos* can mean both "we see ourselves" and "we see each other." Usually, the context of the sentence will reveal the meaning, but there are also ways to clarify your statement—adding *mutuamente* (mutually) or a form of *el uno a otro* (literally "the one to other").

Exercise 9: For Each Other

Choose the correct reciprocal pronoun (*nos, os,* or *se*).

1. *María y José* .... *aman.*

2. *Tú y yo* .... *entendemos.*

3. *Pedro y su socio* .... *necesitan mucho.*

4. *Los amigos* .... *miran en sorpresa.*

5. *Nosotros* .... *queremos mucho.*

6. *¿Vosotros todavía no* .... *habláis?*

7. *Los amantes* .... *besaban bajo la luna.*

8. *Angelina y yo* .... *llamamos todos los días.*

Possessive Adjectives and Pronouns

Possessive adjectives are used in a sentence to signal ownership or possession:

> *el perro de Julia* (**Julia's dog**)
> *su perro* (**her dog**)

In this example, Julia is the possessor and dog is the object of possession. Possessive adjectives have both a singular and plural form:

Singular	Plural	English
mi	*mis*	my
tu	*tus*	your (familiar)
su	*sus*	his, her, its, your (formal)
nuestro/a	*nuestros/as*	our
vuestro/a	*vuestros/as*	your (familiar)
su	*sus*	their, your (formal)

The plural form is used when the object (not the possessor!) is plural: *sus perros* (her dogs), but *su perro* (their dog).

Also, *nuestro* and *vuestro* actually have four forms, because they must match in number and gender with the object: *nuestro perro, nuestra perra, nuestros perros, nuestras perras*.

Possessives have another, alternative form. Instead of saying *mi coche*, you can say one of the following:

> *Es el mío. Es el coche mío.*
> **It's mine. The car is mine.**

In the first case, *mío* is a possessive pronoun, since it no longer modifies anything but stands on its own. In the second example, the adjective has moved to follow the object, which is done for emphasis.

masculine singular	feminine singular	masculine plural	feminine plural	English
el mío	la mía	los míos	las mías	mine
el tuyo	la tuya	los tuyos	las tuyas	yours (informal)
el suyo	la suya	los suyos	las suyas	yours (formal)
el suyo	la suya	los suyos	las suyas	his, hers, its
el nuestro	la nuestra	los nuestros	las nuestras	ours
el vuestro	la vuestra	los vuestros	las vuestras	yours (plural, informal)
el suyo	la suya	los suyos	las suyas	yours (plural, formal)
el suyo	la suya	los suyos	las suyas	theirs

Possessive Pronouns

To choose the right possessive pronoun, you'll need to consider the possessor as well as the object possessed. The correct pronoun will take the form of the possessor but will match the number and gender of the object.

Exercise 10: Whose Is It, Anyway?

Rewrite each sentence using the correct possessive adjective. For example: *Es el libro de Julia. Es su libro.*

1. *Son los problemas del profesor.*

   ....

2. *Es el colchón de mí.*

   ....

3. *Es la corbata de ti.*

   ....

4. *Son las ideas de mí.*

   ....

5. *Es el cuento de ustedes.*

   ....

6. *Son los libros de vosotros.*

   ....

7. *Es la bicicleta de nosotros.*

   ....

8. *Son los zapatos de ti.*

   ....

Exercise 11: Yours and Mine

Fill in the blank with the correct possessive pronoun. Remember that the subject defines which is used and the object determines whether it's singular or plural (and masculine or feminine in certain cases).

1. *Julio trabaja con* .... *padres.*

2. *María y yo vamos a la casa de* .... *amigos.*

3. *Yo estoy buscando* .... *nuevos guantes de lana.*

4. *El estudiante no tiene* .... *mochila.*

5. *Tú nunca olvides* .... *trabajo.*

6. *Ustedes no tienen* .... *boletos.*

7. *Tú no conoces a* .... *nietos.*

8. *Yo sé que es* .... *responsabilidad.*

Exercise 12: In Possession

Fill in all the blanks. **The first column uses possessive adjectives, the second possessive pronouns in the adjective form, and the final column the possessive pronoun form.** The first one is done for you as an example.

1.	*mis amigos*	*los amigos míos*	*los míos*
2.	....	*el coche suyo*	....
3.	*nuestra casa*	....	....
4.	....	....	*el tuyo (libro)*
5.	*sus revistas*	....	....
6.	....	....	*la suya (hermana)*
7.	*nuestros aceites*	....	....
8.	....	*las manzanas tuyas*	....

Demonstrative Pronouns

Demonstrative pronouns point out something or demonstrate. The word "that" in "What is that?" is a good example of a demonstrative pronoun. "That" is a pronoun because it represents something else that's being inquired about. "This," "these," and "those" are the other English demonstrative pronouns.

Demonstrative Pronouns					
Singular Masculine	Singular Feminine	Singular Neuter	Plural Masculine	Plural Feminine	English
éste	*ésta*	*esto*	*éstos*	*éstas*	this/these
ése	*ésa*	*eso*	*ésos*	*ésas*	that/those
aquél	*aquélla*	*aquello*	*aquéllos*	*aquéllas*	that/those

Note that demonstrative pronouns may be masculine, feminine, or neuter. The neuter group is used when the demonstrative pronoun is referring to something general of an unknown gender.

Also, you'll see that *ése* and *aquél* (and all their forms) have the same meanings in English. In Spanish, you use *ése* for things away from the speaker but near the listener. *Aquél* is for something away from both the speaker and listener.

Also, demonstrative pronouns may be used as adjectives—in that case, the accents are dropped: *este coche* (that car).

Exercise 13: In Our Class

Fill in the blank with the correct demonstrative pronoun (a form of *esto, eso,* or *aquello,* as indicated).

1. .... *es el chico más inteligente. (eso)*

2. .... *es el profesor de arte. (aquello)*

3. .... *es imposible. (esto)*

4. .... *son las estudiantes más jóvenes. (esto)*

5. .... *son las profesoras menos simpáticas. (aquello)*

6. *Nunca he visto* .... *(aquello)*

7. .... *es la planta para la clase. (esto)*

8. .... *no son las plantas para la clase. (eso)*

Indefinite Pronouns

Pronombres indefinidos are used in place of nouns but are "indefinite" or unspecific in nature. They can replace a direct object, indirect object, prepositional object, or subject of a sentence. Many indefinite pronouns are commonly used as adjectives ("many" and "some" for example).

Indefinite Pronouns			
one form			
algo	something	*nada*	nothing
alguien	someone	*nadie*	no one
multiple forms			
varios, varias	various	*otro(s), otra(s)*	other
ambos, ambas	both	*todo(s), toda(s)*	all
alguno(s), alguna(s)	some	*uno(s), una(s)*	one (some)
cualquier, cualquiera(s)	whichever	*poco(s), poca(s)*	a little
mucho(s), mucha(s)	a lot	*ninguno(s), ninguna(s)*	none

Words like *mucho* and *poco* may be used to replace nouns (in which case they don't need to follow rules of agreement) or as adjectives (in which case they must agree with the noun).

Exercise 14: Something Indefinite

Listen to each indefinite pronoun and repeat.

TRACK 5

Exercise 15: Which Is Indefinite?

Circle the indefinite pronoun in each sentence. For an added challenge, translate each sentence.

1. *Algunos de los estudiantes están retrasados.*

   ....

2. *Ambos son culpables.*

   ....

3. *La otra es la mía.*

....

4. *Estas cosas son todo lo que vamos a repasar.*

....

5. *Es algo que no puedo explicar.*

....

6. *Muchas todavía no saben conducir.*

....

7. *Es lo poco que tengo.*

....

8. *Nadie sabe la verdad.*

....

9. *Es como cualquiera.*

....

10. *Unos que no saben nada de ese tema.*

....

Relative Pronouns

Pronombres relativos are used in a sentence to introduce a clause that gives more information on a noun or pronoun. Basically, it's a pronoun that combines two sentences or clauses that have a common thread. In English, relative pronouns include "who," "whoever," "whom," "which," "that," and "whose."

This is my car.

I drive this car to work.

This is the car that I drive to work.

In the last example, "that" is the relative pronoun that combines the two sentences.

Relative Pronouns

que	that, which, who
cual(es)	which
quien(es)	who, whom, that
lo que	what, that which

Exercise 16: A Little of That

Fill in the blank with the correct relative pronoun.

1. *María, ... es de España, vive en México.*

2. *.. quiero es un helado.*

3. *Lo mejor es .... pudiéramos descansar muy pronto.*

4. *Lola quiere .... Elena la acompañe.*

5. *Son muchas las razones por las .... deben ayudarme.*

6. *Son profesionales de los negocios, ... han tenido mucho éxito en sus esfuerzos.*

7. *Esto no es .... estoy buscando.*

8. *Vivimos en una época en la .... es posible ser libre.*

Exercise 17: In Combination

Combine each pair of sentences using a relative pronoun. For example: *Yo tengo un coche nuevo. El coche es azul. Yo tengo un coche nuevo que es azul.*

1. *Tengo muchos amigos. Son muy simpáticos.*

   ....

2. *Nosotros miramos la película. La película era muy buena.*

   ....

3. Juego al fútbol. El fútbol es el mejor deporte.

   ....

4. *José es mi amigo. Voy a viajar con José.*

   ....

5. *He leído muchos libros. Los libros son muy interesantes.*

   ....

6. *Trabajo mucho. Es muy cansador.*

   ....

7. *Mi coche es muy viejo. El coche funciona bien.*

   ....

8. *No lo veo. Algo está pasando.*

   ....

Interrogative Pronouns

Pronombres interrogativos are relative pronouns used to form questions. The difference is while relative pronouns connect two clauses, interrogative pronouns are trying to connect a clause with an unknown (by asking the question). You can differentiate between them by looking for the accent: *qué, cuál, cuáles, quién,* and *quiénes* are all interrogative pronouns. Questions in Spanish are also set up with an upside down question mark to start off: *¿Qué es?* (What is it?)

Exercise 18: In the Apartment Building

Fill in the blank with the correct interrogative pronoun.

1. ¿ .... *es él? Es Julio, el inquilino del apartamento en el segundo piso.*

2. ¿ .... *es esto? Es la puerta al apartamento.*

3. ¿ .... *son los responsabilidades de los inquilinos? Cuidar las áreas comunes y pagar la renta.*

4. ¿ .... *son los inquilinos? Son generalmente estudiantes o la gente que trabaja en la universidad.*

5. ¿ .... *es el mejor inquilino? El Señor López, porque siempre paga su renta a tiempo.*

Exclamative Pronouns

Pronombres exclamativos are the same as interrogative pronouns, but used in exclamations. For example: *¡Qúe bonito!* (How pretty!) These can all be exclamative pronouns: *qué, cuán, cuánto, cuánta, cuál, cuáles, quién, quiénes.*

Exercise 19: Full of Exclamations

Translate into English.

1. *¡Qué pena!*

....

2. *¡Qué día!*

....

3. ¡Quién lo diría!

....

4. ¡Qué divertido!

....

5. ¡Cómo cantan!

....

6. ¡Cuán interesante!

....

7. ¡Quién lo sabe!

....

8. ¡Qué cosa más rara!

....

Putting It Together

Now let's see what you've learned!

Exercise 20: Identification, Please

Find the pronouns in the following sentences and indicate which kind of pronoun each one is.

1. *Serena ya lo sabe.* ....

2. *La encuentro muy bella.* ....

3. *El hombre que trabajaba aquí ya se jubiló.* ....

4. *Ellos se quieren mucho.* ....

5. *Susana le compró un regalo.* ....

6. *Su novio es italiano.* ....

7. *¿Quiénes son ellos?* ....

8. *Yo me alegro que no pasó nada malo.* ....

9. *Nadie dijo nada.* ....

10. *Estas cartas son las suyas.* ....

Exercise 21: A Pronoun Pro

TRACK 6

Listen to each sentence and repeat. Then listen to the track again and write down each sentence, circling the pronouns.

1. ....

2. ....

3. ....

4. ....

5. ....

6. ....

7. ....

8. ....

9. ....

10. ....

11. ....

12. ....

13. ....

14. ....

15. ....

16. ....

17. ....

18. ....

19. ....

20. ....

Exercise 22: Another Way of Saying It

Rewrite each sentence, replacing the bolded word or phrase with a pronoun.

1. *María es una chica muy buena.*

   ....

2. *Voy a decirle algo muy importante.*

   ....

3. *¿Quién tiene los libros de ti?*

   ....

4. *Les contamos toda la historia.*

   ....

5. *Es la casa de nosotros.*

   ....

6. *Veo a Marta caminando por la calle.*

   ....

7. *Tú y yo somos muy buenos amigos.*

   ....

8. *¿Dónde está su coche?*

   ....

Exercise 23: Before or After?

The object pronouns (direct, indirect, and reflexive) usually come before the verb they modify. However, when the infinitive (Part 5), present participle (Part 9), and affirmative commands (Part 8) are used, the pronoun can be attached to the end of the verb.

Lo quiero ver.
Quiero verlo.
I want to see it.

Lo estoy comprando.
Estoy comprándolo.
I'm buying it.

In the affirmative command mood, it's only correct to have the pronoun attached at the end.

¡Ayúdame! **(Help me!)**

Identify the type of pronoun used and then translate the sentence into English.

1. *Hay que comprobarlo.*

   ....

2. *No está interesándole el problema.*

   ....

3. *¡Duérmete!*

   ....

4. *Ella va a cantarme una canción de cuna.*

   ....

5. *¡Invítala a la fiesta!*

   ....

Exercise 24: At Work

Write a paragraph describing your job or extracurricular activity, including the people you work with. Use the pronouns you learned in this chapter:

Subject Pronouns: *yo, tú, usted, él, ella, ello, nosotros, nosotras, vosotros, vosotras, ustedes, ellos, ellas.*
Direct Object Pronouns: *me, te, lo, la, nos, os, los, las*
Indirect Object Pronouns: *me, te, le, nos, os, les, se*
Reflexive Pronouns: *me, te, se, nos, os*
Reciprocal Pronouns: *nos, os, se*
Possessive Pronouns: *mi, mis, tu, tus, su, sus, nuestro, nuestra, nuestros, nuestras, vuestro, vuestra, vuestros, vuestras; el mío, la mía, los míos, las mías, el tuyo, la tuya, los tuyos, las tuyas, el suyo, la suya, los suyos, las suyas, el nuestro, la nuestra, los nuestros, las nuestras, el vuestro, la vuestra, los vuestros, las vuestras*
Demonstrative Pronouns: *esto, éste, ésta, éstos, éstas, eso, ése, ésa, ésos, ésas, aquello, aquél, aquélla, aquéllos, aquéllas*
Indefinite Pronouns: *algo, alguien, varios, varias, ambos, ambas, nada, nadie, alguno, alguna, algunos, algunas, cualquier, cualquiera, cualesquieras, muchos, muchas, otro, otra, otros, otras, todo, toda, todos, todas, uno, una, unos, unas, poco, poca, pocos, pocas, ninguno, ninguna, ningunos, nigunas.*
Relative Pronouns: *que, cual, cuales, quien, quienes, lo que*
Interrogative Pronouns: *qué, cuál, cuáles, quién, quiénes*
Exclamation Pronouns: *qué, cuánto, cuánta, cuál, cuáles, quién, quiénes*

....

....

....

....

....

....

....

....

E Part 3
Adjectives and Adverbs

Adjectives and adverbs are parts of speech that modify other parts of speech. Adjectives can modify nouns; qualifying adjectives describe the noun's qualities and traits, and determinant adjectives signal the noun's number, order, or location (determinant adjectives are very similar to determinant pronouns, except in the way they are used in the sentence). An adverb may be used to modify a verb, another adverb, adjective, or verbal phrase.

Noun/Adjective Agreement

As you've already learned, nouns can come in four forms: singular masculine, singular feminine, plural masculine, and plural feminine. An adjective that describes a noun must match it in number. Also, when an adjective ends in an −o in the singular form, it usually changes to match the gender of the noun it is modifying. For example, look at how the adjective *simpático* (nice) changes:

el chico simpático the nice boy	*los chicos simpáticos* the nice boys
la chica simpática the nice girl	*las chicas simpáticas* the nice girls

In dictionaries and vocabularly lists, you will see adjectives listed in the singular masculine form.

Most other adjectives end in −e or a consonant. These usually don't change to match gender, but still must match in number:

el chico pobre	the poor boy	*el chico joven*	the young boy
la chica pobre	the poor girl	*la chica joven*	the young girl
los chicos pobres	the poor boys	*los chicos jóvenes*	the young boys
las chicas pobres	the poor girls	*las chicas jóvenes*	the young girls

Exercise 1: The Right Form

Fill in the correct form of the adjective.

1. *unos edificios* .... *(alto)*

2. *una mujer* .... *(bonito)*

3. *las naranjas* .... *(delicioso)*

4. *un idioma* .... *(difícil)*

5. *mis zapatos* .... (*nuevo*)

6. *las playas* .... (*soleado*)

7. *el helado* .... (*frío*)

8. *la mesa* .... (*rojo*)

9. *la ciudad* .... (*grande*)

10. *el vino* .... (*blanco*)

Exercise 2: In Your Opinion

For each of the following nouns, write down three adjectives that may be used to describe it. Be sure the adjectives agree with noun in number and gender (if applicable).

1. *la opinión* ....

2. *los gatos* ....

3. *las casas* ....

4. *la comida* ....

5. *el estudiante* ....

6. *el profesor* ....

7. *las películas* ....

8. *la esperanza* ....

9. *los trabajadores* ....

10. *el problema* ....

Exercise 3: At the Marketplace

TRACK 7

Listen to the description of the marketplace and then answer the following questions.

1. *¿Cómo son los mercados al aire libre?*

   ....

2. *¿Por qué se esfuerzan los vendedores?*

   ....

3. *¿Cómo son los vendedores que gritan alabanzas?*

   ....

4. *¿Cuáles frutas y vegetales se venden en los mercados?*

   ....

5. *¿De qué color son las manzanas que se venden en el mercado en el otoño?*

   ....

6. *¿Cuáles tipos de calabazas se venden en el mercado en el otoño?*

   ....

7. *¿Cómo es el aire otoñal?*

   ....

8. *¿Qué tipos de productos dulces se venden comúnmente en los mercados?*

   ....

9. *¿Cuáles productos campesinos se venden en los mercados?*

   ....

10. *¿De qué color son los girasoles?*

    ....

Exceptions to the Agreement Rule

Although most adjective endings behave according to the few simple rules already described, there are some exceptions. Some adjectives end in –a whether they modify a feminine or a masculine noun. This is most common in adjectives ending with –ista, –asta, and –ita (except when –ita is used to signal a feminine diminutive):

el chico entusiasta	enthusiastic boy	*el país cosmopolita*	cosmopolitan country
el hombre optimista optimistic man			

As you can see, adjectives *entusiasta, optimista,* and *cosmopolita* end in –a even when they modify masculine nouns like *chico, hombre,* and *país.* In the plural, the ending would be –as.

While most adjectives ending with a consonant only have two forms, another set make up an exception to this rule. Those that end in –dor, –ón, –ín, and –án have four forms:

chico hablador	talkative boy	*chicos habladores*	talkative boys
chica habladora	talkative girl	*chicas habladoras*	talkative girls

Exercise 4: A Gender Switch

In each phrase, switch the gender of the noun and the adjectival ending, if necessary.

1. *el chico charlatán* ....

2. *las empleadas organizadoras* ....

3. *el ayudante personal* ....

4. *el profesor superior* ....

5. *el asesino encubridor* ....

6. *los hermanos inteligentes* ....

7. *la científica optimista* ....

8. *el señor galán* ....

9. *los hombres acusadores* ....

10. *el hijo cortés* ....

Exercise 5: The Right Word for the Occasion

Fill in the correct adjective, changing the ending if necessary. Use the following: *optimista, hablador, rojo, trabajador, cosmopolita, bonito, entusiasta, feliz, interesante, acogedor.*

1. *Yo soy una mujer demasiado* .... *para vivir en el campo.*

2. *Estamos muy* .... *y contentos.*

3. *Él es una persona* .... *: siempre espera lo mejor.*

4. *Vuestra casa es un lugar* ....; *es un placer quedarse allá.*

5. *Ella es una chica muy* .... *: siempre tiene algo que decir.*

6. *Eso es muy* .... *cuéntamelo otra vez.*

7. *Caperucita* .... *fue a visitar a su abuela y fue comida por el lobo.*

8. *Estas joyas no son* .... *, sino feas.*

9. *Tengo mucha energía e interés: soy un hombre* .... *.*

10. *Los estudiantes de nuestra escuela son gente muy* .... *y hacen todas sus tareas a tiempo.*

Qualifying Adjectives

Adjetivo calificativo is an adjective that refers to a quality or characteristic of the noun (or noun phrase or pronoun) it is modifying. Most of the adjectives you've seen thus far in Part 3 have been qualifying adjectives. They generally appear after the noun in Spanish and before the noun in English:

el coche azul	the blue car	*el chico alto*	the tall boy

Adjectives can also appear after a verb:

El coche es azul.   **The car is blue.**
El chico es alto.   **The boy is tall.**

Exercise 6: The Right Color

Fill in the correct qualifying adjective that describes a color. Use the following: *rojo, blanco, azul, negro, café, gris, verde, amarillo, anaranjado, morado.*

1. *El cielo no es rojo, sino* ....

2. *El chocolate no es azul, sino* ....

3. *Las plantas no son negras, sino* ....

4. *El letrero PARE no es azul, sino* ....

5. *La combinación de rojo y amarillo no es morado, sino* ....

6. *Las nubes no son blancas, sino* ....

7. *La nieve no es azul, sino* ....

8. *Las uvas no son amarillas, sino* ....

9. *El sol no es rojo, sino* ....

10. *La tinta no es azul, sino* ....

Exercise 7: A Pretty Picture

In the following paragraph, circle all the qualifying adjectives.

Tamara es una estudiante universitaria. Su clase favorita es el arte. Hoy, ella pinta una pintura muy bonita de un campo. El campo está lleno de flores lindas. En el cielo azul hay unas pocas nubes blancas. En la parte baja de la pintura, hay un perrito alegre. Ésta es la pintura favorita de Tamara. Para terminar, ella espera ganar una buena nota por su trabajo.

Determinant Adjectives

Adjetivos determinativos clarify the noun's number, order, or location. They usually come before the noun. Some determinant adjectives are also referred to as demonstrative adjectives and are very similar to demonstrative pronouns (the difference is in the way they're used; the meanings of the words are the same). These adjectives usually come before the noun they are modifying.

Adjectives of Order			
último	last	*quinto*	fifth
penúltimo	penultimate	*sexto*	sixth
primer	first	*séptimo*	seventh
segundo	second	*octavo*	eighth
tercer	third	*noveno*	ninth
cuarto	fourth	*décimo*	tenth

When used as adjectives, the Spanish words for first and third drop the –o. The first ten adjectives of order match in gender; beyond that most Spanish speakers switch to ordinal numbers, so "the eleventh hour" is most often expressed as *la hora once*.

Adjectives of Quantity			
poco	little, few	*suficiente*	sufficient
mucho	many, much	*tanto*	so much, so many
algún	some, any	*todo*	each, every, all
ambos	both	*unos*	some
bastante	enough	*varios*	various

Any number can also operate as an adjective of quantity. Detailed below are numbers 1 through 20. (For more detailed instructions on numbers in Spanish, see Part 4.)

Numbers 1 – 100			
0	*cero*	11	*once*
1	*uno*	12	*doce*
2	*dos*	13	*trece*
3	*tres*	14	*catorce*
4	*cuatro*	15	*quince*
5	*cinco*	16	*dieciséis*
6	*seis*	17	*diecisiete*
7	*siete*	18	*dieciocho*
8	*ocho*	19	*diecinueve*
9	*nueve*	20	*veinte*
10	*diez*		

Demonstrative Adjectives	
este	this (next to speaker)
ese	that (next to listener)
aquel	that (away from both speaker and listener)

Exercise 8: According to the Calendar

Fill in the adjective of order that best completes the sentence.

1. *El domingo es el* .... *día de la semana.*

2. *Marzo es el* .... *mes del año.*

3. *El jueves es el* .... *día de la semana.*

4. *Septiembre es el* .... *mes del año.*

5. *El viernes es el* .... *día de la semana.*

6. *El sábado es el* .... *día de la semana.*

7. *Octubre es el* .... *mes del año.*

8. *Febrero es el* .... *mes del año.*

9. *Abril es el* .... *mes del año.*

10. *Agosto es el* .... *mes del año.*

Exercise 9: A Quantity of Things

Circle all the adjectives of quantity and translate each sentence in the line provided.

1. *Ambas chicas quieren tener un perrito.*

....

2. *Hay siete días en la semana.*

....

3. *Tengo algún dinero, pero no es bastante para comprarlo.*

....

4. *Tengo treinta y tres años.*

....

5. *No tenemos tanta prisa.*

....

6. *Ella tiene varias razones.*

....

7. *Nos quedábamos aquí todo el tiempo.*

....

8. *Yo sé muchas cosas.*

....

9. *No creo que tengas suficiente valor.*

....

10. *Algún día, vamos a vivir en esta ciudad.*

....

Exercise 10: This or That

Daniel and Sofia are shopping at the grocery store and are speaking to each other from different sides of the aisle. Fill in the blanks with correct demonstrative adjectives, depending on the locations of the object relevant to Daniel and Sofia.

Daniel: *Sofía, ¿Ves* .... *cajas con dulces allá en* .... *balda?*

Sofia: *Sí. Voy a cogerlas. Y tú, coge* .... *galletas cerca de ti, ¿bien?*

Daniel: *Pues, no me gustan* .... *galletas. Prefiero las otras, cerca de ti.*

¿Te parece que compremos .... *galletas?*

Sofia: .... *no me gustan mucho. Vamos a ver. ¿Te gustan* .... *galletas, allá, en las cajitas verdes?*

Daniel: *Sí.* .... *galletas en las cajitas verdes me gustan tanto como* .... *.*

Making Comparisons

Making comparisons in Spanish is very similar to how it's done in English.

más + adjective + *que*	more + adjective + than
menos + adjective + *que*	less + adjective + than
tan + adjective + *como*	as + adjective + as

María es más lista que José.
Maria is smarter than Jose.

Esta lección es menos interesante que la de ayer.
This lesson is less interesting than the one from yesterday.

Ella no es tan loca como parece.
She is not as crazy as she seems.

In addition, you can use *mejor* (better), *peor* (worse), *mayor* (older, larger), and *menor* (younger, smaller) in the same way.

Using a verb like *tener* (to have), you can say something has more of something as well:

María tiene más dinero que Julia.
Maria has more money than Julia.

Exercise 11: Compare and Contrast

Translate each of the following sentences using comparative adjectives.

1. Mexico has more inhabitants than Honduras.

2. This cat is as cute as that one.

3. Alma is less pretty than Hortensia.

4. Mr. Flores is as smart as Mr. Fermoso.

5. My son is younger than yours.

6. Our president is more famous than the president of Ecuador.

7. This news isn't as interesting as the news from yesterday.

8. My idea is better than theirs.

   ....

9. Roberto is less tall than Valentino.

   ....

10. Her suitcase isn't bigger than mine.

    ....

Exercise 12: Who's It Gonna Be?

In each question, take the two sentences and draw a conclusion, using *más, menos,* and *tan/como.* For example:

Yo estoy muy contento. Mi amigo está contento.
Yo estoy más contento que mi amigo./Mi amigo está menos contento que yo.

1. *Mi abuelo tiene setenta años. Mi abuela tiene sesenta y seis años.*

   ....

2. *Carla es inteligente. José no es inteligente.*

   ....

3. *Mi prima Jacinta no es muy linda. Mi otra prima Yazmín es linda.*

   ....

4. *Los elefantes son animales grandes. Las ratas son animales pequeños.*

   ....

5. *El sol es amarillo. Las flores son amarillas.*

   ....

6. *Yo tengo cuatro años. Mi hermana tiene cinco años.*

   ....

7. *Jaime tiene mil pesos. Juana tiene cien pesos.*

   ....

8. *Paco es un asesino. Javier es un tramposo.*

....

9. *Enrique pesa setenta kilogramos. Patricio pesa noventa kilogramos.*

....

10. *Los estudiantes son muy trabajadores. Los obreros son muy trabajadores también.*

....

Superlatives—the Best

A superlative statement simply singles something out as being the most or best or ultimate of all things similar. In English, this is done usually by adding –est, and something most (as in "the most interesting"). In Spanish, adjectives require the use of más (most) and menos (least) to make a superlative:

> *Rusia es el país más grande en el mundo.*
> **Russia is the largest country in the world.**

> *Ella es la empleada menos capaz en la compañía.*
> **She is the least capable employee in the company.**

Exercise 13: The Best and the Brightest

Take each statement and make it superlative. Note that answers will vary. For example: *La chica es bonita. Es la chica más bonita de su clase.*

1. *La ciudad es grande.*

....

2. *El pueblo es pequeño.*

....

3. *La escritora es inteligente.*

....

4. *El libro es interesante.*

....

5. *La torta es deliciosa.*

....

6. *La enfermera es simpática.*

....

7. *El ejercicio es difícil.*

....

8. *La razón es extraña.*

....

9. *La canción es linda.*

....

10. *El hombre es guapo.*

....

Adverbs of Manner

An adverb is a part of speech that modifies a verb, another adverb, or an adjective. Most adverbs are adverbs of manner, which are used in many ways. They basically tell "how" something is done. In Spanish, they typically come after the verb being modified.

Common Adverbs of Manner			
así	like that, thus	*tal*	such
bien	well	*frecuentemente*	frequently
mal	poorly	*lentamente*	slowly

Common Adverbs of Manner continued			
mejor	better	*rápidamente*	rapidly
peor	worse, worst	*raramente*	rarely

As you've probably noticed, the last four have similar endings. In English, many adjectives convert to an adverb by adding –ly. In Spanish, you add –mente to the feminine/singular form of the adjective.

Exercise 14: From Adjective to Adverb

Rewrite each adjective as an adverb.

1. *rápido* ....

2. *efectivo* ....

3. *claro* ....

4. *actual* ....

5. *obvio* ....

6. *feliz* ....

7. *atento* ....

8. *difícil* ....

9. *triste* ....

10. *lento* ....

Exercise 15: The Right Adverb

Fill in the correct adverb using the following: *silenciosamente, lentamente, mal, frecuentemente, bien, contentamente, peor, raramente, mejor, atentamente.*

1. *Juan es un buen conductor. Conduce* ....

2. *El coche no es rápido. Se mueve* ....

3. *Camila está contenta. Se ríe* ....

4. *Los estudiantes están muy interesados. Están escuchando* ....
   ....

5. *No quiero despertar a mamá. Paso por su cuarto* ....

6. *No puedo encontrar mis gafas. Veo mucho* ....

7. *Ellos visitan el parque no más que una vez cada año. Ellos visitan el parque* ....

8. *Yo no canto muy bien. Eduardo canta* ....

9. *Nosotros nos vemos casi todos los días. Nosotros nos vemos* ....
   ....

10. *A Tomás le duele la cabeza. Él se siente* ....

Adverbs of Place

As you could easily guess, an "adverb of place" is an adverb which indicates where something happened. Note that these words also can be used as a preposition or pronoun; it is the context of using the word to modify a verb that makes it an adverb. Adverbs of place can appear before or after the verb.

Common Adverbs of Place			
aquí	here	*cerca*	around
ahí	there	*delante*	before (in position)
allí	there	*adentro*	inside
arriba	up	*detrás*	behind
abajo	down	*lejos*	far away

Aquí, ahí, and *allí* correspond to the demonstratives *este, ese,* and *aquel* in meaning. In some parts of Latin America, you may hear *acá, allá* and *acullá* used instead of (or in addition to) *aquí, allí,* and *ahí.*

Exercise 16: In Place

Some of these sentences feature an adverb of place. Circle these, and then translate each sentence into English.

1. *Siempre comen el desayuno aquí.*

   ....

2. *¿Qué es esto?*

   ....

3. *El restaurante está muy lejos.*

   ....

4. *Estamos cerca de la ciudad.*

   ....

5. *El gorrión está allá, en el árbol.*

   ....

6. *El regalo está dentro de la caja sobre la mesa.*

   ....

7. *Los sombreros están arriba, sobre el armario.*

   ....

8. *El teatro se sitúa detrás de la estación de trenes.*

....

9. *¿Quién está adentro?*

....

10. *Es cierto que los libros necesarios están ahí.*

....

Adverbs of Time

The following adverbs are time-related:

Common Adverbs of Time			
ahora	now	*nunca*	never
antes	before (in order or time)	*pronto*	soon, now
aún	yet	*siempre*	always
ayer	yesterday	*tarde*	late
después	then, after	*temprano*	early
hoy	today	*todavía*	still
luego	later, then	*ya*	now, already
mañana	tomorrow		

Exercise 17: A Timely Matter

For each of the following, choose the most appropriate adverb.

1. *Me gustaría ir a casa* .... *(pronto, ayer, nunca).*

2. *El autobús se fue* .... *(mañana, tarde, todavía).*

3. *Es domingo. Nosotros tenemos que trabajar* .... *(siempre, ayer, mañana).*

4. *No tomé el desayuno* .... *(siempre, ayer, mañana).*

5. *No he comido el almuerzo* .... *(todavía, pronto, siempre).*

6. *Voy a terminar el libro* .... *(nunca, luego, aún), después de la cena.*

7. *No lo he probado* .... *(siempre, temprano, nunca).*

8. *Es demasiado* .... *(temprano, ya, tarde) para dormirse—son solamente las nueve de la noche.*

9. *Ya habrá mejorado* .... *(después, luego, aún) más.*

10. *Es mejor terminar los ejercicios* .... *(temprano, ahora, aún) y no demorar.*

Exercise 18: Language Skills

Circle all the adverbs of place in the following paragraph.

Pedro tiene trece años pero ya habla tres idiomas. Tuvo su clase de francés ayer y mañana tendrá su clase de inglés. Su profesora de francés, la Señora Duprés, normalmente llega tarde, pero ayer ella llegó allá temprano para el repaso antes del examen. Pedro estaba muy sorprendido. Ella nunca lo había hecho antes.

Adverbs of Quantity

Adverbs of quantity control the number or amount of a verb. In Spanish, they are placed before the verb.

Common Adverbs of Quantity			
algo	something	*muy*	very, many
bastante	rather	*nada*	nothing
casi	almost	*poco*	little, few
demasiado	too	*todo*	all, everything
más	more	*sólo*	only
menos	less, fewer	*tan*	as
mucho	many, a lot	*tanto*	so much

Exercise 19: *Not Too Little and Not Too Much*

TRACK 8

Listen to each sentence and repeat out loud. Then listen again and write down the adverbs of quantity used in these sentences.

1. ....

2. ....

3. ....

4. ....

5. ....

6. ....

7. ....

8. ....

9. ....

10. ....

11. ....

12. ....

Putting it Together

Now let's see what you've learned!

Exercise 20: One or the Other

Mark whether the word in bold is an adjective or adverb.

1. *María es **bonita**.* ....

2. ***Ambos** lugares son muy bellos.* ....

3. *No me importa **ya**.* ....

4. *Nada es **peor** que encontrarse completamente solo.* ....

5. *Las muñequitas **pequeñas** son las mejores.* ....

6. *La película resultó **tan** impresionante.* ....

7. *Son mis **primeros** pasos después del accidente.* ....

8. *La música se toca **lentamente**.* ....

9. *Esto es **poco** interesante.* ....

10. *Ya estamos muy **lejos**.* ....

Exercise 21: A Game of Translation

Translate the following into Spanish:

1. There is nothing to see.

   ....

2. I have two pieces of cake.

   ....

3. It's the last day of vacation.

   ....

4. Apples are my favorite fruit.

   ....

5. It's better to stay calm.

   ....

6. It's the fourth time I've seen this.

....

7. He is an enthusiastic player.

....

8. They live in a large house.

....

Exercise 22: A Typical Day at a Typical College

TRACK 9

Listen to Ronaldo's story and write down every adjective and adverb you hear.

Adjectives:

....

....

....

Adverbs:

....

....

....

Part 4

Prepositions, Conjunctions, and More

This section primarily covers prepositions and conjunctions. Prepositions relate a noun or noun equivalent to a verb, an adjective, or another noun. Basically, they connect a noun to the rest of the sentence. Conjunctions are words that connect words or phrases in a sentence. Additionally, this section reviews other (minor) details, including numbers, the alphabet, and use of suffixes to form diminutives, augmentatives, and superlatives.

Introduction to Common Prepositions

A preposition is a word that signals position. In English, "of," "to," "for," "from," "in," "below," and "above" are common prepositions. As you can see, some prepositions may be used to signal physical position (above, below), while others (of and for) are more about the relation of something to something else.

The biggest challenge in learning the prepositions in Spanish is that they do not always have a single simple equivalent in English. To start off, we'll cover five common prepositions: *a, de, en, con,* and *sin.*

You can use *a* like the English preposition "to":

Vamos a la tienda.
We are going to the store.

A may also be used to mean "per," "a," or "at" when describing rate or cost:

Camino veinte millas a la semana.
I walk twenty miles a week.

This often-utilized preposition may also be combined with other words to show spatial location. For example, *a la izquierda* and *a la derecha* mean "to the left" and "to the right."

Placed before a direct object, the preposition *a* shows that the direct object is a person—in this case, it is known as the personal *a.* It's important to understand that the personal *a* does not "mean" anything—its only purpose is grammatical. Here are a few examples:

Encontré a José en su casa.
I found José at his house.

Certain verbs may be followed by the preposition *a,* which connects them to an infinitive. For example:

Este libro te ayuda a entender la gramática española.
This book helps you to understand Spanish grammar.

Here are some other verbs commonly paired with the preposition *a:*

acostumbrarse a	to get used to	*enseñar a*	to teach how to
aprender a	to learn to	*invitar a*	to invite to
apresurarse a	to hurry	*llegar a*	to arrive at
atreverse a	to dare to	*negarse a*	to refuse
ayudar a	to help to	*obligar a*	to force
comenzar a	to begin to	*prepararse a*	to prepare to
contribuir a	to contribute to	*ponerse a*	to start to
dedicarse a	to devote oneself to	*venir a*	to come to
echarse a	to start to	*volver a*	to do again
empezar a	to begin to		

The preposition *de* is usually translated as either "of" or "from," depending on context. It can also express ownership, directly replacing the English construction 's to show possession:

El perro de Miguel es viejo.
Miguel's dog is old.

The preposition *de* can be used as the direct translation of "of":

Dame una taza de té, por favor.
Give me a cup of tea, please.

You can also use *de* in the context of "about":

Hablé de mi madre.
I talked about my mother.

De is used in expressions that show a characteristic, like *lleno de* (full of), *vestido de* (dressed in), *pintado de* (painted), and *harto de* (sick of). Another way this can be done is illustrated in the following example:

el helado de chocolate
chocolate ice cream

The preposition *de* can also mean "from," when indicating someone's origin or the motion "from" place to place:

Soy de España.
I am from Spain.

Another preposition that can be translated as "from" is *desde. Desde* is used to emphasize a specific starting point. For example:

Camino desde mi casa al trabajo todos los días.
I walk from my house to work every day.

The preposition *en* usually means "in," but it may also translate as "on" or "at":

Ellos están en el teatro.
They are at the theater.

La comida está en la mesa.
The food is on the table.

En is not used to mean "in" like "inside." For that, use *dentro de:*

Mis libros están dentro del cajón.
My books are inside the drawer.

And if you want to say "on" in the sense of "on top of," use *sobre:*

Pon el reloj sobre el estante.
Put the clock on the shelf.

You can also use *en* to mean "by" or "via" (a means by which something is done):

Viajaremos al Canadá en coche.
We'll travel to Canada by car.

The preposition equivalent to "with" is *con:*

Voy a la tienda con Marco.
I go to the store with Marco.

The opposite of "with" is "without." In Spanish, the equivalent preposition is *sin:*

Quiero algo sin carne.
I want something without meat.

You can also use *sin* to introduce an infinitive verb:

No puedo estar un minuto sin ayudar a alguien.
I cannot go a minute without helping someone.

Exercise 1: On and Away

Translate into Spanish.

1. We're going by train.

   ....

2. They sleep seven hours a day.

   ....

3. I am from London.

   ....

4. We are going to Marco's house.

   ....

5. I am nothing without you. (singular, formal)

   ....

6. I drink coffee with milk.

   ....

7. He is in the shower.

   ....

8. The girl begins to cry.

   ....

9. We are going to Argentina.

....

10. I know very little about my family.

....

Exercise 2: A, De, En, or Sin

Fill in the blank with *a, de, en,* or *sin.*

1. *Se reunieron* .... *la casa de Pedro.*

2. .... *veces yo no la comprendo.*

3. *Es el collar* .... *oro.*

4. *Ella a menudo anda* .... *zapatos.*

5. *Ayudo* .... *cargar el camión de mudanza.*

6. *Dame un pedazo* .... *pan, por favor.*

7. *El perro duerme* .... *el piso.*

8. *Es posible vivir bien* .... *dinero.*

9. *Ellos no ven* .... *la profesora.*

10. *Déjame* .... *paz.*

Por and Para

These two prepositions are often confusing to people studying Spanish. *Por* and *para* have similar meanings: para may be translated in different contexts as "for," "by," "to," or even "in"; *por* may also mean "in" or "for," or it could mean "on," "through," or "around."

Para most often means "for": for a cause, for (to) a destination, for someone. And you can think of *por* as "by" or "via"—it's a preposition that describes the way or the instrument by which something was accomplished: by car, through the woods, in return for your grades.

Now, let's compare:

Vamos para Nueva York. Vamos por Nueva York.
We're going to New York. We're going through New York.

In this example, *para* is used to point out the destination, whereas *por* places the subject in the city. Compare another example:

La carta fue escrita para el gerente. La carta fue escrita por el gerente.
The letter was written for the manager. The letter was written by the manager.

Para is a preposition that points to someone—the letter is for the manager. *Por,* on the other hand, shows who the action is done by.
Here are other examples of how *para* can be used:

Estudio para ser médico.
I study to become a doctor.

Para ser un niño, él es muy maduro.
For a child, he is very mature.
And here are some examples using *por:*

Compré una camisa por veinte dólares.
I bought a shirt for twenty dollars.

Yo me perdí por el camino.
I got lost on the way.

Lo llevaron preso por robo.
He was arrested for theft.

Also, *por* combines with other prepositions to indicate location:

por encima	over	*por acá*	around here
por detrás	behind	*por dentro*	inside
por debajo	under	*por fuera*	outside

Exercise 3: By and By

Choose either *por* or *para* to complete each sentence.

1. *Los niños corren* .... *la casa.*

2. *En Francia, María tomó el tren* .... *Alemania.*

3. *Gracias* .... *la comida.*

4. *La casa es bella* .... *fuera y* .... *dentro.*

5. *Caminamos* .... *toda la ciudad.*

6. *Estamos aquí* .... *visitar a nuestros abuelos.*

7. *Estábamos en Granada* .... *motivo de las fiestas.*

8. *Este regalo es* .... *mi esposa.*

9. *Se venden las piñas* .... *cuatro dólares cada una.*

10. *La novela fue escrita* .... *el famoso autor.*

Exercise 4: Make It Spanish

Translate the following into Spanish using *por* or *para*.

1. She goes to the post office to buy stamps.

   ....

2. For an American, she is very polite.

   ....

3. We walked all over the place.

   ....

4. The new dishes are for special celebrations.

   ....

5. He paid twenty dollars for his new shirt.

   ....

6. We are going to grandma's house.

....

7. I brought it for you. (singular, informal)

....

8. They take him for a fool.

....

9. Thanks for all your help.

....

10. I need the report by next week.

....

Prepositions of Location

Prepositions of location refer to a physical location of something. They usually follow a verb, especially estar ("to be") when relating to physical location. The two that were just covered, *con* and *en*, are prepositions of location.

Common Prepositions of Location			
al lado de	next to, beside	*dentro de*	inside of
a la derecha de	to the right of	*detrás de*	behind
a la izquierda de	to the left of	*encima de*	on top of
afuera de	outside of	*enfrente de, frente de*	across from, facing
cerca de	near	*entre*	between, among
contra	against	*lejos de*	far from
debajo de	below, under	*sobre*	over, on
delante de	in front of		

Here are some examples of prepositions of location used in a sentence.

Mi casa está enfrente de la biblioteca.
My house is across from the library.

¿Qué está cerca del teatro?
What is near the theater?

Hay un árbol delante de la casa.
There is a tree in front of the house.

La montaña está al lado del océano.
The mountain is next to the ocean.

Estoy dentro del coche.
I am inside the car.

Ella está afuera del coche.
She is outside of the car.

Hay un perro que duerme debajo del árbol.
There is a dog sleeping under the tree.

La silla está detrás del escritorio.
The chair is behind the desk.

La mesa está contra la pared.
The table is against the wall.

Also note that *en contra de* is used in expressions that refer to taking a stand against an idea.

Estoy en contra de comer carne.
I am against eating meat.

Exercise 5: Over and Under

Choose the preposition that best fits the sentence.

1. *El cuaderno está* .... *(sobre, entre) la mesa.*

2. *Javier trabaja* .... *(al lado de, debajo de) Félix en la tienda de deportes.*

3. *El restaurante está* .... *(sobre, cerca de) las tiendas.*

4. *La luna está* .... *(encima de, detrás de) la ciudad.*

5. *En el centro, el parque está a la izquierda y el almacén está* .... *(a la derecha, debajo).*

6. *El túnel corre* .... *(debajo del, sobre el) río.*

7. *Voy a esconderme* .... *(delante de, detrás de) los árboles.*

8. *El cine está* .... *(entre, encima de) la tienda de zapatos y un restaurante tailandés.*

9. *La ciudad de México está* .... *(lejos de, encima de) Nueva York.*

10. *En el coche, la silla del conductor está* .... *(detrás, a la izquierda).*

Exercise 6: Where Is It?

Answer each question using the information provided in the parentheses.

1. *¿Dónde está la escuela?* (near the fire station)

....

2. *¿Dónde está María?* (behind Miguel)

....

3. *¿Dónde están los árboles?* (in front of the windows)

....

4. *¿Dónde está la lavandería?* (opposite the bakery)

....

5. *¿Dónde están tus amigos?* (far from here)

   ....

6. *¿Dónde está el circo?* (next to the river)

   ....

7. *¿Dónde está el hospital?* (across from the dormitories)

   ....

8. *¿Dónde están los zapatos?* (under the bed)

   ....

9. *¿Dónde está la escuela?* (to the right of the playground)

   ....

10. *¿Dónde está el teatro?* (between the museum and the zoo)

   ....

Prepositions of Time

The following are some common prepositions of time:

Common Prepositions of Time			
antes de, antes que	before	*hasta*	until
después de	after		

Note that *antes de* is used before a noun and *antes que* is used before a verb:

La cena terminó antes de su llegada.
Dinner ended before his arrival.

La cena terminó antes que él llegara.
Dinner ended before he arrived.

Here are examples of *después de* and *hasta:*

Voy a verte después de la clase.
I'll see you after class.

Dormiré hasta las siete.
I'll sleep until seven.

Note that *hasta* has another meaning in addition to "until"—it can also mean "even," in which instance it's not a preposition of time at all. For example:

Hasta un niño pequeño conoce la respuesta.
Even a little kid knows the answer.

Exercise 7: In a Timely Fashion

Fill in the blank with the correct preposition of time.

1. *Junio llega* .... *mayo.*

2. *Nosotros nos lavamos las manos* .... *comer.*

3. *No estaremos listos* .... *las ocho.*

4. .... *cine, generalmente vamos al café.*

5. *Tome precauciones* .... *sea tarde.*

6. *Emilio siempre reza* .... *dormir.*

7. *Voy a esperar* .... *que mis hijos lleguen a casa.*

8. *Ellos limpian la cocina* .... *cocinar la cena.*

9. *¡* .... *luego!*

10. *Los jardineros terminan todas sus tareas afuera de la casa* .... *anochezca.*

Prepositional Phrases

A prepositional phrase consists of a preposition and its object and works like a modifier. As you've already noticed, most of the time prepositions are a part of a prepositional phrase. Here are a few examples:

> **behind you**
> **from that area**
> **inside the green car**
> **on my mind**
> **of that kind**

Here are some examples of prepositional phrases serving as the object of the verb:

> *Ella suele bailar en la calle.*
> **She usually dances in the street.**

> *Trabajamos hasta las cinco por la tarde.*
> **We work until five in the afternoon.**

In these sentences, *bailar en la calle* and *hasta cinco por la tarde* are prepositional objects. In other words, they are objects of the verb *bailar* and *trabajamos* and include a preposition.

Exercise 8: Choose the Right Phrase

Choose the correct prepositional phrase to complete the sentence.

1. *Trabajamos* .... *(sobre la cafetería, en la cafetería, de la cafetería).*

2. *Caminamos* .... *(al supermercado, hasta el supermercado, antes que el supermercado.*

3. *Es el coche* .... *(con él, de él, del); es su coche.*

4. *Nadie* .... *(para aquí, dentro aquí, por aquí) sabe jugar al tenis.*

5. *Trabajo aquí* .... *(desde enero, hasta ayer, con ayer).*

6. *¿Conoces* .... *(a Raúl, con Raúl, de Raúl)?*

7. *No oí nada* .... *(en esto, de esto, detrás de esto).*

8. *Este año voy a asistir a muchas fiestas* .... *(por Navidad, de Navidad, debajo de Navidad).*

9. *Voy a completar el proyecto* .... *(con ningunos problemas, de ningunos problemas, sin ningún problema).*

10. *Es el mejor juguete* .... *(sobre los niños, para los niños, por los niños).*

Exercise 9: Where's That Prepositional Phrase?

Circle one or more prepositional phrases in each sentence.

1. *María fue a la tienda en lugar de Miguel.*

2. *Es la casa de nuestros amigos.*

3. *Yo dejé la cartera dentro del coche.*

4. *No podemos irnos hasta las once.*

5. *No hay restaurantes chinos en esta pequeña ciudad.*

6. *La carta con el menú del día está sobre la mesa.*

7. *No pueden quedarse sin ellos.*

8. *Voy a ascender la montaña con tu ayuda.*

9. *Ella es muy cara para nosotros.*

10. *Por eso no puedo decirles nada.*

Coordinating Conjunctions

Coordinating conjunctions are words that are used to relate like terms, whether each term is a single word or a clause.

Common Coordinating Conjunctions			
o (u)	or	*sino*	but
pero	but	*y (e)*	and

One of the most common coordinating conjunctions is *y*. You can use *y* to combine a group of nouns, adjectives, or clauses:

Necesito huevos, pan y leche.
I need eggs, bread, and milk.

Mi hermano y hermana son más jóvenes que yo.
My brother and sister are younger than me.

Another frequently used coordinating conjunction is *o* (or). *O* works similarly to *y*—it may be used to relate single words or clauses:

Me gustaría tener una manzana o una naranja.
I would like to have an apple or orange.

When the word following *y* begins with an *i* sound, the *y* changes to *e* (so you don't have a double *i* (ee) sound. Similarly, the conjunction *o* becomes *u* when it comes before a word that begins with the sound *o*. For example:

Creo que se llama Orlando u Octavio.
I think his name is Orlando or Octavio.

In addition to *y* and *o*, the two other correlative conjunctions are *pero* and *sino*. Both translate as "but," with *sino* used only following a negative clause that is turned around into a positive statement. Take a look at the following example:

Ella no tiene un coche, sino una bicicleta.
She has no car, but (rather) a bicycle.

In this example, "but" negates a negative, so *sino* is used. In all other situations, you must use *pero:*

Quiero esto, pero es demasiado costoso.
I want this, but it is too expensive.

Exercise 10: In Conjunction

In each sentence, circle the coordinating conjunction.

1. *Me siento cansada e irritable.*

2. *Busco alguna comida o por lo menos algo de beber.*

3. *No me gusta, pero estoy feliz.*

4. *¿Es este niño rebelde u obediente?*

5. *Yo no estoy contenta, sino enfadada.*

6. *Hay muchos jóvenes y niños aquí.*

Exercise 11: And, Or, What?

Choose the conjunction that best completes each sentence.

1. *¿Es extraño* .... *(u, y, e) ordinario que no haya nadie en las calles de este pueblo?*

2. *Es muy tarde* .... *(sino, y, e) vamos a acostarnos.*

3. *Las manzanas son rojas* .... *(y, pero, porque) dulces.*

4. *Esta película es poco interesante* .... *(y, e, pero) no es tan aburrida.*

5. *¿Vamos al teatro* .... *(o, pero, sino) al museo?*

6. *No tengo interés en la música rock,* .... *(pero, sino, porque) en la salsa.*

7. *En octubre todavía está templado,* .... *(entonces, pero, sino) llueve mucho.*

8. *Yo hablo español* .... *(porque, y, e) inglés.*

Correlative Conjunctions

Correlative conjunctions come in pairs. In English, these are "either . . . or" and "neither . . . nor," and even native English speakers often have trouble choosing between the two pairs. Here is the basic rule: "Either . . . or" is used in affirmative (positive) sentences—"either one or the other." "Neither . . . nor" is used in negative sentences, when it's "neither one nor the other"—none of them.

In Spanish, use *o . . . o* in the case of "either . . . or" and *ni . . . ni* in the case of "neither . . . nor."

Ella es o doctora o enfermera.
She is either a doctor or a nurse.

Ella no es ni doctora ni enfermera.
She is neither a doctor nor a nurse.

In the second example, there's an extra *no* in the Spanish that is dropped in translation. That's because in Spanish, double negatives are accepted in everyday language (see Part 5 for more information on Spanish negatives).

Exercise 12: Either-Or, Neither-Nor

Take the parts and put them together into complete sentences using a correlative conjunction; for the first four, use *o . . . o;* for the last four, use *ni . . . ni.* For example: *estudiar/trabajar: No prefiero ni estudiar ni trabajar.*

1. *manzanas/peras*

....

2. *coser/tejer*

....

3. *coche/camión*

....

4. *carne de res/tocino*

....

5. *caminar/ir en bicicleta*

....

6. *guitarra/violín*

....

7. *cocinar/comer*

....

8. *azul/verde*

....

Subordinating Conjunctions

Subordinating conjunctions may be used to introduce a dependent clause (a phrase that cannot stand alone) or an independent clause (a phrase that can stand on its own as a sentence). Here are some common words that may be used as subordinating conjunctions:

a menos que	unless	*no obstante*	in spite of, regardless
a pesar de	despite	*para que*	so that
aunque	although	*porque*	because
como	how	*que*	that
con todo	despite, as	*salvo*	except
cuando	when	*si*	if
excepto	except	*sin embargo*	nevertheless
más bien	rather		

Exercise 13: In Subordination

In the following sentences, circle all the subordinating conjunctions.

1. *Si quisiera hacer algo, lo haría.*
2. *Estamos bien a pesar de la situación.*
3. *Estoy muy cansado; sin embargo, continúo caminando.*
4. *Abro la puerta para que ellos puedan entrar.*
5. *Vamos a la playa, a menos que llueva.*
6. *Busco a Elena porque ella me debe dinero.*
7. *Es una persona inteligente, aunque compleja.*
8. *Podemos empezar cuando quieras.*
9. *Nada es imposible, salvo vivir para siempre.*
10. *Ella está muy mal con todo lo que pasó.*

Exercise 14: The Correct Conjunction

Choose the correct subordinating conjunction.

1. *No entiendo* .... *(que, cómo, a pesar de) instalarlo.*

2. *Pienso* .... *(que, como, porque) ellos tienen la razón.*

3. *Ella lo quiere* .... *(si, porque, a pesar de) todo.*

4. *Yo se lo daría a ustedes* .... *(si, no obstante, para que) lo necesitaran.*

5. *Necesito comer* .... *(a pesar de, porque, aunque) tengo mucha hambre.*

6. *Hay que terminar este proyecto* .... *(que, no obstante, aunque) trabajemos toda la noche.*

7. *Es importante ganar,* .... *(que, no obstante, aunque) el obstáculo.*

8. *Tengo todo,* .... *(excepto, que, porque) el honor.*

9. *No hay mucha gente,* .... *(que, salvo, cuando) los turistas.*

10. .... *(Cuando, Que, No obstante) terminó la película, todos sintieron mucho alivio.*

Cardinal Numbers

Knowing your numbers is absolutely essential for even the beginner Spanish speaker. Spanish numbers follow most of the same basic rules of numbers in English. To start counting, here is the first set, starting with zero:

0	cero	6	seis
1	uno	7	siete
2	dos	8	ocho
3	tres	9	nueve
4	cuatro	10	diez
5	cinco		

The next set of numbers includes the teens:

11	*once*	16	*dieciséis*
12	*doce*	17	*diecisiete*
13	*trece*	18	*dieciocho*
14	*catorce*	19	*diecinueve*
15	*quince*		

The numbers 20–29 are also written as one word:

20	*veinte*	25	*veinticinco*
21	*veintiuno*	26	*veintiséis*
22	*veintidós*	27	*veintisiete*
23	*veintitrés*	28	*veintiocho*
24	*veinticuatro*	29	*veintinueve*

Following 30, numbers are written as phrases: *treinta y uno* (31), *treinta y dos* (32), and so on. So all you need to know are the multiples of ten:

30	*treinta*	70	*setenta*
40	*cuarenta*	80	*ochenta*
50	*cincuenta*	90	*noventa*
60	*sesenta*		

After *noventa y nueve* (99), the next one up is *cien* (100). Then, numbers continue up to 199 with *ciento* plus the rest of the number. Here are a few examples:

125	*ciento veinticinco*	189	*ciento ochenta y nueve*
146	*ciento cuarenta y seis*		

The numbers from 200 to 999 work the same. For example, 452 is *cuatrocientos cincuenta y dos.* You just need to know the 100s:

200	*doscientos*	600	*seiscientos*
300	*trescientos*	700	*setecientos*
400	*cuatrocientos*	800	*ochocientos*
500	*quinientos*	900	*novecientos*

The pattern of forming the number by going from hundreds to tens to ones continues the higher you go. For example, 1998 is *mil novecientos noventa y ocho.* Here's the rest of the vocabulary you might need to keep counting up:

1,000	*mil*	1,000,000	*millón*
2,000	*dos mil*	2,000,000	*dos millones*

Using numbers in Spanish is easy. Even when you use a number as an adjective describing how many of something there is, the number's ending does not change according to the gender of the noun. For example: *cuatro hijos* (four sons); *cuatro hijas* (four daughters). However, *uno* and other numbers ending in *uno* do change in gender. For example: *un padre, una madre; veintiún padres; veintiuna madres.* The same is true for hundreds: *doscientos edificios, doscientas casas.*

Exercise 15: One, Two, Three . . .

Listen and repeat each number.

TRACK 10

Exercise 16: In Digits

Fill in the correct number in digits.

1. *dieciocho* ....

2. *veintidós* ....

3. *cincuenta y cuatro* ....

4. *noventa y tres* ....

5. *ciento catorce* ....

6. *doscientos sesenta y nueve* ....

7. *quinientos sesenta y dos* ....

8. *setecientos treinta y cinco* ....

9. *ochocientos noventa y nueve* ....

10. *dos   millones   trescientos   cincuenta   y   dos   mil   seiscientos   trece*

    ....

Exercise 17: Spell It Out

Fill in the correct number by writing it out in Spanish.

1. 17 ....

2. 88 ....

3. 226 ....

4. 355 ....

5. 1.512 ....

6. 3.482.415 ....

Ordinal Numbers

Ordinal numbers don't deal with quantity—they serve to indicate the order of something: first, second, third, and so on. In English, ordinal numbers end with –st, –nd, or –th, so they are easy to recognize. In Spanish, the pattern is only slightly more complicated:

first	*primero*	sixth	*sexto*
second	*segundo*	seventh	*séptimo*
third	*tercero*	eighth	*octavo*
fourth	*cuarto*	ninth	*noveno*
fifth	*quinto*	tenth	*décimo*

The cardinal number should come before the noun it modifies and it should agree with it in gender and number. Here are a few examples: *segunda página* (second page), *terceros términos* (third terms). Also, *primero* and *tercero* drop the –o before a singular, masculine noun: *tercer piso* (third floor).

Exercise 18: What's First?

Fill in the blank for each sentence using an ordinal number.

1. *Marzo es el* .... *mes de la primavera.*

2. *Agosto es el* .... *mes del verano.*

3. *La medalla de plata es galardonada por el* .... *lugar.*

4. *El último día de febrero es generalmente el día* ....

5. *El sentido adicional a los cinco sentidos se llama el* .... *sentido.*

6. *El niño tiene nueve años; tendrá su* .... *cumpleaños en dos semanas.*

7. *Mayo es el* .... *mes del año.*

8. *El último día de los doce días de Navidad es el día* ....

The Alphabet and Spelling

The Spanish alphabet is very similar to the English one, except that letters are pronounced differently and there is an extra letter, ñ.

The Spanish Alphabet			
letter	**pronunciation**	**letter**	**pronunciation**
A	ah	Ñ	EH-nyeh
B	beh	O	oh
C	seh	P	peh
D	deh	Q	koo
E	eh	R	EH-reh
F	EF-eh	S	EH-seh
G	heh	T	teh
H	AH-cheh	U	oo
I	ee	V	veh, beh
J	HOH-tah	W	DOH-bleh veh, DOH-bleh beh
K	kah	X	EH-kis
L	EH-leh	Y	ee GRIEH-gah
M	EH-meh	Z	ZEH-tah, SEH-tah
N	EH-neh		

In some dictionaries "ch" (chay) and "ll" (EL-yay) are recognized as letters, while in others they are not.

Exercise 19: Spell It Out

TRACK 11

Listen to each word as it is spelled out and write it down.

1. ....

2. ....

3. ....

4. ....

5. ....

6. ....

7. ....

8. ....

9. ....

10. ....

11. ....

12. ....

13. ....

14. ....

15. ....

Exercise 20: Spelling Bee

Read the phonetic spellings out loud then write down the word. For more practice, spell out some other words out loud.

1. deh, eh, seh, ee, EH-reh ....

2. HOH-tah, ah, EH-reh, deh, ee con acento, EH-neh ....

3. ee, EH-reh ....

4. ah, EH-meh, ah, EH-reh, ee, EH-leh, EH-leh, oh ....

5. EH-neh, oh, veh, ee, oh ....

6. EH-meh, ah, EH-nyeh, ah, EH-neh, ah ....

7. EH-meh, eh, EH-kis, ee, seh, ah, EH-neh, oh ....

8. peh, eh, EH-reh, EH-reh, oh ....

9. EF-eh, ah, EH-leh, deh, ah ....

10. seh, oh, EH-meh, oo con acento, EH-neh ....

Diminutives, Augmentatives, and Absolute Superlatives

Diminutives, augmentatives, and absolute superlatives are words formed with the addition of the right suffix. These suffixes don't change the meaning altogether—they simply signal additional information like size or the speaker's emotional attitude.

Diminutive suffixes indicate small size, cuteness, or an attitude of endearment. For example, the word *casa* means "house"; *casita* is a little house, maybe a charming little summer cottage. *Gato* is a cat; *gatito* is "kitty." Using a diminutive suffix can allow you to be more descriptive without using an adjective.

The most versatile diminutive suffix in Spanish is *–ito* and its conjugated forms: *–ita, –itos,* and *–itas*. Here are a few other diminutive suffixes commonly used in Spanish:

–cito	*cochecito*	little car
–illo	*abogadillo*	ineffective lawyer
–uete	*amiguete*	pal
–zuelo	*ladronzuelo*	petty thief

Almost any noun (including proper nouns) can take on a diminutive suffix. Even adjectives and adverbs can take on diminutive endings: *pobrecito* (poor), *despacito* (slowly). However, be aware that diminutives are generally used only in informal situations.

Augmentatives are essentially the opposite of diminutives. They indicate large size or the attitude of toughness or importance. For example, *hombre* is "man," but add the augmentative suffix –*ón*, and the result is *hombrón*, "tough guy." Some common augmentative suffixes:

–ote	*librote*	big, heavy book
–ón	*barracón*	a big hut
–azo	*exitazo*	great success

Augmentatives match the gender of the word they modify, with the feminine forms being: –*ona*, –*ota*, and –*aza*. They must also match in number, with the plural forms being: –*ones*, –*onas*, –*otes*, –*otas*, –*azos*, and –*azas*.

Another suffix in Spanish is the absolute superlative. This is like adding extremely, very, or exceptionally before an adjective or adverb. Absolute superlatives are formed by adding the –*ísimo* suffix to an adjective or adverb. Usually, if the adjective or adverb ends in a vowel, you can just drop that letter and add the suffix. For those ending in a consonant, you can just tack the –*ísimo* right on the end.

inteligente	*inteligentísimo*	extremely intelligent
bonita	*bonitísima*	exceptionally pretty

However, if the last consonant is c, g, or z, change that letter to qu, gu, or c in the superlative form. And if it ends in n or r, you form the superlative by adding –*císimo*.

feliz	*felicísimo*	very happy
joven	*jovencísimo*	very young

Exercise 21: Make It Cute

Rewrite each word as a diminutive.

1. *abuela*   ....

2. *momento*   ....

3. *hermana*   ....

4. *pobre*   ....

5. *pedazo*   ....

Exercise 22: Toughen Things Up

Rewrite each as an augmentative.

1. *animal*   ....

2. *grande*   ....

3. *buena*   ....

4. *soltero*   ....

5. *perras*   ....

Exercise 23: The Very Best!

Rewrite each adjective in the absolute superlative form.

1. *fácil* ....

2. *agradable* ....

3. *gordo* ....

4. *alta* ....

5. *rápido* ....

6. *largas* ....

7. *rico* ....

8. *trabajadores* ....

Putting It Together

It's time to find out how much you've retained. Try to complete each exercise in this section without referring to the instructions or any outside materials.

Exercise 24: Preposition Practice

Translate into Spanish.

1. He speaks before listening.

   ....

2. There are two minutes until midnight.

   ....

3. I drink tea with lemon.

   ....

4. She is behind you (singular/formal).

   ....

5. We are near our parents.

   ....

6. It's in the center of the city.

   ....

7. The museum is to the right of the park.

   ....

8. For me, nothing is very important.

   ....

Exercise 25: In Relation to a Pronoun

Fill in the blanks with either *a, de, en, por, para, o con.*

1. *Prefiero comer la sopa* .... *el pan.*

2. *No conozco* .... *Paulina.*

3. *Su novio vive* .... *Canadá.*

4. *Toma las pastillas cuatro veces* .... *día.*

5. *Viajamos* .... *avión.*

6. *Ella es la hermana* .... *Dimitrio.*

7. *Estudiamos* .... *la universidad.*

8. *Busco a Emilio* .... *decirle algo importante.*

Exercise 26: Which Conjunction?

Find and label the conjunction as coordinating, correlative, or subordinating.

1. *Voy a Inglaterra pero no tengo mucho dinero.* ....

2. *Yo me pregunto si me ama.* ....

3. *Me gustaría o el rojo o el azul.* ....

4. *Era tarde cuando regresamos a casa.* ....

5. *Aprender idiomas es algo difícil e interesante.* ....

6. *Es mejor que ella no nos vea.* ....

7. *Yo soy ni bella ni fea.* ....

8. *Me siento feliz a pesar de haber perdido el juego.* ....

Exercise 27: An Interview

TRACK 12

Listen to the following questions and try to answer them. Then listen to the track again and write down your answers.

1. ....

2. ....

3. ....

4. ....

5. ....

6. ....

7. ....

8. ....

9. ....

10. ....

11. ....

12. ....

13. ....

14. ....

15. ....

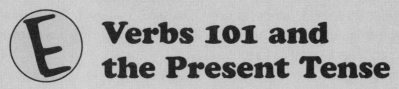

Part 5

Verbs 101 and the Present Tense

Are you excited? You should be—verbs are the last bit you need to form complete sentences! A verb is a word that refers to the action or state of the subject: what it does, what is happening to it, or what it is. In addition to the word's meaning, which remains in the stem (or root) of the verb, verbs in Spanish are conjugated according to person, number, voice, mood, tense, and aspect. This part will cover the present tense and some of the basic ways of conjugating a verb.

Infinitives

Infinitives are used to express a verb at its simplest form. In English, infinitives are usually expressed by adding "to" in front of the verb, such as "to speak." Since a verb in Spanish literally has dozens of different spellings depending on tense, person, number, voice, mood, and aspect, the infinitive is a very useful way of representing the verb at its basic, for instance in dictionaries.

Infinitives fit into three categories of endings: –ar, –er, and –ir. For example, *hablar* (to speak), *beber* (to drink), *asistir* (to attend). This is why Spanish verbs are referred to as AR, ER, or IR verbs. Each group has its own set of regular endings as well as irregularities.

Infinitive forms may be used as nouns. A common example is the phrase *Está prohibido fumar.* (Smoking is forbidden.) In this example, *fumar* is used as a noun, "smoking." When used this way, they are always considered masculine and almost always singular. Infinitives are also used right after conjugated verbs:

Quiero salir.
I want to leave.

Infinitives also come into play with prepositions, which translate into English as the –ing form of the verb. We'll cover this in Part 9, concerning gerunds (or present progressive).

Exercise 1: Look at the Ending

Label whether each is an AR, ER, or IR verb.

1. *comer*   ....

2. *amar*   ....

3. *beber*   ....

4. *asistir*   ....

5. *hablar*   ....

6. *poner*   ....

7. *tutear*   ....

8. *distribuir*   ....

9. *oír*   ....

10. *perder*   ....

Exercise 2: A Verb or a Noun?

Translate each sentence into English.

1. *Beber es poco sano.*

    ....

2. *Necesito comprar unos zapatos.*

    ....

3. *Es importante leer todo el libro.*

    ....

4. *Cantar es un verbo regular.*

    ....

5. *Cocinar es una habilidad muy útil.*

    ....

Present-Tense AR Conjugations

Regular AR verb endings conjugate as follows:

singular		
1st person	*yo*	–o
2nd person	*tú*	–as
3rd person	*él, ella, usted*	–a
plural		
1st person	*nosotros, nosotras*	–amos
2nd person	*vosotros, vosotras*	–áis
3rd person	*ellos, ellas, ustedes*	–an

As you probably remember from the pronoun section, the *tú* and *vosotros* forms are informal forms of the English word "you," while *usted* and *ustedes* are the formal uses.

The verb *hablar* would conjugate like this:

yo hablo	I speak	*nosotros hablamos*	we speak
tú hablas	you speak	*vosotros habláis*	you speak
él habla	he speaks	*ellos hablan*	they speak
ella habla	she speaks	*ustedes hablan*	you speak
usted habla	you speak		

In Spanish, you don't need to say "*yo hablo*" to say "I speak." "*Hablo*" carries the same meaning and is more typically spoken. The "*yo*" is sometimes included for emphasis, but more often by beginner Spanish speakers. The other conjugations often include the pronoun for clarity, or a different subject noun is used:

María habla español.
Maria speaks Spanish.

Common Regular AR Verbs in the Present Tense			
abandonar	to abandon	*fumar*	to smoke
aceptar	to accept	*lavar*	to wash
acuchillar	to cut up (with a knife)	*llevar*	to take, to wear
adaptar	to adapt	*mandar*	to order
adoptar	to adopt	*marchar*	to walk
amar	to love	*mirar*	to look, to watch
andar	to walk	*montar*	to climb
ayudar	to help	*nadar*	to swim
bajar	to go down	*necesitar*	to need

Common Regular AR Verbs in the Present Tense (continued)

bañar	to bathe	*olvidar*	to forget
besar	to kiss	*pagar*	to pay
cambiar	to change	*parar*	to stop
cantar	to sing	*preparar*	to prepare
comprar	to buy	*quedar*	to stay
dejar	to leave, to let	*tirar*	to pull, to draw
entrar	to enter	*tomar*	to take, to drink
esperar	to wait, to hope	*trabajar*	to work
expresar	to express	*viajar*	to travel
ganar	to win, to earn		
gastar	to spend, to waste		
hablar	to speak		

Exercise 3: What It Means

Choose the correct translation for each.

1. *miro (he looks, they look, I look)*
2. *paga (I pay, he pays, we pay)*
3. *miramos (you look, they look, we look)*
4. *entráis (we enter, you enter, she enters)*
5. *viaja (they travel, we travel, she travels)*
6. *entran (he enters, we enter, you enter)*
7. *amo (they love, she loves, I love)*
8. *hablas (we speak, he speaks, you speak)*
9. *lava (I wash, you wash, they wash)*
10. *ganan (they win, he wins, she wins)*

Exercise 4: The Right Form

Fill in the correct form of the given verb for each sentence.

1. *Tú nunca me* .... *(ayudar)*

2. *Nosotros* .... *muy bien. (cantar)*

3. *Usted* .... *tan rápidamente. (nadar)*

4. *Carlos* .... *en la universidad. (trabajar)*

5. *Yo* .... *algo más. (necesitar)*

6. *Ella* .... *frutas en el mercado. (comprar)*

7. *Elena* .... *el autobús al centro de la ciudad. (tomar)*

8. *Nosotros* .... *antes de la estatua. (parar)*

9. *Él* .... *mucho cuando bebe vino. (fumar)*

10. *Vosotras* .... *vestidos al baile. (llevar)*

Present-Tense ER Conjugations

Regular ER verbs conjugate as follows:

singular		
1st person	*yo*	–o
2nd person	*tú*	–es
3rd person	*él, ella, usted*	–e
plural		
1st person	*nosotros, nosotras*	–emos
2nd person	*vosotros, vosotras*	–éis
3rd person	*ellos, ellas, ustedes*	–en

Common Regular ER Verbs in the Present Tense

absorber	to absorb	*leer*	to read
aprender	to learn	*meter*	to put, insert
barrer	to sweep	*poseer*	to own, to possess, to hold
beber	to drink	*prender*	to catch, to turn on
comer	to eat	*proceder*	to proceed
cometer	to commit	*prometer*	to promise
comprender	to comprehend, to understand	*romper*	to break
conceder	to concede, to grant, to award	*sorprender*	to surprise, to promise

Common Regular ER Verbs in the Present Tense (continued)

correr	to run	*suceder*	to succeed, to happen
coser	to sew	*suspender*	to fail, to suspend
creer	to believe	*tejer*	to crochet, weave, knit, braid
deber	to have to, to owe	*temer*	to dread, to fear
depender	to depend	*toser*	to cough
esconder	to hide	*vender*	to sell
exceder	to exceed		

Exercise 5: Depending on the Pronoun

Choose the correct translation for each.

1. *metes* (I put, they put, you put)

2. *comemos* (you eat, we eat, they eat)

3. *tejen* (they knit, I knit, we knit)

4. *leo* (I read, he reads, you read)

5. *corre* (he runs, we run, they run)

6. *aprendéis* (they learn, we learn, you learn)

7. *debe* (we owe, you owe, they owe)

8. *temen* (they fear, we fear, she fears)

9. *vendo* (they sell, I sell, he sells)

10. *prometes* (you promise, we promise, I promise)

Exercise 6: The Right Ending

Fill in the correct form of the given verb for each sentence.

1. *Ella no .... la leche porque le duele el estómago. (beber)*

2. *Yo .... ropa para mi bebé. (coser)*

3. *La tierra está seca y .... el agua muy rápidamente. (absorber)*

4. *Tú .... el suelo cada dos días. (barrer)*

5. *Usted no .... en Dios. (creer)*

6. *Ellos .... de nuestra ayuda. (depender)*

7. *Tú* .... *el riesgo de caer. (correr)*

8. *Ella* .... *mucho; está enferma. (toser)*

9. *Vosotros os* .... *vuestras cabezas por el problema. (romper)*

10. *Nosotros nunca* .... *semejantes errores. (cometer)*

Present-Tense IR Conjugations

Regular IR verbs conjugate as follows:

singular

1st person	*yo*	–o
2nd person	*tú*	–es
3rd person	*él, ella, usted*	–e

plural

1st person	*nosotros, nosotras*	–imos
2nd person	*vosotros, vosotras*	–ís
3rd person	*ellos, ellas, ustedes*	–en

Common Regular IR Verbs in the Present Tense			
abolir	to abolish	*exhibir*	to exhibit
abrir	to open	*existir*	to exist
aburrir	to bore	*gruñir*	to grunt, to growl
admitir	to accept	*imprimir*	to print
añadir	to join, to increase	*incurrir*	to incur

Common Regular IR Verbs in the Present Tense (continued)

aplaudir	to applaud	*inscribir*	to inscribe
asistir	to attend (classes)	*insistir*	to insist
asumir	to assume	*interrumpir*	to interrupt
combatir	to fight, to combat	*invadir*	to invade
confundir	to confuse, to confound	*ocurrir*	to occur
consistir	to consist	*omitir*	to omit
consumir	to consume	*partir*	to divide, to split
convivir	to live together, to coexist	*percibir*	to perceive
cubrir	to cover, to put the lid on	*permitir*	to permit, to allow
cumplir	to complete, to finish	*persistir*	to persist
decidir	to decide	*persuadir*	to persuade
definir	to define	*presidir*	to preside
deprimir	to depress	*presumir*	to presume
describir	to describe	*prohibir*	to prohibit, to forbid
descubrir	to discover, to uncover	*pudrir*	to rot, to decay
discutir	to discuss	*pulir*	to polish, to finish
disuadir	to dissuade	*recibir*	to receive
dividir	to divide	*sobrevivir*	to survive
emitir	to emit	*subir*	to rise, to go up, to board (a bus, etc.)
escribir	to write	*sufrir*	to suffer
escupir	to spit	*transcribir*	to transcribe
		transmitir	to transmit
		unir	to unite
		vivir	to live

Exercise 7: The Right Choice

Choose the correct translation for each.

1. *vivimos* (you live, we live, he lives)

2. *abro* (I open, we open, he opens)

3. *escribe* (we write, they write, you write)

4. *subo* (he goes up, we go up, I go up)

5. *dividís* (you divide, we divide, they divide)

6. *discutimos* (they discuss, we discuss, I discuss)

7. *admite* (she accepts, we accept, they accept)

8. *parten* (we leave, they leave, he leaves)

9. *describe* (I describe, you describe, we describe)

10. *interrumpes* (I interrupt, we interrupt, you interrupt)

Exercise 8: In Translation

Fill in the correct form of the given verb for each sentence.

1. *Yo* .... *regalos cada cumpleaños. (recibir)*

2. *Ella* .... *las escaleras. (subir)*

3. *Ustedes* .... *qué hacer juntos. (decidir)*

4. *Vosotros* .... *la solución. (discutir)*

5. *Yo* .... *el calor. (sufrir)*

6. *Esta película me* .... *(aburrir)*

7. *Nosotros* .... *los mensajes pronto. (recibir)*

8. *Tú* .... *el cambio en la temperatura. (percibir)*

9. *Esto* .... *solo una vez en el siglo. (ocurrir)*

10. *Ellos* .... *en el campo. (vivir)*

Exercise 9: Getting the Endings Down

TRACK 13

Listen to and repeat the present-tense conjugations of three regular verbs, *hablar* (to speak), *beber* (to drink), and *asistir* (to attend).

Spelling Change Verbs

Certain verbs deviate from regular conjugation forms in spelling in order to maintain correct pronunciation. If you know which verbs behave this way, you can figure out correct conjugation forms for new verbs as you learn them. This section reviews verbs that undergo a spelling change in the present tense.

Verbs that end in –uir retain the long "i" sound in all conjugations, which requires changing the spelling of some of the forms from "i" to "y." For example, see how *atribuir* (to attribute) conjugates:

atribuyo	*atribuimos*
atribues	*atribuís*
atribuye	*atribuyen*

Other verbs that follow the same pattern are *concluir* (to conclude), *destruir* (to destroy), *huir* (to flee), *incluir* (to include), *influir* (to influence), and *sustituir* (to substitute).

Verbs that need to retain the hard "h" sound of the "g" at the end of the stem undergo a "g > j" change in the *yo* form of the present indicative. This is true for verbs ending in -ger or –gir, like *coger* (to grab):

cojo	*cogemos*
coges	*cogéis*
coge	*cogen*

Other verbs that follow the same pattern in the *yo* form are *afligir* (to afflict), *dirigir* (to direct), *encoger* (to shrink), *exigir* (to beg), *fingir* (to pretend), *proteger* (to protect), and *recoger* (to gather).

PART 5: VERBS 101 AND THE PRESENT TENSE

Another kind of spelling change is the use of an accent mark. For example, verbs that end in –iar require an accent mark over the "i" in four of the present indicative conjugations (only the *nosotros* and *vosotros* forms remain regular) to signal regular pronunciation. Take a look at *confiar* (to confide):

confío	*confiamos*
confías	*confiáis*
confía	*confían*

Other verbs that follow the same pattern are *enviar* (to send), *espiar* (to spy), *guiar* (to guide), and *variar* (to vary).

The same pattern also applies to –uar verbs, except it's the "ú" that requires the accent mark. See, for example, the conjugated forms of the verb *actuar* (to act):

actúo	*actuamos*
actúas	*actuáis*
actúa	*actúan*

Other verbs that follow the same pattern are *continuar* (to continue), *evaluar* (to evaluate), and *insinuar* (to suggest).

Verbs that end in –ecer need to maintain the "s" sound at the end of the stem. Because the *yo* form, *apareco,* won't work, there's a change in pronunciation with the addition of a "z": *aparezco.* The other present tense forms remain regular:

aparezco	*aparecemos*
apareces	*aparecéis*
aparece	*aparecen*

Other verbs that follow the same pattern are *agradecer* (to thank), *conocer* (to know), *crecer* (to grow), *establecer* (to establish), *merecer* (to deserve), *obedecer* (to obey), *ofrecer* (to offer), *parecer* (to seem), *permanecer* (to remain), and *pertenecer* (to belong). Additionally, the same change applies to –ucir verbs like *traducir* (to translate):

traduzco	traducimos
traduces	traducís
traduce	traducen

Other verbs that follow the same pattern are *conducir* (to drive), *deducir* (to deduce), *lucir* (to shine) *producir* (to produce), and *reproducir* (to reproduce).

Exercise 10: Choose Well

Choose the correct translation for each.

1. *encojo* (she shrinks, I shrink, we shrink)

2. *estableces* (he establishes, I establish, you establish)

3. *espiamos* (I spy, you spy, we spy)

4. *concluyo* (I conclude, you conclude, they conclude)

5. *lucen* (I shine, we shine, they shine)

6. *afligimos* (he afflicts, we afflict, they afflict)

7. *reproduce* (I reproduce, he reproduces, they reproduce)

8. *huyo* (I flee, we flee, they flee)

9. *deducís* (we deduce, you deduce, they deduce)

10. *pertenecen* (I belong, we belong, you belong)

Exercise 11: Conjugation Conundrum

Fill in the correct form of the given verb for each sentence.

1. *Yo* .... *a este grupo también. (to belong)*

2. *Tú no* .... *a tus padres.* (to obey)

3. *Nosotros* .... *dinero a nuestros abuelos en el Perú. (to send)*

4. *Ellos no* .... *este galardón.* (to deserve)

5. *Yo no* .... *la enfermedad.* (to pretend)

6. *Vosotros* .... *coches italianos.* (to drive)

7. *Usted* .... *aprendiendo español.* (to continue)

8. *Marisa* .... *mi página de Internet.* (to evaluate)

9. *Yo* .... *toda su confianza.* (to destroy)

10. *Ustedes probablemente los* .... *a ellos.* (to know)

Stem Changing Verbs

Some groups of Spanish verbs undergo a stem change—that is, the verb's root changes spelling and pronunciation in four of the six conjugation forms (excluding nosotros and vosotros). The most common changes occur in the stem's vowel: "e" may change to "ie" or "i" and "o" may change to "ue" or "u."

Many AR and ER verbs undergo an "e > ie" change in the stem when the "e" is in the stressed syllable. For example, this is the conjugation of the verb *pensar* (to to think):

pienso	*pensamos*
piensas	*pensáis*
piensa	*piensan*

Other verbs that follow the same pattern:

infinitive	yo form	English
apretar	*aprieto*	I grip
ascender	*asciendo*	I go up
atravesar	*atravieso*	I cross
cerrar	*cierro*	I close
comenzar	*comienzo*	I commence

infinitive	yo form	English
defender	defiendo	I defend
descender	desciendo	I go down
empezar	empiezo	I begin
entender	entiendo	I understand
pensar	pienso	I think
perder	pierdo	I lose
querer	quiero	I want
recomendar	recomiendo	I recommend
sentar	siento	I sit down

A similar change occurs with IR verbs. In the conjugations where the "e" is accented, it is replaced with "i." For example, *repetir* (to repeat) conjugates as follows:

repito	repetimos
repites	repetís
repite	repiten

Other verbs in this category are:

infinitive	yo form	English
gemir	gimo	I moan
impedir	impido	I prevent
medir	mido	I measure
pedir	pido	I ask
seguir	sigo	I follow
servir	sirvo	I serve
vestir	visto	I dress

A few IR verbs do have an "e > ie" stem change:

infinitive	yo form	English
mentir	miento	I lie
preferir	prefiero	I prefer
sentir	siento	I feel

Just as stressed "e" may undergo a change to "i" or "ie," a stressed "o" in some irregular verbs changes to "u" or "ue." For example, *dormir* (to sleep) conjugates:

duermo	dormimos
duermes	dormís
duerme	duermen

Other verbs that follow the "o > ue" stem change include the following:

infinitive	yo form	English
almorzar	almuerzo	I have lunch
contar	cuento	I tell
costar	cuesto	I cost
doler	duelo	I hurt
encontrar	encuentro	I find
jugar	juego	I play
morir	muero	I die
mostrar	muestro	I show
poder	puedo	I can
probar	pruebo	I try

recorder	recuerdo	I remember
soler	suelo	I am accustomed to
volar	vuelo	I fly
volver	vuelvo	I return

Exercise 12: Up to You

Choose the right translation for each conjugated Spanish verb.

1. *almuerzan (we eat lunch, he eats lunch, they eat lunch)*

2. *siento (I feel, you feel, she feels)*

3. *quebramos (we break, you break, they break)*

4. *sigues (I follow, you follow, he follows)*

5. *contáis (we count, you count, they count)*

6. *gimes (I moan, you moan, he moans)*

7. *miente (I lie, she lies, they lie)*

8. *muero (I die, you die, it dies)*

9. *medís (I measure, you measure, he measures)*

10. *muestra (I show, we show, you show)*

Exercise 13: What It Means

Fill in the blank with the correct form of the given infinitive.

1. *Ella* .... *perdón por ofender a la profesora.*
   (pedir)

2. *Tú* .... *poco para un niño de tu edad.*
   (dormir)

3. *Él raramente* .... *nuevas cosas. (probar)*

4. *Nosotros* .... *la verdad. (decir)*

5. *Ustedes* .... *beber ocho vasos de agua por día. (recomendar)*

6. *Usted* .... *que todo está bien. (pensar)*

7. *Yo* .... *huevos y pan tostado para el desayuno. (servir)*

8. *Nosotros* .... *a casa muy tarde. (volver)*

9. *Tú* .... *escribir con talento. (comenzar)*

10. *¿Vosotros* .... *a Teresa? (recordar)*

Irregular Verbs

There are other groups of irregular verbs as well. For instance, the following group of verbs gains a "g" in the *yo* form. For example, take a look at the conjugations of the verb *hacer* (to do):

hago	*hacemos*
haces	*hacéis*
hace	*hacen*

Other verbs that take on a "g" in the *yo* form:

infinitive	yo form	English
poner	*pongo*	I put
salir	*salgo*	I leave
venir	*vengo*	I come

Additionally, a group of verbs gain a "g' plus have an additional irregularity. The verb *tener* (to have) is also an "e > ie" verb:

tengo	tenemos
tienes	tenéis
tiene	tienen

And so is *venir* (to come):

vengo	venimos
vienes	venís
viene	vienen

The verb *decir* (to say) is a "e > i" verb:

digo	decimos
dices	decís
dice	dicen

And some verbs with an added "g" are also spelling change verbs:

infinitive	yo form	English
caer	caigo	I fall
decaer	decaigo	I decline
traer	traigo	I bring

As you can see, a lot of verbs have an irregular *yo* form in the present tense. Here are some others (their other five forms are regular):

infinitive	yo form	English
caber	quepo	I fit
dar	doy	I give

entrever	entreveo	I glimpse
prever	preveo	I forecast
infinitive	**yo form**	**English**
saber	sé	I know
ver	veo	I see

The rest of the verbs are singular in terms of their particular irregularity.

Verbs Irregular in the Present Tense					
errar (to stray, to wander, to err)					
yerro	erramos	yerras	erráis	yerra	yerran
estar (to be)					
estoy	estamos	estás	estáis	está	están
haber (to have)					
he	hemos	has	habéis	ha	han
ir (to go)					
voy	vamos	vas	vais	va	van
oír (to hear, to listen)					
oigo	oímos	oyes	oís	oye	oyen
oler (to smell, to sniff)					
huelo	olemos	hueles	oléis	huele	huelen
reír (to laugh)					
río	reímos	ríes	reís	ríe	ríen
ser (to be)					
soy	somos	eres	sois	es	son

Exercise 14: One out of Three

Choose the right translation for each conjugated Spanish verb.

1. *doy (I give, he gives, we give)*

2. *sabes (I know, he knows, you know)*

3. *son (I am, we are, they are)*

4. *estoy (I am, you are, she is)*

5. *sonreís (I smile, you smile, they smile)*

6. *hueles (I smell, you smell, we smell)*

7. *hemos (I have, you have, we have)*

8. *sé (I know, you know, we know)*

9. *vas (I go, we go, you go)*

10. *oigo (I hear, he hears, they hear)*

Exercise 15: The Right Version

Fill in the blank with the correct form of the given infinitive.

1. *Nosotros .... italianos. (ser)*

2. *... treinta personas aquí. (haber)*

3. *Ellos .... al restaurante para cenar. (ir)*

4. *Usted .... este color. (ver)*

5. *Su energía .... lentamente. (decaer)*

6. *Yo .... cuando empiezas a hacer chistes. (reír)*

7. *Tú .... en tus cálculos. (errar)*

8. *Yo no .... en esta pequeña silla. (caber)*

9. *Vosotros .... demasiado lejos. (estar)*

10. *Yo no .... en este cuartito. (caber)*

In the Negative

The Spanish word for "no" isn't hard to remember—it's *no*. A simple statement can be made negative by adding *no* in front of the verb.

Hablo español.	I speak Spanish.
No hablo español.	I do not speak Spanish.

When answering a question in the negative, it is typical to use *no* twice:

¿Habla español?	Do you speak Spanish?
No, no hablo español.	No, I do not speak Spanish.

But we know that there are several other negative modifiers:

nunca	never	*por/en ninguna parte*	nowhere
jamás	never	*por/en ningún lado*	nowhere
ninguna vez	never once	*tampoco*	neither, not either
nada	nothing	*ni ... ni*	neither ... nor
nadie	no one		

These negatives can be used alone:

Nadie escucha.
Nobody listens.

Ella nunca come.
She never eats.

Tampoco sabe lo que pasó.
He doesn't know what happened either.

In Spanish, double negatives are very common (and grammatically correct). Sometimes even more than two negatives appear:

No lo hago nunca.
I never do it.

No necesitas nada.
You don't need anything.

No compro nada nunca.
I never buy anything.

Exercise 16: Yes and No

Rewrite each sentence as a negative statement.

1. *Siempre me despierto temprano.*

   ....

2. *Hablo español.*

   ....

3. *Siempre se viste bien.*

   ....

4. *Me gustaría o café o té.*

   ....

5. *Conozco a todos aquí.*

   ....

6. *Ella está en algún sitio.*

   ....

7. *Los hermanos Martín juegan afuera.*

   ....

8. *Su interés en el arte es algo impresionante.*

   ....

9. *Yo estoy muy contento también.*

....

10. *Voy a decírselo alguna vez.*

....

Exercise 17: The Answer Is "No"

Answer each question using the negative.

1. *¿Tienen hambre los niños?*

....

2. *¿Tenéis algo que decirme?*

....

3. *¿Conoces a alguien en esta fiesta?*

....

4. *¿Están aquí los mariachis?*

....

5. *¿Hay alguien en el coche?*

....

6. *¿Hay algo para beber?*

....

7. *¿Es que ustedes necesitan algo?*

....

8. *¿Y tú, también vas con nosotros?*

....

9. *¿Quién tiene algunos dulces?*

....

10. *¿Con quiénes va usted?*

....

Exercise 18: It's Either One or the Other

Add a follow-up sentence to each of the following phrases to create a negative statement that makes logical sense. For example: *Él es mecánico. No es profesor.* Note that answers will vary.

1. *El restaurante chino está en la calle Green.*

2. *Pienso que tienes razón.*

3. *María es brasileña.*

4. *El perro come poco.*

5. *Compramos frutas y vegetales en el mercado.*

6. *Los médicos escuchan música clásica.*

7. *Viajas a España todos los años.*

8. *Tenemos muchos libros.*

Exercise 19: No Way, No How!

TRACK 14

Listen to each sentence and repeat. Then, play the track again, write each sentence down, and circle the words that make it a negative statement.

1. ....

2. ....

3. ....

4. ....

5. ....

6. ....

7. ....

8. ....

9. ....

10. ....

Active and Passive Voice

A verb may be in active voice or passive voice. Active-voice verbs are tied to, and express, the action of the subject:

Yo hablo español. Hablo español.
I speak Spanish.

Passive voice drops the subject of the verb from the sentence by moving the object up in its place and substituting the active verb with the correct form of *ser* and a past participle (more about past participles in Part 7).

The passive voice works the same in English and Spanish. Here is how to turn an active-voice sentence into a passive-voice one:

María lee la lección.
Maria reads the lesson.

La lección es leída.
The lesson is read.

As you can see, the switch to passive voice makes it possible to have the lesson, and not Maria, as the subject of the sentence, even though it's the object of the verb's action. It's possible to add Maria back in by using the prepositional phrase with *por* (by):

La lección es leída por María.
The lesson is read by Maria.

Another way of using the passive voice is to incorporate the reflexive pronoun *se* (this will be covered in the Reflexive Verbs section of Part 6).

Exercise 20: Make It Passive

Rewrite the sentence using the passive voice. The correct past participle of the verb is given. For example: *Miguel escribe la carta. (escrita) La carta es escrita por Miguel.*

1. *Elena compra la chaqueta. (comprada)*

   ....

2. *El supermercado vende la comida para cocinar. (vendida)*

   ....

3. *Yo paro el coche en la calle. (parado)*

   ....

4. *Yo veo la torre. (vista)*

   ....

5. *Nosotros comprendemos esta idea. (comprendida)*

   ....

6. *Los sacerdotes hacen sacrificios. (hechos)*

   ....

7. *Nosotros escuchamos la música. (escuchada)*

   ....

8. *Los soldados nos garantizan la seguridad. (garantizada)*

   ....

9. *Nunca siento estos sentimientos. (sentidos)*

   ....

10. *Ellos beben cerveza. (bebida)*

    ....

Introduction to Verb Moods

Parts 8 and 9 will go into verb moods in detail, but an introduction is helpful to at least learn to differentiate between them. In addition to tenses, verbs are also conjugated according to mood. English and Spanish both have three moods:

Indicative mood: Used to make ordinary, objective statements. This is the most commonly used mood, particularly in English.

Subjunctive mood: Used to express statements that are in doubt or hypothetical. In the following sentence, the verb "were" is in the subjunctive mood: "If I were younger, I would be able to run quickly." The subjunctive mood is not used a lot in English, but it is common in Spanish.

Imperative mood: The mood of command. Examples: Take this one! Give me the rest! Don't put it there! Notice that in giving commands, you drop the subject "you." The same is true in Spanish, but the verb is conjugated differently.

Exercise 21: In the Mood

Determine the mood of each sentence.

1. I saw the movie yesterday. ....

2. Let's go out to the movies. ....

3. If I were the owner, I'd expand the menu. ....

4. I would love it if she were my boss. ....

5. We went yesterday. ....

6. I insist that he leave. ....

7. Turn down the volume. ....

8. I need a new car. ....

9. Please close the window. ....

10. We recommended that he fill out the form. ....

Using Ser and Estar

Both *ser* and *estar* mean "to be" in English, but they are anything but interchangeable. The generalized difference is that *ser* describes permanent state and *estar* refers to temporary condition or location.

Ser means "is" in the sense that something *is* the way it is. It's also used to describe nationality, and in combination with *de* it may be used to say where someone is from. It is also used with other permanent characteristics that describe a person's status, such as profession, religion, or family relationship.

Characteristics that are relatively permanent—that don't change from day to day—are described with *ser*. These might be physical features like eye color or height, or personality features like intelligence or kindness. Features that don't change over a short period of time, such as being young or old, are also described with *ser*. Possessive constructions in Spanish rely on *ser* to establish the relationship between the possessor and the possessed.

The one exception to the idea of *ser* being used to describe what is permanent is that this verb is employed in expressions of time—to say what day, week, month, and year it is, and also what time it is. Examples of sentences using *ser:*

Usted es alto y soy bajo.
You are tall and I am short.

Patrizio es de Inglaterra. Es inglés.
Patrizio is from England. He is English.

Angelina y Alberto son estudiantes.
Angelina and Alberto are students.

Éste es mi abuelo.
This is my grandfather.

Somos católicos.
We are Catholic.

Ellos son jóvenes.
They are young.

María es bonita.
Maria is pretty.

El libro es de Julia.
The book is Julia's.

Son las nueve de la mañana.
It's nine in the morning.

Hoy es domingo.
Today is Sunday.

Ser may be used to say where you are from, but *estar* is the verb of choice when you need to explain where you are, geographically or physically. *Estar* is sometimes translated as "to be located," but its role is not limited to indicating location. *Estar* is also the verb "to be" used to describe temporary states of being. States of boredom, tiredness, or happiness all come with the verb *estar*. This verb is also used to describe a temporary condition—being open, closed, off, etc.

Some examples:

Ella está en casa.
She is at home.

Mis padres están en México.
My parents are in Mexico.

Clara está enferma.
Clara is sick.

¿Cómo están? Estamos bien.
How are you? We're fine.

One way to understand how *ser* and *estar* differ is by comparing pairs of phrases where the only difference is the verb:

Nosotros somos aburridos.
We are boring.

Nosotros estamos aburridos.
We are bored.

In the first sentence, the adjective reflects a characteristic of the subject, "we." In the second sentence, the adjective describes the temporary mood or condition of the subject.

Ser and *estar* are also used in verbal constructions. *Ser* is used in the Spanish passive voice, and *estar* combines with a present participle to form the present progressive tense. Both of these constructions are described in other sections.

Exercise 22: To Be or Not to Be

Fill in the blank with the correct form of *ser* or *estar*.

1. *No .... verdad.*

2. *Esta semana nosotros .... en Buenos Aires.*

3. *Yo .... francés.*

4. *Hoy .... martes.*

5. *Mientras ellos .... en la calle, no saben las nuevas noticias.*

6. *Jane .... de Australia.*

7. *... las cinco y media de la tarde.*

8. *Tú .... muy cansado.*

9. *Clara, tú .... la hermana de Enrique, ¿no es así?*

10. *La tienda .... abierta hoy.*

Exercise 23: The Right "Be"

Translate each sentence.

1. I am in the train, waiting to arrive.

....

2. My mom and dad are lawyers.

   ....

3. The bank is closed.

   ....

4. Those things are theirs.

   ....

5. My grandmother is very old.

   ....

6. Rosa's dress is green and white.

   ....

7. We are very confused.

   ....

8. You (informal, singular) are very smart.

   ....

9. Carolina's eyes are blue.

   ....

10. You (informal, plural) are sad.

   ....

Putting It Together

Now let's see what you've learned.

Exercise 24: Conjugation Practice

Conjugate the following infinitives in the present tense:

1. *cantar (regular AR verb)*

   ....

   ....

   ....

2. *vivir (regular IR verb)*

   ....

   ....

   ....

3. *meter (regular ER verb)*

   ....

   ....

   ....

4. *mostrar (stem-changing verb)*

   ....

   ....

   ....

5. *coger (spelling-change verb)*

   ....

   ....

   ....

6. *tener (stem-changing, spelling-change verb)*

   ....

   ....

   ....

7. *ser (irregular verb)*

   ....

   ....

   ....

Exercise 25: A Hard Day of Work

TRACK 15

Listen to the following questions and try to answer them. Then listen to the track again and write down your answers.

1. ....

2. ....

3. ....

4. ....

5. ....

6. ....

7. ....

8. ....

9. ....

10. ....

Exercise 26: Regular or Not?

Fill in the blank with the correct form of the verb in parentheses.

1. *Usted* .... *mucho en su vida. (encontrar)*

2. *Yo no* .... *las cosas en la oscuridad sin mis gafas. (distinguir)*

3. *Ustedes no me* .... *(amar)*

4. *Nosotros* .... *las barreras. (romper)*

5. *Él* .... *su invitación. (aceptar)*

6. *Yo la* .... *amando a pesar de todo. (seguir)*

7. *Ella* .... *sus estudios el próximo día. (empezar)*

8. *Tú* .... *nuestros gastos; eres muy generoso. (cubrir)*

Exercise 27: Hear the Voice

Label whether each sentence is using the passive or active voice.

1. *La carta ya está escrita.* ....

2. *Ella es artista.* ....

3. *Yo he escrito la carta.* ....

4. *Toda la ciudad es vista.* ....

5. *Soy muy inteligente.* ....

6. *Ellos son encerrados en la cárcel.* ....

7. *El libro es muy interesante.* ....

8. *El libro es colocado aquí por el estudiante.* ....

Part 6

Verbs and Objects

Now that you've been introduced to objects and to verbs, this is your opportunity to look at them together. This part reviews verbs that take on direct objects, indirect objects, and reflexive objects.

Direct and Indirect Objects

The direct object of a sentence is the word or phrase that receives the action of a transitive verb. For example, take the sentence, "He buys ice cream." The direct object here is "ice cream."

The indirect object is generally a person that is indirectly affected by the action of the verb; it answers the question "to whom" or "for whom" an action is done. For example, in the sentence, "He buys his friend ice cream," "his friend" is the indirect object. Here is another example, using Spanish:

María le da una carta a Miguel.
Maria gives a letter to Michael.

In this sentence, *una carta* is the direct object and *a Miguel* is the indirect object.

And as explained in Part 2, direct and indirect objects may be expressed as pronouns. In Spanish, sentences with indirect objects must include an indirect object pronoun (hence the *le* in the previous example). The phrase *a Miguel* is actually optional, added for clarity; without it, the above example would translate as "Maria gives him a letter," and if we didn't know *le* referred to Michael, it could also mean "her" or "it."

As you may remember, the direct object and indirect object usually follow the verb, but when the pronouns are used, they are moved up front, in between the subject and the verb:

María se la da.
Maria gives it to him.

However, when a conjugated verb is followed by an infinitive or the present progressive (covered in Part 9), an object pronoun can be placed either before the verbs or attached to the second verb (the infinitive or present participle). For example:

Le quiero comprar unas flores para mi novia.
Quiero comprarle unas flores para mi novia.

Both mean "I want to buy some flowers for my girlfriend," and both are grammatically correct.

Exercise 1: The Object of This Lesson

Mark whether the underlined word or words in each sentence is the direct object or indirect object.

1. *Julia le escribe <u>una carta</u>.* ....

2. *Yo se lo compro <u>a ella</u>.* ....

3. *Nunca me <u>los</u> dan.* ....

4. *Voy a decir<u>les</u> la verdad.* ....

5. *<u>Lo</u> cantan en voz alta.* ....

6. *<u>Me</u> ocurre algo interesante.* ....

7. *Quiero dár<u>selas</u>.* ....

8. *Estoy aprendiéndo<u>lo</u>.* ....

Exercise 2: Objectively Speaking

TRACK 16

Listen to each sentence and repeat. Then, play the track again and write each sentence down, circling the direct object.

1. ....

2. ....

3. ....

4. ....

5. ....

6. ....

7. ....

8. ....

9. ....

10. ....

Exercise 3: Indirectly Necessary

Circle the indirect object pronouns and translate each sentence.

1. *Ella me habla en español.*

   ....

2. *María les compra dulces a sus niños.*

   ....

3. *La compañía le ofrece el trabajo a usted.*

   ....

4. *Su madre quiere traeros alguna comida.*

   ....

5. *Él se las manda a ella.*

   ....

6. *Yo se lo doy a ustedes.*

   ....

7. *Su novia no le contesta a él.*

   ....

8. *Tú me escribes cartas cada semana.*

   ....

Reflexive Verbs

Reflexive verbs are verbs that take on a specific kind of direct object pronoun—a reflexive pronoun—which refers back to the verb's subject. In English, adding "myself," "yourself," etc. to a sentence makes the verb reflexive: "I hurt myself." "She hurt herself." In the infinitive, reflexive verbs appear with –se tacked on at the end:

Common Reflexive Verbs

aburrirse	to get bored	*enfermarse*	to get sick
acostarse	to go to bed	*enojarse*	to get angry
afeitarse	to shave	*lastimarse*	to hurt oneself
alegrarse	to be happy	*lavarse*	to wash
arreglarse	to get ready	*levantarse*	to get up
bañarse	to bathe	*peinarse*	to comb
calmarse	to calm down	*ponerse*	to put on, to dress
caerse	to fall (down)	*preocuparse*	to worry
cansarse	to get tired	*probarse*	to try on
cepillarse	to brush (hair, teeth)	*quebrarse*	to break (arm, leg)
colocarse	to get a job	*quedarse*	to stay, remain
cortarse	to cut (hair, nails)	*quemarse*	to burn (oneself, one's body)
decidirse	to make up one's mind	*quitarse*	to take off (clothes)
despedirse	to say goodbye to	*romperse*	to tear (clothes), to break (arm, leg)

Common Reflexive Verbs

despertarse	to wake up	*sentarse*	to sit down
divertirse	to have a good time	*sentirse*	to feel
dormirse	to fall asleep	*sorprenderse*	to be surprised
ducharse	to take a shower	*vestirse*	to get dressed

Here's an example of how a reflexive verb is conjugated in present tense:

lavarse	to wash
me lavo	I wash (myself)
te lavas	you wash (yourself)
se lava	he/she washes (himself/herself); you wash (yourself)
nos lavamos	we wash (ourselves)
os laváis	you wash (yourselves)
se lavan	they/you wash (themselves/yourselves)

While only some Spanish verbs can be reflexive, many reflexive verbs also have non-reflexive forms. In the following, compare *lavar* and *lavarse:*

María lava el coche.
Maria washes the car.

María se lava las manos.
Maria washes her hands.

Exercise 4: Test Your Reflexes

Fill in the correct reflexive verb and pronoun:

1. Yo .... (cepillarse) los dientes todos los días.

2. *En pocos días ellos* .... *(mudarse) a California.*

3. *Nosotros no* .... *(afeitarse) ya.*

4. *Vosotros* .... *(enterarse) de la verdad.*

5. *Tú* .... *(vestirse) mal, con ropa sucia.*

6. *Ustedes no* .... *(quedarse) aquí.*

7. *Usted* .... *(alegrarse) de que todo vaya bien.*

8. *¿Yo no* .... *(acordarse) de nada?*

Exercise 5: Build Your Own Sentence

In each sentence, fill in the correct subject, choosing from one of the following answers: *yo; tú; Elena y tú; María y su hermana mayor; la abuelita.*

1. .... *se levantan a las seis de la mañana.*

2. .... *me pongo la ropa.*

3. .... *os cansáis de mis quejas.*

4. .... *se enferma mucho durante los inviernos.*

5. .... *te cepillas los dientes.*

The Impersonal Se Construction

In Spanish, the reflexive *se* constructions may be used as an equivalent of the English passive voice. (Passive voice constructions are covered in Part 5.) Compare the following:

La carta es escrita.
The letter is written.

En España se habla español.
Spanish is spoken in Spain.

In the first example, both English and Spanish sentences are written in passive voice. In the second example, the English passive voice is rendered as a reflexive *se* construction in Spanish.

Exercise 6: Passive Constructions

The following sentences rely on the impersonal *se* construction to indicate passive voice. Translate them into English, keeping in mind that a word-for-word translation won't always work best.

1. *Aquí se venden frutas y vegetales.*

   ....

2. *Se dice que la verdad siempre gana.*

   ....

3. *No se come carne de vaca en India.*

   ....

4. *No se puede usar el secador del pelo en la bañera.*

   ....

5. *Se ven los elefantes en el zoológico.*

   ....

Exercise 7: The Big Date

TRACK 17

Listen to each sentence and repeat. Note that each of these sentences includes a reflexive verb.

Transitive and Intransitive Verbs

Transitive verbs require a direct object to form a complete sentence. For example, *yo amo* (I love) requires a direct object—what or whom I love—to be complete. Transitive verbs form a "transition" between the subject and direct object.

Intransitive verbs are just the opposite. These verbs do not refer to—or need—a direct object. For example, the verb *dormir* (to sleep) doesn't make sense with a direct object (you can't "sleep" something):

La chica duerme.
The girl sleeps.

If you want to elaborate on the intransitive verb, you can add a prepositional phrase:

La chica duerme en su cuarto.
The girl sleeps in her room.

Some verbs can only be transitive. Others can only be intransitive. However, some can be either, depending on the context:

La chica estudia para el examen.
The girl studies for the exam. (intransitive)

La chica estudia el impacto de la sequía.
The girl studies the impact of drought. (transitive)

Exercise 8: In Transit

TRACK 18

Listen to each sentence and repeat. Then listen to the track again, write down each sentence, and see if you can figure out whether the verb in the sentence is used transitively or intransitively.

1. ....

2. ....

3. ....

4. ....

5. ....

6. ....

7. ....

8. ....

9. ....

10. ....

Exercise 9: Label That Verb

For each verb, label whether it can be used in a sentence as a transitive verb, an intransitive verb, or both.

1. *nadar (to swim)*   ....
2. *tener (to have)*   ....
3. *salir (to leave)*   ....
4. *correr (to run)*   ....
5. *oler (to smell)*   ....
6. *tomar (to take, to play, to drink)*   ....
7. *ver (to see)*   ....
8. *viajar (to travel)*   ....

Putting It Together

Complete these exercises without referring to the book or any outside sources.

Exercise 10: Look for the Clues

Fill in the missing piece in each sentence and label it as a direct object or an indirect object. Answers will vary.

1. *Ella limpia* ....

2. *Le voy a regalar las rosas* ....

3. *Tomamos* .... *en el desayuno.*

4. *Nosotros les escribimos mensajes* ....

5. *No le metas miedo* ....

Exercise 11: Reflexive Challenge

In this exercise, you are given two infinitive choices—one is reflexive and the other is not. Figure out which you should use and then fill in the appropriate form of the verb.

1. *Patricio no* .... *(sentir / sentirse) bien hoy.*

2. *Tú* .... *(levantar / levantarse) las manos cuando hablas.*

3. *Ustedes* .... *(dormir / dormirse) en la cama.*

4. *Nosotros no* .... *(lastimar / lastimarse) a ustedes, ¿verdad?*

5. *Yo* .... *(divertir / divertirse) a los niños con chistes.*

6. *Mariana* .... *(colocar / colocarse) los libros en el estante.*

7. *Vosotros* .... *(sentar / sentarse) en el sofá.*

8. *Usted* .... *(decidir / decidirse) demasiado rápido.*

9. *Los empleados* .... *(poner / ponerse) el dinero en el banco.*

10. *Yo* .... *(duchar / ducharse) al menos una vez al día.*

Exercise 12: Translate It!

Translate each sentence. Note that each one uses a reflexive verb.

1. *Miguel se levanta.*

   ....

2. *Yo me visto para la ocasión.*

   ....

3. *Nosotros nos caemos en la nieve.*

   ....

4. *Ella se quemó el brazo.*

   ....

5. *Usted se prueba la camisa.*

   ....

6. *Vosotros os arregláis para la fiesta.*

   ....

7. *Ellos se enojan cuando no entienden la lección.*

   ....

8. *Tú te sientes muy bien.*

   ....

Exercise 13: Getting Up

Describe your morning routine, using as many reflexive verbs as you can.

....

....

....

....

....

Part 7

Past, Future, Conditional, and Perfect Tenses

What happened? What will happen? What might have happened? You'll be able to answer these types of questions once you master this section. In addition, Part 7 covers the five perfect tenses—tenses that indicate a completion of an action. In English, we form perfect tenses by using a form of the verb "to have" followed by the past participle. In Spanish, the equivalent of "to have" is *haber*.

Preterite Past

The preterite is one of the two main past tenses. The tense is used for actions that occurred—and were completed—in the past:

Yo terminé el trabajo ayer.
I finished the work yesterday.

The following are preterite conjugations of AR, ER, and IR verbs, as exemplified by verbs *hablar* (to speak), *beber* (to drink), and *asistir* (to attend). As you can see, ER and IR verbs have identical endings in the preterite.

AR Verbs: hablar (to speak)

*yo habl**é*** (I spoke)	*nosotros/nosotras habl**amos*** (we spoke)
*tú habl**aste*** (you spoke)	*vosotros/vosotras habl**asteis*** (you spoke)
*él/ella/Ud. habl**ó*** (he/she/you spoke)	*ellos/ellas/Uds. habl**aron*** (they/you spoke)

ER Verbs: beber (to drink)

*yo beb**í*** (I drank)	*nosotros/nosotras beb**imos*** (we drank)
*tú beb**iste*** (you drank)	*vosotros/vosotras beb**isteis*** (you drank)
*él/ella/Ud. beb**ió*** (he/she/you drank)	*ellos/ellas/Uds. beb**ieron*** (they/you drank)

IR Verbs: asistir (to attend)

*yo asist**í*** (I attended)	*nosotros/nosotras asist**imos*** (we attended)
*tú asist**iste*** (you attended)	*vosotros/vosotras asist**eis*** (you attended)
*él/ella/Ud. asist**ió*** (he/she/you attended)	*ellos/ellas/Uds. asist**ieron*** (they/you attended)

Here are some verbs that are regular in the preterite:

abandonar	to abandon	*hablar*	to speak
aceptar	to accept	*fumar*	to smoke
acuchillar	to cut up (with a knife)	*lavar*	to wash
adaptar	to adapt	*llevar*	to take, to wear
adoptar	to adopt	*mandar*	to order
amar	to love	*marchar*	to walk
ayudar	to help	*mirar*	to look, to watch
bajar	to go down	*montar*	to climb
bañar	to bathe	*nadar*	to swim
besar	to kiss	*necesitar*	to need
cambiar	to change	*olvidar*	to forget
cantar	to sing	*parar*	to stop
comprar	to buy	*preparar*	to prepare
dejar	to leave, to let	*quedar*	to stay
entrar	to enter	*tirar*	to pull, to draw
esperar	to wait, to hope	*tomar*	to take, to drink
expresar	to express	*trabajar*	to work
ganar	to win, to earn	*viajar*	to travel
gastar	to spend, to waste		

Additionally, AR and ER verbs that have an e > ie or o > ue stem change in the present tense remain regular in the preterite. These verbs include:

apretar	to grip	*entender*	to understand
ascender	to go up	*gobernar*	to govern
atravesar	to cross	*pensar*	to think

cerrar	to close	*perder*	to lose
defender	to defend	*recomendar*	to recommend
descender	to go down	*sentar*	to sit down
encender	to light		

However, IR verbs that have an e > i or e > ie change in the present tense do have an e > i change in the third-person forms (both singular and plural). For example, take a look at the conjugations of the verb *pedir* (to ask for, to request):

pedí	*pedimos*
pediste	*pedisteis*
pidió	*pidieron*

To refresh your memory, other IR verbs in this category include the following:

gemir	to moan	*seguir*	to follow
impedir	to prevent	*sentir*	to feel
medir	to measure	*servir*	to serve
mentir	to lie	*vestir*	to dress
preferir	to prefer		

Similarly, IR verbs that include an o > u change in the present have an o > u third-person irregularity in the preterite. Take a look at *dormir* (to sleep):

dormí	*dormimos*
dormiste	*dormisteis*
durmió	*durmieron*

There is also a group of verbs that undergo a spelling change in the first person singular *(yo)* form of the preterite. These are verbs with a stem that ends in c, g, or z.

In AR verbs with a stem ending in a hard "c," the change is c > qu, like in *sacar* (to take out):

saqué	*sacamos*
sacaste	*sacasteis*
sacó	*sacaron*

In AR verbs with a stem ending in "g," a "u" is added to the ending of the *yo* form. For example, the following is a conjugation of *llegar* (to arrive):

llegué	*llegamos*
llegaste	*llegasteis*
llegó	*llegaron*

Finally, in AR verbs with a stem ending in "z," the stem ending changes to "c," as in *abrazar* (to hug):

abracé	*abrazamos*
abrazaste	*abrazasteis*
abrazó	*abrazaron*

Spelling changes also occur in ER and IR verbs that have a stem ending in a vowel, such as the *–uir* verbs. The "i" at the end changes to a "y" in the third-person conjugations (both singular and plural). For example, take a look at the conjugation of *huir* (to run away):

huí	*huimos*
huiste	*huisteis*
huyó	*huyeron*

Other verbs with a stem ending in a vowel include *creer* (to believe), *leer* (to read), *poseer* (to own), *oír* (to hear), and *desoír* (to ignore). These verbs also have an "i" to "y" change in the third person. In addition, they require extra accent marks. For example, here's how to conjugate *creer* (to believe):

creí	creímos
creíste	creísteis
creyó	creyeron

An entire set of verbs—including AR, ER, and IR verbs—have an irregular stem and modified preterite endings in the preterite. The endings are:

e	imos
iste	isteis
o	ieron

Note that these endings are similar to the ER and IR verb endings, except for the *yo* form and the absence of accent marks in some of the forms. The modified stems are:

infinitive	preterite stem	translation
andar	anduv–	to walk
caber	cup–	to fit
decir	dij–	to say
estar	estuv–	to be
hacer	hic– (hiz–)	to do
poder	pud–	to be able to
poner	pus–	to put
producir	produj–	to produce
querer	quis–	to want
saber	sup–	to know
tener	tuv–	to have
traer	traj–	to bring

venir	vin–	to arrive

For example, here's the conjugation of the verb *producir:*

produje	*produjimos*
produjiste	*produjisteis*
produjo	*produjeron*

Other verbs ending in *–ucir* will follow the same irregularity as *producir.* Some of these verbs may also follow additional stem and spelling change forms as well. For example, *hacer* (to do) becomes *hizo* in the third-person singular conjugation.

Some verbs are simply irregular in the preterite:

dar (to give)

di	*dimos*
diste	*disteis*
dio	*dieron*

ver (to see)

vi	*vimos*
viste	*visteis*
veio	*vieron*

ser (to be) and ir (to go)

fui	*fuimos*
fuiste	*fuisteis*
fue	*fueron*

?rcise 1: Memorizing Preterite Endings

Listen to and repeat the preterite-tense conjugations of three regular verbs, *hablar* (to speak), *beber* (to drink), and *asistir* (to attend).

TRACK 19

Exercise 2: Choose or Lose

Choose the correct translation for each.

1. *adaptaron (they adapted, we adapted, she adapted)*

2. *pidió (he asked for, we asked for, I asked for)*

3. *tuve (I had, we had, you had)*

4. *llevó (I wore, we wore, you wore)*

5. *escribió (we wrote, they wrote, he wrote)*

6. *fuiste (I went, he was, you went)*

7. *comisteis (they ate, we ate, you ate)*

8. *tomé (you took, I took, he took)*

9. *oímos (I heard, he heard, we heard)*

10. *durmieron (he slept, you slept, we slept)*

Exercise 3: What's Done Is Done

Fill in the correct form for the given verb for each sentence.

1. *Nosotros* .... *la televisión. (mirar)*

2. *Ustedes* .... *sandías en el mercado. (vender)*

3. *Enrique* .... *con Elena ayer. (hablar)*

4. *Yo* .... *las maletas al camarero. (dar)*

5. *Tú* .... *en conducir el coche. (insistir)*

6. *El señor Ochoa y su esposa* .... *a su vecino. (creer)*

7. *Vosotros* .... *que ella no estuvo muy contenta. (sentir)*

8. *Yo* .... *en la casa y cerré la puerta. (entrar)*

9. *Usted* .... *admitir la verdad. (omitir)*

10. *Marina* .... *que nunca volvería a aquel lugar. (decir)*

Imperfect Past

The imperfect is another tense used to refer to the past. It's used to describe ongoing past actions, or actions that occurred regularly:

En los fines de semana, visitábamos la playa.
On weekends, we used to go to the beach.

The imperfect tense can also be used to talk about the time or date when a certain event takes place. For example:

Era diciembre cuando nosotros vimos la nieve por primera vez.
It was December when we first saw the snow.

Conjugating verbs in the imperfect past is very straightforward. You simply drop the infinitive ending and add the imperfect ending:

AR Verbs

–aba	–ábamos
–abas	–abais
–aba	–aban

ER and IR Verbs

–ía	–íamos
–ías	–íais
–ía	–ían

The only irregular verbs in the imperfect past are:

ir (to go)

iba	*íbamos*
ibas	*ibais*
iba	*iban*

ser (to be)

era	*éramos*
eras	*erais*
era	*eran*

ver (to see)

veía	*veíamos*
veías	*veíais*
veía	*veían*

Exercise 4: Complete Conjugations

Conjugate each verb in the imperfect past tense.

hablar (to speak):

....

....

....

beber (to drink):

....

....

....

asistir (to attend):

....

....

....

Exercise 5: Imperfect Endings, Perfectly

Choose the correct translation for each verb.

1. *fumaba (we smoked, they smoked, I smoked)*

2. *cometía (we committed, he committed, you committed)*

3. *iba (we went, you went, they went)*

4. *dormían (we slept, he slept, they slept)*

5. *vendía (you sold, we sold, they sold)*

6. *pagabais (we paid, he paid, you paid)*

7. *leías (we read, he read, you read)*

8. *veías (we saw, he saw, you saw)*

9. *traducía (she translated, we translated, they translated)*

10. *trabajábamos (they worked, we worked, you worked)*

Exercise 6: It Used to Be . . .

Fill in the correct form for the given verb for each sentence.

1. .... *las dos cuando la clase terminó. (ser)*

2. *Ella siempre me* .... *miedo. (dar)*

3. *Nosotros nunca* .... *la oportunidad de hablar con él. (tener)*

4. *Yo* .... *por el camino cada día. (andar)*

5. *Ustedes* .... *pagar la renta. (prometer)*

6. *El hombre* .... *del aburrimiento. (morir)*

7. *Tú y yo* .... *a la discoteca los sábados por la noche. (ir)*

8. *Cuando era joven, usted* .... *los dulces baratos. (comprar)*

9. *Vosotros* .... *todo lo posible para evitar la separación. (hacer)*

10. *En aquellos días, tú* .... *a bailar con la Señora Serrano. (aprender)*

Future Tense

El futuro is used to express actions that will take place in the future. The future tense conjugations are the same for AR, ER, and IR verbs:

hablar (to speak)

*hablar**é***	*hablar**emos***
*hablar**ás***	*hablar**éis***
*hablar**á***	*hablar**án***

beber (to drink)

beber**é**	beber**emos**
beber**ás**	beber**éis**
beber**á**	beber**án**

asistir (to attend)

asistir**é**	asistir**emos**
asistir**ás**	asistir**éis**
asistir**á**	asistir**án**

The only irregularity in this verb tense is that a few verbs have an irregular stem change. All the endings remain regular.

Irregular Future Verbs		
infinitive	**future stem**	**translation**
caber	cabr–	to fit
decir	dir–	to say, to tell
haber	habr–	to have
hacer	har–	to do, to make
oír	oir–	to hear
poder	podr–	to be able
poner	pondr–	to put, to place
querer	querr–	to want
reír	reir–	to laugh
saber	sabr–	to know
salir	saldr–	to leave
tener	tendr–	to have

valer	valdr–	to cost
venir	vendr–	to come

Después de la clase, ya sabré conjugar los verbos en el futuro.
After class, I'll already know how to conjugate verbs in the future (tense).

The future tense may also be used for guessing or hypothesizing about actions in the present tense. For example:

Ellos estarán enojados.
They will be angry. They are probably angry.

This example has two possible translations, depending on context; in the second translation, the future tense is used to express uncertainty.

Exercise 7: Future Actions

Fill in the correct form of the given verb.

1. *Nosotras* .... *a Europa en otoño. (viajar)*

2. *Yo* .... *la puerta para ustedes. (abrir)*

3. *Ella* .... *por la ventana en un momento. (mirar)*

4. *Vosotros* .... *los platos en la lavadora después de comer. (poner)*

5. *Usted* .... *el riesgo de perder. (correr)*

6. *Tú me* .... *las notas a mí más tarde. (dar)*

7. *Ellos* .... *buenos padres para el bebé. (ser)*

8. *Yo* .... *la respuesta a todos ustedes. (decir)*

9. *Ellos* .... *lo que hacer sin usted. (decidir)*

10. *Él* .... *mejor con el uso del audífono. (oír)*

Exercise 8: Back to the Future

Rewrite each sentence so that it is in the future tense.

1. *Los músicos podían tocar sonatas.*

   ....

2. *¿Quiere usted comer el desayuno?*

   ....

3. *Marilena generalmente estaba en casa antes que yo.*

   ....

4. *Cuando te conocí, ya sabía bailar.*

   ....

5. *Tú no trabajaste ayer.*

   ....

6. *La torta consiste en harina, huevos, y otros ingredientes.*

   ....

7. *La semana pasada, yo aprendí los verbos irregulares.*

   ....

8. *Nosotros tuvimos la oportunidad de conocer a una estrella del teatro.*

   ....

9. *Ustedes cantan muy bien.*

   ....

10. *Vosotros dormís todo el día.*

    ....

Exercise 9: In Twenty Years

TRACK 20

Listen to the questions and try to answer them. Then listen to the track again and write down your answers.

1. ....

2. ....

3. ....

4. ....

5. ....

6. ....

7. ....

8. ....

9. ....

10. ....

Conditional Tense

The conditional tense in English is expressed with the verb "would," but in Spanish, it's a simple tense that works similarly to the future tense, except with different endings. The following are the conditional-tense endings; note that verbs with the irregular stem in the future tense have the same irregularity in the conditional.

hablar (to speak)

hablaría	*hablaríamos*
hablarías	*hablaríais*
hablaría	*hablarían*

beber (to drink)

*beber**ía***	*beber**íamos***
*beber**ías***	*beber**íais***
*beber**ía***	*beber**ían***

asistir (to attend)

*asistir**ía***	*asistir**íamos***
*asistir**ías***	*asistir**íais***
*asistir**ía***	*asistir**ían***

The conditional refers to the potential of something that would happen on the condition of something else taking place:

Me gustaría descansar.
I would like to rest.

Podría ser mejor.
It could be better.

The conditional is also used to express guessing or conjecture in the past tense. For example:

Ellos estarían enojados.
They would be angry. They were probably angry.

Exercise 10: Potentially Right

Choose the correct translation for each verb.

1. *gustarían (I would like, we would like, they would like)*

2. *metería (you would put, we would put, they would put)*

3. *salía (I would leave, we would leave, they would leave)*

4. *comeríamos (I would eat, you would eat, we would eat)*

5. *decidíais (I would decide, you would decide, they would decide)*

6. *cabría (you would fit, it would fit, they would fit)*

7. *nadarías (I would swim, you would swim, we would swim)*

8. *bañarían (I would bathe, you would bathe, we would bathe)*

9. *vendría (I would come, we would come, they would come)*

10. *escribiríamos (I would write, you would write, we would write)*

Exercise 11: A Tricky Condition

Fill in the blanks with the verb conjugated in the conditional tense.

1. *Si pudiera, yo* .... *adentro. (ir)*

2. *Ellas* .... *la pregunta otra vez. (repetir)*

3. *Él* .... *lo que le gusta. (hacer)*

4. *Usted* .... *perdón si él lo hubiera hecho primero.* *(pedir)*

5. *Yo* .... *la puerta; no estoy segura. (cerrar)*

6. *Si salierais, vosotros* .... *vuestro lugar en la fila.* *(perder)*

7. *Si hiciera frío, tú te* .... *con la manta. (cubrir)*

8. *Usted* .... *aquí y no a su propia casa. (volver)*

9. *Estos vestidos* .... *más con camisetas a juego. (valer)*

10. *En este lugar nosotros* .... *más tarde. (almorzar)*

Present Perfect

The rest of Part 7 covers the perfect tenses. Each perfect tense has two verbs: the auxiliary verb haber and a past participle. Forming a past participle from an infinitive is easy: drop the ending and add *–ado* for AR verbs or *–ido* for ER and IR verbs:

infinitive	past participle
hablar	hablado
beber	bebido
asistir	asistido

Only a few verbs have irregular past participle forms:

infinitive	past participle	English
abrir	abierto	opened
caer	caído	fallen
creer	creído	believed
cubrir	cubierto	covered
decir	dicho	said, told
descubrir	descubierto	discovered
deshacer	deshecho	undone
escribir	escrito	written
hacer	hecho	done, made
imponer	impuesto	imposed
imprimir	impreso	printed
ir	ido	gone
leer	leído	read
morir	muerto	died

infinitive	past participle	English
oír	oído	heard
poner	puesto	put
rehacer	rehecho	redone, remade
reír	reído	laughed
resolver	resuelto	resolved, solved
romper	roto	broken
traer	traído	brought
ver	visto	seen
volver	vuelto	returned

The most common of the perfect tenses is the present perfect, and it uses the present-tense form of the auxiliary verb *haber*. The present perfect is used to talk about actions that occurred in the recent past and may continue into the present. In English, the equivalent relies on the verb "to have": *he hecho* (I have done); *hemos visto* (we have seen); and so on.

Here are the present-tense conjugations of *haber*:

he	hemos
has	habéis
ha	han

Exercise 12: The Participle Form

Fill in the past participle of each verb.

1. *pensar* ....
2. *decidir* ....
3. *hacer* ....
4. *ganar* ....

5. *abrir*   ....

6. *comer*   ....

7. *decir*   ....

8. *pagar*   ....

9. *vender*   ....

10. *escribir*   ....

Exercise 13: A Perfect Conjugation

Fill in the blank with the correct present perfect form of the given verb.

1. *Yo* .... *la puerta. (abrir)*

2. *Usted* .... *mucho. (trabajar)*

3. *Vosotros* .... *tantos libros. (leer)*

4. *Cristina* .... *los zapatos afuera del dormitorio. (poner)*

5. *Tú* .... *arriba antes. (subir)*

6. *Ustedes* .... *el perro al veterinario. (traer)*

7. *Los camareros* .... *a los clientes. (servir)*

8. *Nosotros ya* .... *esta canción. (cantar)*

9. *Yo* .... *tres años en Nueva York. (pasar)*

10. *Pedro* .... *esas cosas muchas veces. (ver)*

Pluperfect Tense

The pluperfect tense, sometimes called the past perfect, describes an action that occurred before another past-tense action. In English, the tense uses the past tense of "to have" plus the past participle: "I had left," "she had started." In Spanish, the imperfect form of *haber* is used. First, a review of the past-perfect conjugations of *haber*:

había	*habíamos*
habías	*habíais*
había	*habían*

Now, here are some examples:

Carolina no había terminado de lavarse cuando se acabó el agua caliente.
Carolina hadn't finished washing when the hot water run out.

Nosotros habíamos leído esta novela en la escuela secundaria.
We had read this novel in high school.

Exercise 14: Past and Perfect

Choose the correct translation for each pluperfect verb pair.

1. *habían vuelto (I had returned, we had returned, they had returned)*

2. *habíais sorprendido (they had surprised, we had surprised, you had surprised)*

3. *había andado (we had walked, they had walked, I had walked)*

4. *habías ido (he had gone, you had gone, I had gone)*

5. *habíamos salido (we had left, they had left, she had left)*

6. *había escuchado (we had listened, I had listened, they had listened)*

7. *había enseñado (we had taught, you had taught, they had taught)*

8. *había dicho (they had said, we had said, I had said)*

9. *habías fumado (I had smoked, we had smoked, you had smoked)*

10. *habían mirado (I had watched, you had watched, we had watched)*

Exercise 15: Had to Be Right

Fill in the blank with the correct pluperfect form of the given verb.

1. *Yo me* .... *antes que ellos me llamaran. (levantar)*

2. *Ustedes* .... *allá. (estar)*

3. *Marco no* .... *en Dios hasta el accidente. (creer)*

4. *Verónica les* .... *que la llevaran con ellos. (pedir)*

5. *Nosotros les* .... *a ellos organizar una fiesta en el apartamento. (prohibir)*

6. *Aquel día, vosotros* .... *en la casa por la ventana. (entrar)*

7. *Ellos no lo* .... *el año pasado. (aprender)*

8. *Tú no lo* .... *a tiempo. (decir)*

9. *Las flores* .... *mucha fragrancia. (tener)*

10. *Usted nos* .... *cierto interés. (mostrar)*

Preterite Perfect

The preterite perfect is used less often than the past perfect. It is similar to the past perfect—it refers to actions that had occurred before other actions that occurred in the past. However, in the case of the preterite perfect, the action had to have happened just prior to the main event. The preterite perfect is generally accompanied by words like *apenas* (scarcely), *en cuanto* (as soon as), and *cuando* (when).

The preterite perfect uses preterite conjugations of the verb *haber* as the auxiliary verb:

hube	*hubimos*
hubiste	*hubisteis*
hubo	*hubieron*

Él apenas hubo comido cuando oyó el ruido afuera.
He had barely finished eating when he heard the noise outside.

En cuanto hube rendido el examen, regresé a casa.
As soon I had taken the exam, I returned home.

Exercise 16: In the Distant Past

Choose the correct translation for each preterite perfect verb pair.

1. *hubimos viajado (I had traveled, you had traveled, we had traveled)*

2. *hubieron muerto (you had died, we had died, they had died)*

3. *hube resuelto (I had resolved, she had resolved, they have resolved)*

4. *hubiste ido (I have gone, you had gone, they have gone)*

5. *hubisteis escrito (I had written, you had written, we had written)*

6. *hubo demostrado (I had demonstrated, you had demonstrated, they had demonstrated)*

7. *hubieron impuesto (I had imposed, you had imposed, they had imposed)*

8. *hubo traído (I had brought, he had brought, we had brought)*

9. *hube concedido (I had conceded, she had conceded, we had conceded)*

10. *hubo amado (I had loved, she had loved, we had loved)*

Future Perfect

The future perfect uses the future tense conjugations of *haber* along with the past participle. This tense can be used to discuss an event or action that will have happened before another event, action, or particular point in the future. Here are the future tense conjugations of *haber,* followed by some examples:

habré	*habremos*
habrás	*habréis*
habrá	*habrán*

Tú habrás completado el libro en tres horas.
You will have completed the book in three hours.

Yo habré preparado la torta antes que ellos lleguen.
I will have prepared the cake before they will arrive.

Exercise 17: In the Perfect Future

Choose the correct translation for each future perfect verb pair.

1. *habrán terminado (I will have finished, we will have finished, they will have finished)*

2. *habrá ocurrido (I will have occurred, it will have occurred, they will have occurred)*

3. *habréis bañado (I will have bathed, you will have bathed, they will have bathed)*

4. *habremos descrito (he will have described, we will have described, they will have described)*

5. *habrás traído (I will have brought, you will have brought, they will have brought)*

6. *habré comprendido (I will have understood, she will have understood, we will have understood)*

7. *habrán esperado (I will have waited, you will have waited, we will have waited)*

THE EVERYTHING SPANISH PRACTICE BOOK

8. *habré ido (I will have gone, he will have gone, they will have gone)*

9. *habrás barrido (I will have swept, you will have swept, we will have swept)*

10. *habrá pagado (I will have paid, you will have paid, they will have paid)*

Exercise 18: Will and Will Have

Fill in the blank with the correct future perfect form of the given verb.

1. *Mañana Mauricio* .... *su ropa. (lavar)*

2. *Usted* .... *a Madrid en marzo. (volver)*

3. *Yo* .... *en frente del café. (parar)*

4. *Vosotros* .... *el sonido. (oír)*

5. *A ciento veinte millas por hora, el coche* .... *la velo-cidad máxima. (exceder)*

6. *Nosotros no lo* .... *. (permitir)*

7. *Los empleados nos* .... *las mercancías. (enviar)*

8. *A ti te* .... *correr después de mucha práctica. (gustar)*

9. *Yo lo* .... *en el banco. (poner)*

10. *Ustedes* .... *en no cambiarlo. (insistir)*

Conditional Perfect

The conditional perfect describes actions that didn't take place, but would have if a particular condition had been met: "she would have left," "she would have won." Here are the conditional tense conjugations of the verb haber, plus some examples:

habría	habríamos
habrías	habríais
habría	habrían

Exercise 19: The Perfect Condition

Translate each sentence.

1. *Yo no le habría contestado.*

   ....

2. *Pedro la habría ayudado a ella de todas maneras.*

   ....

3. *Vosotros habríais abierto todas las ventanas.*

   ....

4. *Usted habría bebido todo el jugo.*

   ....

5. *Catalina no los habría conocido aquí.*

   ....

6. *Nosotros no habríamos tomado el ultimo pedazo.*

   ....

7. *Tú habrías escrito todo el ensayo aquella noche.*

   ....

8. *Ustedes habrían cosido mucha ropa.*

   ....

9. *Yo me habría bañado antes.*

   ....

10. *Los soldados habrían subido a tiempo.*

    ....

Exercise 20: Answers, Unconditionally

Choose the correct translation for each conditional perfect verb pair.

1. *habría tenido (I would have had, we would have had, they would have had)*

2. *habríamos impreso (she would have printed, we would have printed, they would have printed)*

3. *habría resuelto (he would have resolved, we would have resolved, they would have resolved)*

4. *habríais prometido (we would have promised, you would have promised, they would have promised)*

5. *habría rehecho (you would have remade, we would have remade, they would have remade)*

6. *habrías compensado (we would have compensated, you would have compensated, they would have compensated)*

7. *habríamos resuelto (it would have resolved, we would have resolved, they would have resolved)*

8. *habrían ganado (I would have won, we would have won, you would have won)*

9. *habrían perdido (I would have lost, we would have lost, they would have lost)*

10. *habría vuelto (I would have returned, we would have returned, they would have returned)*

Putting It Together

Now let's see what you've learned!

Exercise 21: Lost in Time, Lost in Thought

TRACK 21

Listen to each sentence and repeat. Then listen to the track again, write down each sentence, and identify the verb tense of the verb *pensar.*

1. ....

2. ....

3. ....

4. ....

5. ....

6. ....

7. ....

8. ....

9. ....

10. ....

Exercise 22: Two Pasts, One Answer

Choose the correct conjugation of the verb or verbs in parentheses; choose between the preterite and imperfect tense.

1. *¿(Usted)* .... *(descansar) un rato?*

2. *Hace unos días que nosotros* .... *(regresar) de las vacaciones.*

3. *Yo nunca* .... *(terminar) de hacer preguntas.*

4. *Generalmente ustedes* .... *(caminar) a casa.*

5. *Ellos* .... *(pensar) encontrarla en el parque, pero*

   Lisa no .... *(llegar) allá a la hora predeterminada.*

6. *Mientras mi padre* .... *(cortar) el césped, mi madre*

   .... *(cocinar) los bistecs.*

7. *Ya vosotros le* .... *(contar) a su madre toda la historia.*

8. *La clase se* .... *(acabar) a las dos.*

9. *Tú* .... *(estar) escribiendo una carta cuando ella* .... *(llamar) por teléfono.*

Exercise 23: Lost in Time

Label the tense of each of the following verbs.

1. *comerán* ....

2. *vivieron* ....

3. *he hecho* ....

4. *podrá* ....

5. *escribiríamos* ....

6. *amaba* ....

7. *dio* ....

8. *habíais pedido* ....

9. *habría entrado* ....

10. *habrán vendido* ....

Exercise 24: Haber Revisited

For the perfect tenses to come naturally, you'll need to know all the corresponding conjugations of *haber*. Fill in the correct conjugations for each tense.

1. Present

....

....

....

2. Past

....

....

....

3. Preterite

....

....

....

4. Future

....

....

....

5. Conditional

....

....

....

Part 8

Subjunctive and Imperative Moods

The verb tenses covered to this point have all been in the indicative mood. The indicative is used to express objective statements. It is the most common verb mood used in both Spanish and English. The two other verbal moods in both Spanish and English are the subjunctive and the imperative. Subjunctive mood is used for expressions that are potential or uncertain. The imperative, also called the command mood, is for making direct commands.

The Present Subjunctive

The subjunctive mood may be used to express a feeling, opinion, or attitude—to say how things may be as opposed to how they really are.

Present subjunctive conjugations are similar to the present indicative tense (covered in Part 5), with some key differences. Most significantly, the endings are reversed: AR verbs have endings beginning with "e," and ER and IR verbs have endings that start with "a." Another difference is that the *yo* and *él/ella/usted* forms are the same. Here are some examples:

hablar (to speak)

hable	*hablemos*
hables	*habléis*
hable	*hablen*

beber (to drink)

beba	*bebamos*
bebas	*bebáis*
beba	*beban*

asistir (to attend)

asista	*asistamos*
asistas	*asistáis*
asista	*asistan*

In the majority of cases, the stem used in the subjunctive is the same as the *yo* form of the present indicative. So if a verb is irregular in the *yo* form of the present indicative, it has the same stem irregularity in all the conjugations of the present subjunctive. For example, the *yo* present indicative form of the verb *tener* (to have) is *tengo*. Therefore, the stem *teng*– is used as the stem for all the present subjunctive conjugations:

*teng**a***	*teng**amos***
*teng**as***	*teng**áis***
*teng**a***	*teng**an***

The stem remains the same in all six conjugations, and the subjunctive endings are regular.

Exercise 1: At the Root

For each verb, write down the stem which would be used in the present subjunctive conjugations.

1. *comprar* ....

2. *describir* ....

3. *prometer* ....

4. *concluir* ....

5. *venir* ....

6. *deber* ....

7. *repetir* ....

8. *caer* ....

Exercise 2: A Subjunctive Matter

Fill in the correct form of the given verb for each sentence.

1. *Le contaré la historia mientras usted me .... a lavar los platos. (ayudar)*

2. *Es necesario que vosotros .... a los culpables. (coger)*

3. *Espero que tú ya los .... a ellos. (conocer)*

4. *Ellos me aconsejan que yo .... con mis padres para ahorrar el dinero. (vivir)*

5. *Vosotros dudáis que nosotros........................... el ruido. (oír)*

6. *Mis padres me exigen que yo* .... *italiano antes del viaje. (aprender)*

7. *Ustedes necesitan que ellos* .... *a la escuela por la puerta detrás de la cafetería. (entrar)*

8. *Tenemos dudas que las maletas* .... *en el maletero del coche. (caber)*

Irregular Present Subjunctive Verbs

There are three groups of present subjunctive irregularities. The first group uses the *yo* form of the present indicative as its model, but only in four of the six conjugations—the *nosotros* and *vosotros* forms either retain the infinitive's stem or undergo a different stem change altogether.

This group includes some AR and ER verbs that experience a stem change (e > ie, o >ue) in the *yo* form of the present indicative. For example, look at the following conjugation:

pensar (to think)

piense	*pensemos*
pienses	*penséis*
piense	*piensen*

Other e > ie verbs that follow the same pattern in the present subjunctive are *atravesar* (to cross), *cerrar* (to close), *defender* (to defend), *encender* (to light), *gobernar* (to govern), *perder* (to lose), *querer* (to want), and *sentar* (to sit).

AR and ER verbs with the o > ue stem change follow the same pattern. For example:

volver (to return)

vuelva	*volvamos*
vuelvas	*volváis*
vuelva	*vuelvan*

Other o > ue verbs that follow the same pattern in the present subjunctive are *contar* (to count, to tell), *costar* (to cost), *doler* (to hurt), *mostrar* (to show), *poder* (to be able to), *recordar* (to remember), and *volar* (to fly).

Stem-changing IR verbs are a little different. For the *nosotros* and *vosotros* forms, the stem vowel changes as follows: e > i, o > u. For example:

dormir (to sleep)

duerma	*durmamos*
duermas	*durmáis*
duerma	*duerman*

Others that follow the same pattern are *mentir* (to lie), *morir* (to die), *preferir* (to prefer), and *sentir* (to feel).

The second group of irregular verbs undergoes a spelling change to retain stem pronunciation. The letters involved in the modification are "c," "g," and "z," and they are found at the end of the stem, where their interaction with the endings results in the change. When you're conjugating an AR verb in the present subjunctive, the "e" in the endings requires the following changes:

c > qu   **g > gu**   **z > c**

For example:

sacar (to take out)

saque	*saquemos*
saques	*saquéis*
saque	*saquen*

pagar (to pay)

pague	*paeguemos*
pagues	*paguéis*
pague	*paguen*

cazar (to hunt)

cace	cacemos
caces	cacéis
cace	cacen

This pattern will hold true for verbs ending in –car, –gar, and –zar. However, if there is a spelling change in one of the vowels of such a verb, like in *empezar* (to begin), you must make both changes:

empiece	empecemos
empieces	empecéis
empiece	empiecen

The third group of irregular verbs in the present subjunctive has stems that are unique to this tense. The following verbs have an irregular stem but regular endings:

infinitive	present-subjunctive stem	yo form
haber (to have)	hay–	haya
ir (to go)	vay–	vaya
saber (to know)	sep–	sepa
ser (to be)	se–	sea

However, there are three other verbs with both irregular stems and irregular endings in the present subjunctive: *dar* (to give), *estar* (to be), and *oler* (to smell). The conjugations are here:

dé	demos
des	deis
dé	den

esté	estemos
estés	estéis
esté	estén

huela	olamos
huelas	oláis
huela	huelan

Exercise 3: Irregular Conjugations

Fill in the correct present-subjunctive form of the verb for each subject.

1. tú .... (sacar)

2. nosotros .... (ir)

3. yo .... (defender)

4. ella .... (dormir)

5. usted .... (estar)

6. ellos .... (querer)

7. él .... (dar)

8. vosotros .... (costar)

Using and Choosing the Subjunctive

When choosing between the indicative and subjunctive moods, determine whether the verb is used to describe a state or action that is concrete (past, present, or future tenses don't matter), or if it is something that's only potential and/or subjective. Compare the two statements:

Nosotros sabemos que nuestros amigos están allá.
We know our friends are there.

Nosotros esperamos que nuestros amigos estén allá.
We hope our friends are (may be) there.

The first sentence states a fact—our friends are there—but the second sentence lacks certainty: we only hope they are there. We don't know for certain. In Spanish, this kind of uncertainty requires the use of the subjunctive. When translating into English, the subjunctive mood will sometimes include the word "may" or "might."

The present subjunctive is often used within a *que* (that) clause. For example, take a look at the following sentence:

Yo no estoy seguro que ella esté contenta.
I am not sure that she is happy.

The main clause of the sentence is in the indicative mood: "I am not sure." It's the second *estar* in the *que* clause that's in the subjunctive. The following are groups of verbs that take on a subjunctive *que* clause:

Doubt or Uncertainty			
dudar	to doubt	*imaginarse*	to expect
no estar seguro	not to be sure		

Hope or Necessity			
esperar	to hope, to expect	*querer*	to want
necesitar	to need	*preferir*	to prefer

Emotional State			
alegrar	to make happy	*gustar*	to like
enojar	to make angry	*sentir*	to feel

Telling or Asking			
aconsejar	to advise	*pedir*	to ask
decir	to say	*prohibir*	to forbid
exigir	to beg	*rogar*	to beg
insistir	to insist		

Here are some examples:

Dudamos que usted tenga suficiente valor.
We doubt that you have enough courage.

Ellos prefieren que nieve.
They prefer that it snows.

Me enojo que vosotros todavía no vayáis a la escuela.
It makes me angry that you still don't go to school.

Ojalá que el próximo año sea mejor.
Let's hope that next year is better.

If the main clause uses an impersonal construction without a defined subject, the *que* clause can be in the subjunctive mood to express a hypothetical or potential, or to demonstrate attitude or emotion. Common impersonal phrases that are used with the subjunctive include the following:

es bueno que	it's good that	*es necesario que*	it's necessary that
es dudoso que	it's doubtful that	*es probable que*	it's probable that
es importante que	it's important that	*es triste que*	it's sad that
es malo que	it's bad that	*es una lástima que*	it's a pity that
es mejor que	it's better that		

Some examples:

Es triste que ellos no tengan padres.
It's sad that they don't have parents.

Es probable que tú estés equivocado.
It's probable that you are mistaken.

The verb within the *que* clause must have a subject (in the previous examples, *ellos* and *tú* are the subjects) in impersonal constructions. If no subject is present, then the infinitive is used instead:

Es importante que nosotros sepamos la respuesta.
It's important that we know the answer.

Es importante saber la respuesta.
It's important to know the answer.

Another situation in which the subjunctive mood is sometimes used is in adverbial clauses that include a verb. (An adverbial clause is a clause that modifies a verb.) For example:

Voy a darle medicinas para que ella no se enferme.
I'm going to give her medicine so that she doesn't get sick.

The phrase *ella no se enferme* is introduced by the conjunction *para que* and not *que*. Other conjunctions that make adverbial phrases subjunctive include:

a fin de que	in order that	*como*	as
a menos que	unless	*cuando*	when
antes (de) que	before	*en caso de que*	in case
con tal (de) que	provided that	*sin que*	without

Additionally, the following conjunctions might use the subjunctive in the adverbial clause, depending on context:

aunque	although	*donde*	where
como	how	*mientras*	while
de manera que	so that	*según*	according to

Here are two examples to show the difference. The first has an adverbial clause that uses a verb in the indicative; the second includes a verb in the subjunctive.

Según los médicos, yo estoy sana.
According to the doctors, I am healthy.

Según los médicos, yo podría estar sana.
According to the doctors, I may be healthy.

Again, you can see how in the first example, the statement is definite, where as the second example shows uncertainty.

Exercise 4: An Approximate Translation

Translate the following sentences into English.

1. *Limpio la casa a fin de que esté limpia.*

   ....

2. *Preparo la cena en caso de que los niños tengan hambre.*

   ....

3. *Es probable que ellos no sepan la verdad.*

   ....

4. *Es dudoso que nosotros podamos correr con tanta prisa.*

   ....

5. *Voy al cine con tal que ellos vayan conmigo.*

   ....

6. *Ellos se sienten tristes cuando te quejas de tus problemas.*

   ....

7. *Vamos a la playa a menos que llueva.*

   ....

8. *Es necesario que ustedes vuelvan a casa a tiempo.*

   ....

Exercise 5: Right or Wrong?

Each of these sentences includes a verb in the present subjunctive mood. However, in some cases the use of subjunctive is incorrect. Mark the sentences that should be in the indicative mood.

1. *Ella siempre escucha el disco que repita la misma canción.*

2. *Es importante que nosotros aprendemos a tocar la guitarra.*

3. *Se alegran de que ella vuelva a trabajar con ustedes.*

4. *Es cierto que ustedes no duerman suficientemente.*

5. *Ellos van a comer donde yo quiera.*

6. *Prefiero que no describas a ella con semejantes palabras.*

7. *Yo quiero que me tomen en serio.*

8. *Ella está en el restaurante donde sirvan el mejor bistec.*

Exercise 6: The Perfect Ending

Fill in the correct form for the given verb for each sentence. Note that some should be in the present indicative while others in the present subjunctive.

1. *Yo sé que este empleo no* .... *mucho. (pagar)*

2. *Es malo que nosotros no* .... *listos. (estar)*

3. *Según este periódico, el presidente no* .... *en la Casa Blanca, pero no lo creo. (estar)*

4. *Me gusta* .... *en este vecindario. (vivir)*

5. *Los estudiantes piden que el director de la escuela*

   .... *al nuevo profesor por algún otro. (sustituir)*

6. *Yo dudo que* .... *posible entrar por esta puerta sin ningún ruido. (ser)*

7. *No hay duda de que la película* .... *en un momento. (empezar)*

8. *Es interesante que vosotros* .... *tanto dinero por estos boletos. (pagar)*

Perfect Tenses in the Subjunctive

The subjunctive mood has two perfect tenses: the present perfect and past perfect. The rules for using subjunctive in the perfect tenses are the same as in the present subjunctive for the most part. Like all perfect tenses, perfect subjunctives (past and present) pair haber with the past participle (covered in Part 7).

The present-perfect subjunctive is used when the main verbal clause is in the present tense, and the present-perfect conjugations of *haber* are:

haya	*hayamos*
hayas	*hayáis*
haya	*hayan*

Here are examples of how the present-perfect subjunctive may be used:

Quiero que hayan terminado el examen.
I want them to have finished the test.

Ella busca a una persona que haya visitado a este museo.
She is looking for a person who has visited this museum.

The past-perfect subjunctive is the subjunctive equivalent of a perfect past tense, and it is often used when the main verbal clause of the sentence is in preterite, imperfect, or conditional tense. First, the past perfect subjunctive conjugations of *haber*. (Note these are the imperfect subjunctive endings; this tense is covered in the next section.)

hubiera	*hubiéramos*
hubieras	*hubierais*
hubiera	*hubieran*

And some examples:

Era posible que ustedes no hubieran sabido la verdad.
It was possible that you hadn't known the truth.

Si yo me hubiera escondido, ellos no me habrían encontrado.
If I had hidden myself, they wouldn't have found me.

Exercise 7: Perfect Subjunctives

Fill in the correct present perfect subjunctive form of the verb given in parentheses.

1. *Es dudoso que yo* .... *por la casa mientras dormía. (caminar)*

2. *Espero que vosotros ya lo* .... *(decir)*

3. *Es probable que él no* .... *casi nada. (beber)*

4. *Es bueno que nosotros lo* .... *en un lugar seguro. (poner)*

5. *Muchos se consideran bien educados sin que ellos*

   .... *al teatro. (ir)*

6. *No es bueno nadar aquí, a menos que tú* .... *aquí en el pasado. (nadar)*

7. *Ojalá que usted ya* .... *muchas novelas. (escribir)*

Exercise 8: The Subjunctive Past

Fill in the correct past perfect subjunctive form for the given verb for each sentence.

1. *Fue desafortunado que ella* .... *algo mal cocido y se sintiera muy mal. (comer)*

2. *Ojalá que nosotros* .... *una tienda para vender joyas. (abrir)*

3. *En aquellos tiempos, quiso que ustedes me*

   .... *(agradecer)*

4. *No era cierto que tú la* .... *en la playa aquel día. (ver)*

5. *Si ellos me* .... *por el collar, no los hubiera perseguido. (pagar)*

6. *Usted piensa que yo* .... *en California. (vivir)*

7. *Prefirió que vosotros* .... *lo que había pedido. (hacer)*

Exercise 9: The English Version

Translate each sentence. Note that some feature the present-perfect subjunctive and others the past perfect.

1. *Yo pensaba que hubieras sentido algo.*

   ....

2. *Era posible que yo hubiera estado aquí una vez.*

   ....

3. *Busco a una persona que haya tenido éxito con esta dieta.*

   ....

4. *Ellos niegan que nosotros hayamos llegado a un acuerdo.*

   ....

5. *Yo hubiera querido poder quererte para siempre.*

   ....

6. *Es terrible que el programa se haya repetido dos o tres veces.*

   ....

7. *Si ellos hubieran podido hablar, habrían gritado.*

   ....

8. *Es posible que nuestro amor se haya ido.*

   ....

Imperfect Subjunctive

The imperfect subjunctive (commonly called the past subjunctive) is used similarly to the present subjunctive, except in the past tense. The imperfect subjunctive appears in que clauses introduced by a verb in the preterite, imperfect, past perfect, or conditional tense.

A unique trait of the imperfect subjunctive is it has two different sets of endings. Both are correct, and choosing one over the other will not change the meaning of a sentence. Fortunately, even though there are two sets of endings, each set applies to AR, ER, and IR verbs:

–ra	*–´ramos*
–ras	*–rais*
–ra	*–ran*
–se	*–´semos*
–ses	*–seis*
–se	*–sen*

To conjugate a verb in the imperfect subjunctive, take the third-person plural *(ellos)* form of the preterite and drop the –ron ending to get the stem. Then, add the correct imperfect subjunctive ending. For example, the preterite *ellos* form of *beber* is *bebieron*. Removing the *–ron* ending will leave *bebie–* as a stem. All that's left is adding the imperfect subjunctive ending, either the *–ra* or the *–se* set:

bebiera, bebiese	*bebiéramos, bebiésemos*
bebieras, bebieses	*bebierais, bebieseis*
bebiera, bebiese	*bebieran, bebiesen*

If a verb has an irregular *ellos* conjugation in the preterite, the same irregularity will remain in the imperfect subjunctive forms. For example, the preterite *ellos* form of *poder* (to be able to) is *pudieron,* so in the imperfect subjunctive the stem of each form should be *pudie–.*

In sentences where the imperfect subjunctive is used, the main verb that introduces the *que* clause may be in the imperfect, preterite, past perfect, or conditional tenses. If you need to brush up on the rules for these tenses, they are all covered in Part 7. The following are examples incorporating the imperfect subjunctive with these four indicative tenses.

The imperfect indicative with an imperfect subjunctive clause:

Era dudoso que lo volviera a ver otra vez.
It was doubtful that I would see him again.

The preterite with an imperfect subjunctive clause:

Luego ellos insistieron que nosotros prometiéramos olvidar todo.
Then they insisted that we promise to forget everything.

The past perfect indicative with an imperfect subjunctive clause:

Habíamos querido que ellos se relajaran.
We had wanted them to relax.

The conditional with an imperfect subjunctive clause:

Si pudiera leer todos los libros, sería un sabio.
If I could read all the books, I'd be a wise man.

Exercise 10: Seeing Double

TRACK 22

Listen to and repeat the two different forms of the imperfect subjunctive conjugations of three regular verbs, *hablar* (to speak), *beber* (to drink), and *asistir* (to attend).

Exercise 11: Give Me a Ra!

Fill in the blank with the correct imperfect subjunctive form of the given verb. Use only the set that includes the *–ra* ending.

1. Fernando habló en voz baja, como si se .... a sí mismo. *(hablar)*

2. *Quien* .... *que ellos regresarían a este pueblo, estaba equivocado (pensar)*

3. *Nosotros* .... *que alguien nos*

.... *aquí. (querer, esperar)*

4. *Si ellos* .... *, tendrían ya veinte años. (vivir)*

5. *El alcalde sugirió que el pueblo* .... *el nuevo ayuntamiento. (construir)*

6. *Si nosotros* .... *la verdad, nunca consentiríamos a este proyecto. (saber)*

7. *Si yo* .... *quince años, podría conseguir tantas cosas. (tener)*

8. *Si usted* .... *una novela, ella me serviría como inspiración. (escribir)*

Exercise 12: Give me a Se!

Again, fill in the blank with the correct imperfect subjunctive form of the given verb, but this time use only the *–se* endings.

1. *Fernando habló en voz baja, como si se* .... *a sí mismo. (hablar)*

2. *Quien* .... *que ellos regresarían a este pueblo, estaba equivocado. (pensar)*

3. *Nosotros* .... *que alguien nos*

.... *aquí. (querer, esperar)*

4. *Si ellos* .... *, tendrían ya veinte años. (vivir)*

5. *El alcalde sugirió que el pueblo* .... *el nuevo ayuntamiento. (construir)*

6. *Si nosotros* .... *la verdad, nunca consentiríamos a este proyecto. (saber)*

7. *Si yo* .... *quince años, podría conseguir tantas cosas. (tener)*

8. *Si usted* .... *una novela, ella me serviría como inspiración. (escribir)*

The Imperative Mood

The third mood (besides indicative and subjunctive) is the imperative—or command—mood. As its name indicates, the imperative expresses commands and requests. Because of this, the imperative mood is mostly limited to the second person, "you" (*tú, usted, vosotros, ustedes*). It also works with nosotros (it's the equivalent of the phrase "let's" in English). The imperative may also be used to ask or suggest, as long as it's done in a direct address. Some examples:

¡Dame tu cartera!
Give me your wallet!

Conteste usted la pregunta, por favor.
Please answer the question.

Visitemos a nuestros abuelos.
Let's visit our grandparents.

Conjugating verbs in the imperative mood is a little complicated. Some forms look like indicative conjugations, others are identical to subjunctive conjugations, and still others are unique to the imperative mood. In addition, the endings may change depending on whether the statement is positive (do!) or negative (don't!). Let's review each possibility in order.

A positive command directed at *tú* is identical to the third person singular form of the present indicative. Compare:

Él toma agua.
He drinks water.

Toma un sorbo.
Drink a sip.

However, there are some exceptions to this simple rule. Some verbs drop the ending in the positive *tú* command:

decir (to say)	*di*
hacer (to do)	*haz*
ir (to go)	*ve*
poner (to put)	*pon*

salir (to leave)	*sal*
ser (to be)	*sé*
tener (to have)	*ten*
venir (to come)	*ven*

The negative form of the *tú* command is identical to the second person singular subjunctive form. Compare the following:

No es bueno que tú mires la televisión.
It's not good that you watch TV.

No mires la televisión.
Don't watch TV.

When addressing *usted,* the conjugation is the same as to the third-person singular of the subjunctive. Similarly, if *ustedes* is the addressee, the conjugation is identical to the third-person plural of the subjunctive. This rule is true in both positive and negative commands. Here are examples of each:

Escuche, por favor.
Listen, please. (to *usted*)

Empiecen, por favor.
Begin, please. (to *ustedes*)

No lo discuta más, por favor.
Don't discuss it any more, please. (to *usted*)

No griten dentro de la casa, por favor.
Don't yell inside the house, please. (to *ustedes*)

Note that saying *usted* or *ustedes* following the command verb makes the sentence more polite.

There is also a *vosotros* form for the imperative mood. To make a positive *vosotros* command, drop the final "r" of the verb's infinitive and replace it with a "d." For example:

Tomad un café.
Drink some coffee.

The only exception to this rule is the verb *ir* (to go), which uses *idos*:

¡Idos a casa ahora mismo!
Go home immediately!

To make negative *vosotros* commands, use the *vosotros* present subjunctive form:

¡No me contradigáis!
Don't contradict me!

The one other imperative conjugation goes with *nosotros*. To form positive and negative commands, you can use the *nosotros* form of the subjunctive:

Comamos la cena ya.
Let's eat supper now.

No esperemos más.
Let's not wait any longer.

The exception to that rule is that *vamos* is used instead of *vayamos* for positive commands:

Vamos a la escuela. No vayamos al campo.
Let's go to school. Let's not go to the countryside.

In statements using the imperative, there are some differences in the placement of reflexive and object pronouns. They behave as usual in negative commands (they precede the verb). In positive commands, however, the pronouns are attached to the end of the verb:

Tómalo.
Take it. (to *tú*)

Váyanse, por favor.
Please leave. (to *ustedes*)

When this happens, some verbs (like *tomar* and *irse* in the previous examples) require an accent mark to retain correct pronunciation. Also, the *nosotros* and *vosotros* forms have a change in the ending. The final "s" of the ending is dropped in positive *nosotros* commands when the verb includes the reflexive pronoun *nos* or the indirect object pronoun *se:*

Despertémonos temprano hoy.
Let's wake up early today.

Prestemos estas joyas a la novia. Prestémoselas.
Let's lend these jewels to the bride. Let's lend them to her.

This is done to simplify the pronunciation of the compound words. Similarly, you drop the "d" in positive *vosotros* commands that end with the reflexive pronoun *os:*

Controlaos, por favor.
Please control yourselves.

Exercise 13: It's a Command

Translate the following commands into Spanish.

1. Let's stay.

    ....

2. Don't shout! (to tú)

    ....

3. Open your notebooks, please. (to ustedes)

    ....

4. Eat your cookies. (to vosotros)

    ....

5. Don't give it to me. (to usted)

    ....

Exercise 14: Make It Positive

Rewrite each of the following negative commands as a positive.

1. *No lo pongas allá.*

....

2. *No salgáis de aquí.*

....

3. *No se los manden.*

....

4. *No lo hagas.*

....

5. *No les diga nada.*

....

Exercise 15: A Suggestion, a Command

TRACK 23

The sentences you will hear illustrate the imperative mood. Write down each sentence and then translate it into English.

1. ....

2. ....

3. ....

4. ....

5. ....

6. ....

7. ....

8. ....

9. ....

10. ....

Putting It Together

Now let's see what you've learned!

Exercise 16: In Tense

For each verb's conjugation, label what tense/mood it's in.

1. *preferamos* ....

2. *hubiera olido* ....

3. *cerrad* ....

4. *sepáis* ....

5. *describieran* ....

6. *ven* ....

7. *haya dicho* ....

8. *mentid* ....

Exercise 17: In the Mood

TRACK 24

Listen to each sentence and repeat. Then listen to the track again, write down each sentence, and identify whether it is in the subjunctive, imperative, or indicative mood.

1. ....

2. ....

3. ....

4. ....

5. ....

6. ....

7. ....

8. ....

9. ....

10. ....

Exercise 18: Your Wish Is My Command

Translate each command into English.

1. *¡No grites!*

   ....

2. *No vayamos a la playa.*

   ....

3. *No lo hagan con tanta fuerza.*

   ....

4. *¡Cállate la boca!*

   ....

5. *Cerrad las puertas ahora mismo.*

   ....

6. *Póntelos.*

   ....

7. *Por favor, no le preste dinero.*

   ....

8. *No penséis en las consecuencias.*

   ....

Exercise 19: If It's Any Indication

Fill in the correct conjugation of the verb given in parentheses. You'll have to determine whether the verb should be conjugated in the subjunctive, command, or indicative mood.

1. *Es posible que ella no* .... *allá. (estar)*

2. *Ojalá que no* .... *problemas con esto. (haber)*

3. *¡No me* .... *aquí! (dejar)*

4. *Yo* .... *que todo está bien. (saber)*

5. *Ellos no me* .... *(conocer)*

6. *Chico, no* .... *un imbécil. (ser)*

7. *Es cierto que ellos lo* .... *(tener)*

8. *Nosotros se las* .... *(escribir)*

Part 9

EVerbal Constructions and More

This part covers the remaining verbal constructions, as well as some other bits essential for a comprehensive practice of Spanish. From the progressive forms to talking about the weather, this part helps round out your Spanish skills. Also included in this part are some topics that will help you out in daily Spanish conversations.

Present Progressive

Ongoing actions are described by using a progressive tense. In English, progressive tenses are formed with the verb "to be" followed by the present participle (a verbal construction ending in "ing": laughing, going, running, etc., also called the verb's gerund). In Spanish, progressive tenses also rely on the verb "to be"—in this case estar—and the present participle.

Like the past participles, Spanish present participles are formed by dropping the infinitive ending and adding the correct present participle ending:

verb group	present participle ending	example	English
AR verbs	–ando	hablando	speaking
ER verbs	–iendo	corriendo	running
IR verbs	–iendo	viviendo	living

There are a few irregular forms as well. If the stem of an ER or IR verb ends in a vowel, its present participle ending is –*yendo*. For example:

caer	cayendo	falling
creer	creyendo	believing
leer	leyendo	reading
oír	oyendo	hearing
traer	trayendo	bringing

IR verbs with a stem change in the third person singular form of the preterite tense (covered in Part 7) retain that stem change in the present participle:

infinitive	preterite	present participle	English
decir	dijo	diciendo	saying
dormir	durmió	durmiendo	sleeping
morir	murió	muriendo	dying

infinitive	preterite	present participle	English
pedir	pidió	pidiendo	asking
repetir	repitió	repitiendo	repeating
sentir	sintió	sintiendo	feeling
servir	sirvió	sirviendo	serving
venir	vino	viniendo	coming

The only other irregulars are the present participle forms of these two:

ir	yendo	going
poder	pudiendo	being able

The most frequently used progressive tense is the present progressive. This tense uses the present-indicative conjugations of *estar:*

estoy	estamos
estás	estáis
está	están

In English, we often use the present progressive to talk about things that are going on right now, as opposed to regularly. Compare:

He walks to work. (in general)
He is walking to work. (right now)

In Spanish, actions taking place "right now" can also be described with the present indicative form: *Él camina al trabajo.* However, if the fact that the action is occurring at that very moment and you want to highlight that fact, the present progressive form is preferable: *Él está caminando al trabajo.*

It is also possible to use the verb *seguir* (to follow, to continue) in progressive constructions. For example:

Sigo bailando.
I keep on dancing./I am dancing.

Exercise 1: Assembling Participles

For each verb, fill in the correct present participle.

1. *escribir* ....

2. *cantar* ....

3. *servir* ....

4. *pensar* ....

5. *hacer* ....

6. *crear* ....

7. *dormir* ....

8. *ir* ....

Exercise 2: This Very Second

Fill in the correct form of *estar* + the present participle in each blank.

1. *Ella me* .... *a mí. (mirar)*

2. *Nosotros* .... *algo muy importante.*
   (decir)

3. *Usted* .... *el libro. (leer)*

4. *Yo* .... *la ventana. (abrir)*

5. *Vosotros* .... *tantas cosas. (sentir)*

6. *Tú no* ...., *eres sincero. (actuar)*

7. *Marco* .... *por la calle. (andar)*

8. *Ustedes nos* .... *un gran favor.*
   (pedir)

Exercise 3: Make It Right Now

Rewrite each sentence in the present progressive tense.

1. *Yo me lavo las manos.*

....

2. *Usted toma agua.*

....

3. *Elena compra un vestido y pantalones.*

....

4. *Los atletas practican natación.*

....

5. *Nosotros lo escuchamos a él.*

....

6. *Yo voy a la escuela.*

....

7. *Carlos baila en la discoteca.*

....

8. *Vosotros cocináis paella.*

....

Past Progressives

There are two past progressive forms: the preterite progressive and the imperfect progressive. They are formed in the same way as the present progressive, except that *estar* is conjugated in the preterite and the imperfect, respectively:

imperfect conjugations

| estaba | estábamos | estabas | estabais | estaba | estaban |

preterite conjugations

| estuve | estuvimos | estuviste | estuvisteis | estuvo | estuvieron |

The imperfect progressive is a more commonly used past progressive. This tense is used to describe ongoing actions in the past:

Yo estaba cantando mientras cocinaba.
I was singing while I cooked dinner.

Ellos estaban caminando por la calle.
They were walking down the street.

The more infrequently needed preterite progressive does have some uses. It refers to an action that was in progress in the past but was then completed:

Ella estuvo leyendo hasta que el teléfono sonó.
She was reading until the phone rang.

Exercise 4: A Time of Imperfections

Fill in the correct imperfect progressive conjugation of the verb in parentheses.

1. *Las enfermeras* .... *al médico. (ayudar)*

2. *Vosotros* .... *algo mover por la pantalla. (ver)*

3. *Yo* .... *a la fiesta. (venir)*

4. *Nosotros* .... *del arte. (hablar)*

5. *Usted* .... *perdón. (pedir)*

6. *Patricia* .... *cuando su marido llegó a casa. (almorzar)*

7. *El autobús* .... *a la estación. (volver)*

8. *Yo* .... *a cada su palabra. (repetir)*

Exercise 5: Up to a Point

Now fill in the correct form of *estar* in the preterite progressive + the present participle in each blank.

1. *Tú* .... *hasta que el cigarillo se extinguió.* (fumar)

2. *Vosotros* .... *algo incomprensible.* (temer)

3. *Yo* .... *hasta que no pude comer más.* (comer)

4. *Enrique* .... *en algo importante cuando oyó el grito.* (pensar)

5. *Nosotros* .... *cuando sonó el despertador.* (dormir)

Hay and Its Other Forms

The phrases "there is" and "there are" are equivalent to the Spanish word *hay. Hay* can be used when referring to a single object or multiple objects:

Hay un libro en la mesa.
There is a book on the table.

Hay muchos libros en la mesa.
There are many books on the table.

The tense of *hay* is present indicative, but there are forms for the other tenses as well—all you need to do is conjugate *haber* in the third-person singular form:

the right conjugation	English	tense
hay	there is/are	present
hubo	there was/were	preterite
había	there was/were	imperfect
habrá	there will be	future

the right conjugation	English	tense
habría	there would be	conditional
haya	there may be	subjunctive
hubiera	there may have been	past subjunctive

Exercise 6: There Is a Way

Translate each sentence.

1. *Hay un mercado en la calle Verde.*

   ....

2. *Habrá frutas y vegetales para comprar.*

   ....

3. *Había un problema con el coche.*

   ....

4. *En este caso habría algo que hacer.*

   ....

5. *Había una razón para su rechazo.*

   ....

6. *Hubo algo para cada persona.*

   ....

7. *Hay dulces en el paquete.*

   ....

8. *Hubieron errores en su liderazgo.*

   ....

Heading into the Future with Ir A

The construction *ir a* in the present tense can be used to talk about things that will happen in the future—something that is "going to be" done. It is formed by using the appropriate present indicative conjugation of *ir*, followed by *a*, and then the infinitive of the main action verb:

> *Voy a escuchar música y relajarme.*
> **I'm going to listen to music and relax.**

> *Vamos a aprender el español.*
> **We're going to learn Spanish.**

Remember, here is how *ir* is conjugated in the present indicative:

voy	*vamos*
vas	*vais*
va	*van*

Exercise 7: Finish It Already

Rewrite each to make the action occur in the future by using *ir a*.

1. *Tú compras jabón.*

   ....

2. *Yo viajo por avión.*

   ....

3. *Ustedes trabajan en el salón de automóviles.*

   ....

4. *Vosotros miráis el programa deportivo.*

   ....

5. *Ella come una pera.*

   ....

Exercise 8: What Are You Going to Do?

Given each situation, explain what you are going to do.

1. *Tienes hambre. Voy a* ....

2. *Hace mucho calor. Voy a* ....

3. *Es el día del cumpleaños de tu amiga. Voy a* ....

4. *No te gusta tu trabajo. Voy a* ....

5. *Estás enfermo. Voy a* ....

Exercise 9: It Must Be Done

TRACK 25

Listen to each statement of what someone has to do and then rewrite using the *ir a* form to explain what the person is going to do. For example: *Tienes que limpiar la casa. Vas a limpiar la casa.*

1. ....

2. ....

3. ....

4. ....

5. ....

6. ....

7. ....

8. ....

9. ....

10. ....

Just Finished

Another useful verbal expression to know is *acabar de* + infinitive. *Acabar* is "to finish," but the expression can be used to refer to an action that was just completed. Here is an example:

> *Acabo de leer este libro.*
> **I just finished reading this book.**

The expression *acabar de* + infinitive need not to be in the present tense:

> *Acabé de escuchar esta canción.*
> **I had just finished listening to this song.**

Exercise 10: Blast from the Recent Past

Rewrite each sentence to make it refer to an action that just happened, using *acabar de*.

1. *Usted lee la revista.*

   ....

2. *Yo veo la imagen.*

   ....

3. *Vosotros fingís alegría.*

   ....

4. *La tienda cierra.*

   ....

5. *El señor muere.*

   ....

Exercise 11: What Did You Just Do?

Given each situation, complete the sentence with what you just did.

1. *La casa está muy limpia. Acabo de* ....

2. *No puedes comer más. Acabo de* ....

3. *El público aplaude con entusiasmo. Acabo de* ....

4. *Tu cabello está peinado. Acabo de* ....

5. *Eres muy alegre. Acabo de* ....

Saber Versus Conocer

Non-native Spanish speakers often have trouble deciding whether to use *saber* or *conocer*. Both translate as "to know"; *saber* can also mean "to be able to do," and *conocer* sometimes means "to meet." In some situations, the distinction isn't very clear. Here's a quick review.

Saber is used to express knowledge or ignorance of a fact, and when talking about knowing or not knowing how to do something:

¿Sabes nadar?
Do you know how to swim?

Yo sé la respuesta.
I know the answer.

Ella sabe cuál es la capital de Francia.
She knows what's the capital of France.

Conocer is used to express an acquaintance with a person, place, or thing. *María conoce a José* means "Maria knows José" in the sense that she's met him, not merely that she knows of him.

Él no conoce a ninguno de sus vecinos.
He doesn't know any one of his neighbors.

Conozco San Francisco—pasé muchos años viviendo allá.
I know San Francisco—I spent many years living there.

Exercise 12: What You Know, You Know

TRACK 26

Listen to each sentence and repeat. Then listen to the track again and write down English translations of these sentences. Note that all of these are examples of correctly using *saber* and *conocer*.

1. ....

2. ....

3. ....

4. ....

5. ....

6. ....

7. ....

8. ....

9. ....

10. ....

Exercise 13: You Either Know It or Know It

Fill in the blank with the correct form of either *conocer* or *saber*.

1. *Carmen* .... *a David ayer en la escuela.*

2. *Hasta hoy, ellos no* .... *los detalles de esta historia.*

3. *Cuando vea la respuesta, yo* .... *si tenía la razón.*

4. *Yo la* .... *a ella, es la novia de Felipe.*

5. *Es probable que vosotros no* .... *a aquel hombre.*

Past Participles as Adjectives

In Spanish, past participles (introduced in Part 7) can be used as adjectives. When used this way, the past participle must agree in number and gender with the noun it modifies. For example:

La casa tiene dos puertas abiertas.
The house has two open doors.

Exercise 14: A Verb Unverbed

Insert the correct past-participle adjective form of the verb.

1. *La casa tiene dos puertas* .... *(abrir)*

2. *Ponte la chaqueta* .... *en la tienda La Ropa de Marco. (comprar)*

3. *Son los libros más* .... *por la Red. (vender)*

4. *Ellos leyeron las palabras* .... *en la pared. (escribir)*

5. *Por favor acepten nuestras más* .... *palabras. (sentir)*

6. *Es la carta* .... *por Ramón. (enviar)*

7. *No es el ensayo* .... , *es la misma versión. (rehacer)*

8. *Ya veo el edificio* .... *por los viajeros a este lugar. (describir)*

9. *El coche* .... *allá es el mío. (parar)*

10. *No me des los lápices* .... *(romper)*

How About That Weather?

Talking about the weather in Spanish doesn't always directly translate well into English. English speakers usually use a form of the verb "to be" to discuss the weather: "it's rainy out," "it's going to be snowing," etc. In some cases, you can use *estar* to talk about the weather in Spanish:

¿Cómo está el tiempo?
How is the weather?

Está lloviendo.
It's raining.

Está nublado.
It's cloudy.

Está nevando.
It's snowing.

As you can see, you can use present and past participles with the verb *estar.* Another verb to use is *hacer* (to make):

¿Qué tiempo hace?

The direct literal translation of this sentence is "What does the weather do?" The actual meaning, however, is: "What is the weather like?" Some common answers:

Hace sol.
It's sunny.

Hace viento.
It's windy.

Hace mucho frío.
It's very cold.

Hace mucho calor.
It's very hot.

Note that in these examples, *hacer* is matched with nouns *(viento, lluvia, sol, frío, calor)*.

Exercise 15: The Weather Report

Translate each sentence into Spanish.

1. It is going to snow tomorrow.

   ....

2. Is it raining?

   ....

3. Yesterday was colder than today.

   ....

4. It's cloudy out.

   ....

5. The weather is bad today.

   ....

6. It is sunny at the beach.

   ....

7. What is the weather like in your country?

   ....

8. I am cold.

   ....

Talking Time

Saying what time it is in Spanish is fairly simple. See the chart.

Telling Time in Spanish	
1:00	*Es la una.*
2:00	*Son las dos.*
4:00	*Son las cuatro.*
11:00	*Son las once.*
2:03	*Son las dos y tres.*
2:15	*Son las dos y cuarto.*
3:45	*Son las cuatro menos cuarto.*
3:55	*Son las cuatro menos cinco.*
10:30	*Son las diez y media.*
Noon	*Son las doce del día. / Es el mediodía.*
Midnight	*Son las doce de la noche. / Es la medianoche.*

To say "half past" the hour, simply add "*y media*"; "quarter past" is "*y cuarto*"; and quarter of is "*menos cuarto.*" To clarify day or night, add *de la mañana/de la tarde/de la noche:*

Son las siete de la mañana.
It's seven in the morning. / It's seven a.m.

Es la una de la tarde.
It is one in the afternoon.

Son las ocho y media de la noche.
It is eight thirty at night.

Exercise 16: What Time Is It?

Write in the correct time in the blank.

1. 3:00 ....
2. 11:15 ....
3. 3:45 ....
4. 1:05 ....
5. 8:22 ....
6. 6:50 ....
7. 5:30 ....
8. 2:02 ....
9. 6:00 a.m. ....
10. 9:33 p.m. ....

Putting It Together

Now let's see what you've learned!

Exercise 17: Many Blanks to Fill In

As you've noticed, knowing the conjugations of *estar* is essential to form progressives. See if you can fill in the correct conjugations for each tense.

Present Indicative:

....
....
....

Imperfect:

Preterite:

Exercise 18: Living in the Moment

TRACK 27

Listen to the statements and rewrite them using the appropriate progressive tense form. For example: *María come panqueques. María está comiendo panqueques.*

1. ....
2. ....
3. ....
4. ....
5. ....
6. ....
7. ....
8. ....
9. ....
10. ....

Exercise 19: Playing with Time

Rewrite each sentence twice—once with *acabar de* and once with *ir a*.

1. *El ave vuela al techo de la casa.*

    ....

2. *Mi hermana está caminando a la escuela.*

    ....

3. *Nosotros leemos el periódico.*

    ....

4. *Tú tomas el jugo de naranja para el desayuno.*

    ....

5. *Ustedes cierran las ventanas.*

    ....

Exercise 20: Hope You Were Paying Attention

Translate each sentence. Some use multiple elements from this part.

1. *Acaba de llover.*

    ....

2. *Voy a hacerlo a las cinco y media.*

    ....

3. *Vosotros no la conocéis a ella muy bien.*

    ....

4. *Hacía demasiado frío ayer.*

....

5. *Yo estaba caminando a la escuela cuando empezó a nevar.*

....

6. *La mujer cansada acaba de terminar su proyecto.*

....

7. *Hizo sol toda la semana pasada.*

....

8. *Voy a dormirme a las once y cuarto de la noche.*

....

(E) *Part 10*

The Final Exam

This part pulls everything together. In it you'll find reviews of individual parts of speech plus exercises concerning how different parts of speech interact. Some of these exercises will be more challenging, but try and complete each exercise with as little outside help as possible. Once you determine where you're struggling, then go back and review the appropriate sections.

Basic Understanding

Having all the grammar rules crammed into your head isn't enough—you have to bring that knowledge into practice. In reality, the only way to really get there is to go out and talk to people (preferably in Spanish). However, there are some exercises that can help you along the way.

Other things you can do include reading any printed materials you can in Spanish and seeing how well you understand the content. Children's books are an excellent start. Spanish music, movies, and television programs will also help you get used to spoken Spanish.

Exercise 1: Common Questions

Below are some common questions you may encounter or need to ask. Translate them into English in the space provided.

1. *¿Puede ayudarme, por favor?*

   ....

2. *¿Cómo está?*

   ....

3. *¿Cuánto cuesta esta cosa?*

   ....

4. *¿Cuántos años tiene?*

   ....

5. *¿Podría repetirlo, por favor?*

   ....

6. *¿Podría escribirlo, por favor?*

   ....

7. *¿Qué hora es?*

   ....

8. *¿Dónde está el baño?*

   ....

Exercise 2: Speak Up

TRACK 28

Listen to the following questions and try to answer each one quickly. You can practice several times until the answers come to you naturally and you don't have to think about it too much.

Exercise 3: At the Doctor's Office

Read the conversation, then answer the questions below.

Q: **El doctor:** *Buenos días, Carlos. ¿Cómo estás?*
A: **El paciente:** *Buenos días, doctor. Desafortunadamente no estoy muy bien.*

Q: **El doctor:** *¿Qué te pasa, Carlos?*
A: **El paciente:** *Pues, me siento muy mal.*

Q: **El doctor:** *Dime qué síntomas tienes.*
A: **El paciente:** *Ay, doctor, tengo tantos. Me duele la cabeza. Me duele la garganta y no puedo tragar. Moqueo mucho. Y además tengo una formidable tos. Me siento muy débil.*

Q: **El doctor:** *Carlos, ¿cuándo empezaron estos síntomas?*
A: **El paciente:** *Hace tres días que empezó el dolor de garganta. Era el lunes. Luego, el martes, empezó el moqueo. Era algo terrible, no terminaba de sonarme la nariz. Y hoy, ya tengo dolor de cabeza.*

Q: **El doctor:** *Parece que también tienes fiebre.*
A: **El paciente:** *Sí. Ya la he tenido durante dos días.*
Q: **El doctor:** *Carlos, parece que de verdad estás muy enfermo. Tienes bronquitis. Tienes que tomar unas medicinas. Aquí están.*
A: **El paciente:** *Gracias, doctor. Pero, estas medicinas, ¿tienen efectos secundarios?*

Q: **El doctor:** *Éstas, no. Pero debes tomarlas todas, hasta que las termines. Si no, la enfermedad regresará.*
A: **El paciente:** *Entiendo. Voy a tomarlas todas. Muchas gracias.*

Q: **El doctor:** *De nada. Ojalá que te sientas muy bien pronto.*
A: **El paciente:** *Espero que sí. Adiós.*

1. *¿Quiénes están hablando?*

   ....

2. *¿Cómo se siente Carlos?*

   ....

3. *¿Cuáles son sus síntomas?*

   ....

4. *¿Cuándo empezó a sentirse mal?*

   ....

5. *¿Cuándo empezó a sonarse la nariz?*

   ....

6. *¿Cuántas días ha tenido fiebre?*

   ....

7. *¿Cuál es el diagnóstico del doctor?*

   ....

8. *¿Qué debe hacer Carlos para recuperarse?*

   ....

9. *¿Quién espera que Carlos se recupere pronto?*

   ....

Matching Nouns with Articles and Adjectives

The following exercises will sharpen your skills in properly matching nouns with other parts of speech. For a review of what nouns and adjectives are, refer back to Part 1 and Part 3, respectively.

Exercise 4: The Articles

For 1–5, fill in the correct definite article before each noun; for 6–10, fill in the correct indefinite article.

1. .... *banco*

2. .... *coches*

3. .... *días*

4. .... *mano*

5. .... *hijas*

6. .... *paquete*

7. .... *postales*

8. .... *hotel*

9. .... *naranja*

10. .... *pepinos*

Exercise 5: Hard Decisions

TRACK 29

Listen to Pedro's story and then try to recount it in your own words.

....

....

....

....

....

....

....

Exercise 6: How Best to Describe It

Circle the adjective that matches the noun, both grammatically and in sense.

1. *helado (delicioso, caldo, naranja)*

2. *fotos (interesante, impresionantes, simpáticos)*

3. *jardín (dulce, nueva, grande)*

4. *madre (cierta, cariñoso, indulgente)*

5. *coches (rápidas, nuevos, duras)*

6. *canción (bella, fría, tibia)*

7. *ciudad (ruidoso, pequeña, bastante)*

8. *idiomas (largas, difíciles, bellas)*

9. *calles (anchas, estrechos, tibios)*

10. *libros (interesantes, rojas, mojados)*

Exercise 7: In Color

Fill in the correct adjective by describing the color of each object.

Colors			
blanco	white	*anaranjado*	orange
negro	black	*amarillo*	yellow
gris	gray	*marrón*	brown
rojo	red	*verde*	green
azul	blue	*morado*	purple

1. *Las manzanas son* .... ,

   .... , *y* ....

2. *El cielo es* ....

3. *Los gorriones son* ....

4. *El papel es comúnmente* ....

5. *El agua del mar es* ....

6. *Las berenjenas son* ....

7. *En el otoño, las hojas de los árboles se vuelven* .... ,

   .... , *y* ....

8. *La noche es* ....

Pronoun Review

Spanish pronouns were covered in depth in Part 2. Many students of Spanish have trouble with the many kinds of pronouns, especially since so many are very similar in usage and spelling. The following exercises will challenge your ability to use and identify the many types of this essential part of speech.

Exercise 8: Not Naming Names

Rewrite each sentence. Replace the word or phrase in bold with a pronoun.

1. **Los hermanos Márquez** *eran los mejores jugadores de fútbol en nuestro vecindario.*

   ....

   ....

2. *Es el dinero **de los hombres de negocios**.*

   ....

   ....

3. *Estas noticias no interesan **a los estudiantes**.*

....

....

4. *Manda la carta **a Elena y a mí**.*

....

....

5. *Patricio es el hermano **de Clarisa y mío**.*

....

....

6. ***Esas cosas** son las más interesantes.*

....

....

7. *Ponte **el sombrero**, hace frío.*

....

....

8. *Son los problemas **de ti**.*

....

....

Exercise 9: Pronoun Mastery

In each sentence, circle all pronouns. Then translate these sentences into English.

1. *Nos casaremos en su casa.*

....

....

2. *Luego ustedes estarán comprándoselas.*

....

....

3. *Quién sabe cómo ella logró escapar de aquí.*

....

....

4. *No te duermas sin cepillarte los dientes y lavarte la cara.*

....

....

5. *Nadie lo hace como tú.*

....

....

6. *¡Levántate a pie!*

....

....

7. *No sé a quién se lo digo.*

....

....

8. *Mi mamá me las regaló cuando yo tenía doce años.*

....

....

Using Adverbs

In Part 3, you learned about adverbs of manner, adverbs of place, adverbs of time, and adverbs of quantity. Now you can test your knowledge of these types of adverbs and get extra practice using them correctly.

Exercise 10: Proper Adverb Manners

Fill in the correct adverb of manner in each blank. Choose from the following adverbs: *descuidadamente, altamente, dudosamente, fuertemente, bonitamente, fácilmente, bien, tristemente.*

1. *Los músicos cantan en voz alta.*

   Cantan ....

2. *Nosotros somos buenos estudiantes.*

   Estudiamos ....

3. *Ustedes trabajan con mucha fuerza.*

   Trabajan ....

4. *Yo estoy llorando, llena de tristeza.*

   Lloro ....

5. *Tú trabajas sin cuidado.*

   Trabajas ....

6. *Ella se viste con ropa bonita.*

   Se viste ....

7. *Para vosotros, es fácil aprender idiomas.*

   Los aprendéis ....

8. *Usted habla con duda.*

   Usted habla ....

Exercise 11: In the Right Place

Circle all adverbs of place and then translate the sentences into English.

1. *Ahora vamos abajo.*

   ....

2. *El ruido se oye desde muy lejos.*

   ....

3. *No podemos quedarnos cerca.*

   ....

4. *Creo que no están delante de la casa, sino detrás.*

   ....

5. *Mira qué está pasando allí.*

   ....

6. *Vamos adentro.*

   ....

7. *Es posible que puedas encontrarlos arriba.*

   ....

8. *Nadie está aquí.*

   ....

Exercise 12: Questions of Quantity

Fill in the correct adverb of quantity. The adverbs to choose from are: *algo, casi, bastante, demasiado, más, menos, mucho, muy, poco,* and *tan.*

1. *La nieve está tan sucia, está* .... *negra.*

2. *La explicación no es clara. Es* .... *precisa.*

3. *No entiendo este libro, es* .... *difícil para mí.*

4. *No es nada rara. Es* .... *típica.*

5. *Prefiero el café. El té me gusta* ....

6. *Es más que bonita. Es* .... *bella.*

7. *No creo que ella sea estúpida.*
   Parece que es .... *inteligente.*

8. *Pedro es* .... *elegante como Paco.*

9. *El precio de veinte dólares no es* .... *mejor que el de dieciocho dólares.*

10. *Mi tía tiene cuarenta años y su marido tiene cuarenta y dos;*
    él es .... *viejo que ella.*

Prepositions and Conjunctions

Mastering prepositions and conjunctions will help you form complete thoughts and complex statements. Part 4 gave you an introduction to the most common prepositions and conjunctions, as well as their proper usage. The exercises below are your chance to review them again.

Exercise 13: Prep Work

Choose the preposition that best completes each sentence.

1. *No quiero salir* .... *ella.*
   (a, de, sin)

2. *Esta carta es* .... *ustedes.*
   (por, para, con)

3. *No lo he visto a él* .... *ayer.*
   (de, en, desde)

4. *Las semillas son sembradas* .... *la tierra.*
   (cerca de, al lado de, debajo de)

5. *Puedes encontrar la información* .... *la Red.*
   (en, sobre, entre)

6. *Van a estar ocupados* .... *las tres de la tarde.*
   (hasta, a, con)

7. *Es la opinión* .... *la mayoría de la gente.*
   (delante de, de, en)

8. *No te inclines* .... *el vidrio.*
   (contra, entre, con)

9. *La montaña está muy* .... *la ciudad.*
   (después de, lejos de, entre)

10. *Las revistas están* .... *la mesa.*
    (hasta, por, sobre)

Exercise 14: And, Or, What?

Choose the conjunction that best completes each sentence.

1. *Él va a esperar,* .... *que ya es muy tarde.*
   (por, a pesar de, cuando)

2. *Fui invitada a su casa,* .... *no puedo visitarlos porque tengo mucho que hacer.*
   (sino, excepto, pero)

3. *Está enojada* .... *tiene que lavar los platos sucios que sus compañeras de cuarto han dejado en el fregadero.*
   (porque, salvo, aunque)

4. *No estamos cansados,* .... *hemos pasado toda la noche bailando.*
   (porque, sino, aunque)

5. *El mejor amigo es alguien simpático* .... *sincero.*
   (o, y, e)

6. *Estoy gritando* .... *te fijes en mí.*
   (para que, y, excepto)

7. *Este restaurante es tan bueno* .... *el que está cerca de nuestra oficina.*
(que, como, pero)

8. *Ellos están aburridos* .... *no pasa nada.*
(cuando, para que, salvo)

9. *No llegas temprano,* .... *tarde.*
(pero, sino, o)

10. *Puedo comer cualquier carne,* .... *el tocino.*
(sino, salvo, porque)

Choosing the Correct Verb Tense

It takes a great deal of discipline and energy to even master the regular forms of all the verb tenses. Add in figuring out which to use when and where and things get tricky. And if that's not difficult enough, there are still the many irregularities and spelling changes to memorize. Get through this part without help and you'll have earned a nice pat on the back.

Exercise 15: Conjugation Frustration

On a separate piece of paper, conjugate the verbs *hablar, beber,* and *asistir* in the following tenses. Check your answers in Appendix A.

1. Present indicative
2. Preterite
3. Imperfect
4. Future
5. Conditional
6. Present subjunctive
7. Imperfect subjunctive
8. Imperative

9. Past participle

10. Present participle

Exercise 16: Know Your Tenses

Translate each of the following verb forms into English, including one pronoun that would fit.

1. *empezamos*

2. *pondrían*

3. *caminaba*

4. *volveréis*

5. *dejas*

6. *haz*

7. *miren*

8. *sufrí*

9. *veremos*

10. *pudiéramos*

Exercise 17: Basic Tenses

Translate each sentence into English, paying special attention to the tense.

1. *Vosotros estáis muy cansados.*

2. *Esperemos. Mauricio llegará pronto.*

3. *Llovía todo el día.*

....

4. *A mí me gusta despertarme temprano.*

....

5. *Ella tendría dinero si pudiera trabajar.*

....

6. *Usted se graduó de la universidad en el año 1994.*

....

7. *Si tuvieras suerte, podrías ganar el premio.*

....

8. *Por favor no se ofendan.*

....

9. *Nosotros repasaremos aquellos problemas.*

....

10. *Es posible que ellos no tengan la responsabilidad.*

....

Exercise 18: Perfect Tenses in Review

Translate each of the following verb forms into English, including one pronoun that would fit.

1. *hayas comprendido* ....

2. *han producido* ....

3. *hube tratado* ....

4. *hemos ganado* ....

5. *hubiera hecho* ....

6. *había sido* ....

7. *hayan vendido* ....

8. *hubiésemos dicho* ....

9. *habrán manejado* ....

10. *habríais visto* ....

Exercise 19: Traveling in Time

Fill in the blank with the correct form of the given verb.

Present Indicative Tense

1. *Yo no* .... *nada de esto. (entender)*

2. *Nosotros* .... *un futuro mejor. (emprender)*

3. *Ustedes* .... *a su nuevo compañero por su buen trabajo. (felicitar)*

Preterite Tense

1. *La persona que te* .... *por teléfono no* .... *ella. (llamar, ser)*

2. *Tú* .... *muchos errores. (cometer)*

3. *Las chicas* .... *muchas cosas antes de comprar algo. (probarse)*

Imperfect Tense

1. *Aunque Dora* .... *inteligente,* .... *como una tonta. (ser, comportarse)*

2. *Nosotros* .... *que hacer algo muy impor-tante. (tener)*

3. *Vosotros* .... *enojados todo el día. (parecer)*

Future Tense

1. *Yo* .... *a todas tus preguntas. (responder)*

2. *Tú no* .... *que yo sea engañada. (dejar)*

3. *Ellos* .... *cuando oigan tu voz. (aplaudir)*

Conditional Tense

1. *Si ella pudiera, lo* .... *a él con el dedo. (señalar)*

2. *Me* .... *tomar el desayuno ahora. (gustar)*

3. *Los nietos* .... *a sus abuelos si eso fuera posible. (visitar)*

Present Perfect Tense

1. *Yo ya* .... *las pastillas. (tomar)*

2. *Tú* .... *a casa muy tarde. (regresar)*

3. *Nosotros* .... *por un rato. (platicar)*

Pluperfect Tense

1. *Él* .... *su secreto. (descubrir)*

2. *Vosotros* .... *aquí demasiado tarde. (volver)*

3. *Ellos* .... *a otra casa. (mudarse)*

Preterite Perfect Tense

1. *Yo* .... *el borde. (demarcar)*

2. *Tú* .... *algo terrible. (hacer)*

3. *Vosotros no* .... *nada. (ver)*

Future Perfect Tense

1. *Tú* .... *en la trampa. (caer)*

2. *Usted* .... *muchos esfuerzos. (intentar)*

3. *Nosotros* .... *un guión. (escribir)*

Conditional Perfect

1. *Usted* .... *una multa. (imponer)*

2. *Nosotros* .... *de aquí. (irse)*

3. *Ellos nos* .... *algo para comer. (traer)*

Getting In the Mood

As you know, Spanish has three verbal moods, which are covered in Part 8. These exercises will test your ability to use each one correctly.

Exercise 20: What Mood?

Below are ten things you might want to say to or ask someone. In the blank, fill in what mood you'd use when translating your statement into Spanish.

1. I want something to eat. ....

2. Go away, please. ....

3. I think it may be okay. ....

4. I would have done better if I had gotten more sleep.

    ....

5. Give me a coffee. ....

6. We will be there soon. ....

7. I am looking for the train station. ....

8. Could you close the window? ....

9. It's okay that you're tired. ....

10. I hope the lecture ends soon. ....

Exercise 21: A Wish or a Command

Identify which mood is used and translate into English.

1. *Sea lo que sea.*

    ....

2. *Descansemos por un rato.*

    ....

3. *Es cierto que nada se ha cambiado.*

    ....

4. *Lamento que ellos no me estimen.*

    ....

5. *Dame la mano.*

    ....

Exercise 22: More Moodiness

Switch the mood of each of the following sentences. If the mood is indicative, switch to subjunctive, and vice versa.

1. *Están alegres que tú vayas a visitarlos mañana.*

   ....

2. *Van a la fiesta aunque no tienen mucho tiempo.*

   ....

3. *Es cierto que no tenemos problemas con él.*

   ....

4. *Dudamos que ella haya hecho algo importante.*

   ....

5. *Espero que lleguen a tiempo.*

   ....

Exercise 23: Traveling in Time

Fill in the blank with the correct form of the given verb.

Present Subjunctive

1. Que te .... algo en la cabeza. (caer)

2. Yo deseo ganar, por supuesto, pero que .... lo mejor. (ser)

3. Son estúpidos los que .... ser exitosos sin hacer ningún esfuerzo. (pensar)

Present Perfect Subjunctive

1. *Es importante que tú* .... *esta información. (obtener)*

2. *Él duda que vosotros* .... *este libro. (leer)*

3. *No estamos seguros que ellos* .... *lo que paso. (ver)*

Past Perfect Subjunctive

1. *Ojalá que ustedes* .... *la felicidad que tenía yo cuando vivía allá. (tener)*

2. *Si la gente* .... *que se les manipulaba, él* .... *sus manipulaciones. (percibir, terminar)*

3. *Cualquier persona* .... *lo mismo. (hacer)*

Imperfect Subjunctive

1. *Mis padres llegaron al acuerdo que yo* .... *viajar a Canadá con mis amigos. (poder)*

2. *Es como si usted no* .... *en nosotros. (confiar)*

3. *Sentí la música como si* .... *por mis venas. (correr)*

Making Sense of Spanish

As your skills get better and better, you'll pick up some of the nuances of the language. The following exercises provide some more grammar challenges.

Exercise 24: One Thing Wrong

TRACK 30

Each sentence in this track has one grammatical mistake. Find the mistake and write the sentence down correctly.

1. ....

2. ....

3. ....

4. ....

5. ....

6. ....

7. ....

8. ....

9. ....

10. ....

Exercise 25: Final Corrections

Each sentence has one mistake in it, some sentences have two mistakes. Rewrite it in the space provided so that it's correct.

1. *Mis hermanas jóvenas se llaman Astrid y Elena.*

2. *Cuando fui una niña, me gustó jugar con muñecas.*

3. *Le estudio para mejorar la gramática.*

4. *Eres mi amigo, jamás no te daría daño.*

5. *Cuando pondré la ropa, estaré listo para salir.*

6. *Las tortas fue hecho por la mamá.*

7. *Siento muy embarazada que no te reconocí.*

8. *El viernes pasado hicieron mucho viento.*

9. *Ojalá que hace sol hoy todo el día.*

10. *Le la daré mañana.*

11. *Tenía nada para comer.*

12. *Pona usted el libro en la mesa.*

13. *Ya me limpié la casa.*

14. *Estoy poniendolos en la maleta.*

15. *Ella claromente tiene toda la razón.*

Appendix A
Verb Tables

hablar—regular AR verb	estar
beber—regular ER verb	hacer
asistir—regular IR verb	ir
haber—compound tense verb	oír
	oler
aparecer	reír
cerrar	saber
conocer	seguir
dar	ser
decir	tener
dormir	venir
enviar	ver

Hablar (to speak)

REGULAR –AR VERB

	PRESENT	SUBJUNCTIVE
yo	hablo	hable
tú	hablas	hables
él	habla	hable
nosotros	hablamos	hablemos
vosotros	habláis	habléis
ellos	hablan	hablen
	PRETERITE	IMPERFECT
yo	hablé	hablaba
tú	hablaste	hablabas
él	habló	hablaba
nosotros	hablamos	hablábamos
vosotros	hablasteis	hablabais
ellos	hablaron	hablaban
	FUTURE	CONDITIONAL
yo	hablaré	hablaría
tú	hablarás	hablarías
él	hablará	hablaría
nosotros	hablaremos	hablaríamos
vosotros	hablaréis	hablaríais
ellos	hablarán	hablarían
IMPERFECT SUBJUNCTIVE	FORM 1	FORM 2
yo	hablara	hablase
tú	hablaras	hablases
él	hablara	hablase
nosotros	habláramos	hablásemos
vosotros	hablarais	hablaseis
ellos	hablaran	hablasen
	COMMAND	PRESENT PARTICIPLE
(tú)	habla	hablando
	no hables	
(Ud.)	hable	
(nosotros)	hablemos	**Past Participle**
(vosotros)	hablad	hablado
	no habléis	
(Uds.)	hablen	

Beber (to drink)

Regular –ER verb

	PRESENT	SUBJUNCTIVE
yo	bebo	beba
tú	bebes	bebas
él	bebe	beba
nosotros	bebemos	bebamos
vosotros	bebéis	bebáis
ellos	beben	beban
PRETERITE	IMPERFECT	
yo	bebí	bebía
tú	bebiste	bebías
él	bebió	bebía
nosotros	bebimos	bebíamos
vosotros	bebisteis	bebíais
ellos	bebieron	bebían
FUTURE	CONDITIONAL	
yo	beberé	bebería
tú	beberás	beberías

él	beberá	bebería
nosotros	beberemos	beberíamos
vosotros	beberéis	beberíais
ellos	beberán	beberían
IMPERFECT SUBJUNCTIVE	FORM 1	FORM 2
yo	bebiera	bebiese
tú	bebieras	bebieses
él	bebiera	bebiese
nosotros	bebiéramos	bebiésemos
vosotros	bebierais	bebieseis
ellos	bebieran	bebiesen
	COMMAND	PRESENT PARTICIPLE
(tú)	bebe	bebiendo
	no bebas	
(Ud.)	beba	
(nosotros)	bebamos	Past Participle
(vosotros)	bebed	bebido
	no bebáis	
(Uds.)	beban	

Asistir (to attend)

Regular –IR verb

	PRESENT	SUBJUNCTIVE
yo	asisto	asista
tú	asistes	asistas
él	asiste	asista
nosotros	asistimos	asistamos
vosotros	asistís	asistáis
ellos	asisten	asistan
	PRETERITE	IMPERFECT
yo	asistí	asistía
tú	asististe	asistías
él	asistió	asistía
nosotros	asistimos	asistíamos
vosotros	asististeis	asistíais
ellos	asistieron	asistían
	FUTURE	CONDITIONAL
yo	asistiré	asistiría
tú	asistirás	asistirías
él	asistirá	asistiría
nosotros	asistiremos	asistiríamos
vosotros	asistiréis	asistiríais
ellos	asistirán	asistirían
IMPERFECT SUBJUNCTIVE	FORM 1	FORM 2
yo	asistiera	asistiese
tú	asistieras	asistieses
él	asistiera	asistiese
nosotros	asistiéramos	asistiésemos
vosotros	asistierais	asistieseis
ellos	asistieran	asistiesen
	COMMAND	PRESENT PARTICIPLE
(tú)	asiste	asistiendo
	no asistas	
(Ud.)	asista	
(nosotros)	asistamos	Past Participle
(vosotros)	asistid	asistido
	no asistáis	
(Uds.)	asistan	

Haber ("to have" in compound tenses; there is/are)

Irregular verb

	PRESENT	SUBJUNCTIVE
yo	he	haya
tú	has	hayas
él	ha	haya
nosotros	hemos	hayamos
vosotros	habéis	hayáis
ellos	han	hayan
	PRETERITE	IMPERFECT
yo	hube	había
tú	hubiste	habías
él	hubo	había
nosotros	hubimos	habíamos
vosotros	hubisteis	habíais
ellos	hubieron	habían
	FUTURE	CONDITIONAL
yo	habré	habría
tú	habrás	habrías
él	habrá	habría
nosotros	habremos	habríamos
vosotros	habréis	habríais
ellos	habrán	habrían
IMPERFECT SUBJUNCTIVE	FORM 1	FORM 2
yo	hubiera	hubiese
tú	hubieras	hubieses
él	hubiera	hubiese
nosotros	hubiéramos	hubiésemos
vosotros	hubierais	hubieseis
ellos	hubieran	hubiesen
	COMMAND	PRESENT PARTICIPLE
(tú)	he	habiendo
	no hayas	
(Ud.)	haya	
(nosotros)	hayamos	Past Participle
(vosotros)	habed	habido
	no hayáis	
(Uds.)	hayan	

Aparecer (to appear)

Spelling-change (C > ZC) –ER verb

	PRESENT	SUBJUNCTIVE
yo	aparezco	aparezca
tú	apareces	aparezcas
él	aparece	aparezca
nosotros	aparecemos	aparezcamos
vosotros	aparecéis	aparezcáis
ellos	aparecen	aparezcan
	PRETERITE	IMPERFECT
yo	aparecí	aparecía
tú	apareciste	aparecías
él	apareció	aparecía
nosotros	aparecimos	aparecíamos
vosotros	aparecisteis	aparecíais
ellos	aparecieron	aparecían
	FUTURE	CONDITIONAL
yo	apareceré	aparecería
tú	aparecerás	aparecerías
él	aparecerá	aparecería
nosotros	apareceremos	apareceríamos
vosotros	apareceréis	apareceríais
ellos	aparecerán	aparecerían
IMPERFECT SUBJUNCTIVE	FORM 1	FORM 2
yo	apareciera	apareciese
tú	aparecieras	aparecieses
él	apareciera	apareciese
nosotros	apareciéramos	apareciésemos
vosotros	aparecierais	aparecieseis
ellos	aparecieran	apareciesen
	COMMAND	PRESENT PARTICIPLE
(tú)	aparece	apareciendo
	no aparezcas	
(Ud.)	aparezca	
(nosotros)	aparezcamos	Past Participle
(vosotros)	apareced	aparecido
	no aparezcáis	
(Uds.)	aparezcan	

Cerrar (to close)

Stem-changing (E > IE) –AR verb

	PRESENT	SUBJUNCTIVE
yo	cierro	cierre
tú	cierras	cierres
él	cierra	cierre
nosotros	cerramos	cerremos
vosotros	cerráis	cerréis
ellos	cierran	cierren
	PRETERITE	IMPERFECT
yo	cerré	cerraba
tú	cerraste	cerrabas
él	cerró	cerraba
nosotros	cerramos	cerrábamos
vosotros	cerrasteis	cerrabais
ellos	cerraron	cerraban
	FUTURE	CONDITIONAL
yo	cerraré	cerraría
tú	cerrarás	cerrarías
él	cerrará	cerraría
nosotros	cerraremos	cerraríamos
vosotros	cerraréis	cerraríais
ellos	cerrarán	cerrarían
IMPERFECT SUBJUNCTIVE	FORM 1	FORM 2
yo	cerrara	cerrase
tú	cerraras	cerrases
él	cerrara	cerrase
nosotros	cerráramos	cerrásemos
vosotros	cerrarais	cerraseis
ellos	cerraran	cerrasen
	COMMAND	PRESENT PARTICIPLE
(tú)	cierra	cerrando
	no cierres	
(Ud.)	cierre	
(nosotros)	cerremos	Past Participle
(vosotros)	cerrad	cerrado
	no cerréis	
(Uds.)	cierren	

Conocer (to know)

Spelling-change (C > ZC) –ER verb

	PRESENT	SUBJUNCTIVE
yo	conozco	conozca
tú	conoces	conozcas
él	conoce	conozca
nosotros	conocemos	conozcamos
vosotros	conocéis	conozcáis
ellos	conocen	conozcan
	PRETERITE	IMPERFECT
yo	conocí	conocía
tú	conociste	conocías
él	conoció	conocía
nosotros	conocimos	conocíamos
vosotros	conocisteis	conocíais
ellos	conocieron	conocían
	FUTURE	CONDITIONAL
yo	conoceré	conocería
tú	conocerás	conocerías
él	conocerá	conocería
nosotros	conoceremos	conoceríamos
vosotros	conoceréis	conoceríais
ellos	conocerán	conocerían
IMPERFECT SUBJUNCTIVE	FORM 1	FORM 2
yo	conociera	conociese
tú	conocieras	conocieses
él	conociera	conociese
nosotros	conociéramos	conociésemos
vosotros	conocierais	conocieseis
ellos	conocieran	conociesen
	COMMAND	PRESENT PARTICIPLE
(tú)	conoce	conociendo
	no conozcas	
(Ud.)	conozca	
(nosotros)	conozcamos	Past Participle
(vosotros)	conoced	conocido
	no conozcáis	
(Uds.)	conozcan	

Dar (to give)

Irregular –AR verb

	PRESENT	SUBJUNCTIVE
yo	doy	dé
tú	das	des
él	da	dé
nosotros	damos	demos
vosotros	dais	deis
ellos	dan	den
	PRETERITE	IMPERFECT
yo	di	daba
tú	diste	dabas
él	dio	daba
nosotros	dimos	dábamos
vosotros	disteis	dabais
ellos	dieron	daban

	FUTURE	CONDITIONAL
yo	daré	daría
tú	darás	darías
él	dará	daría
nosotros	daremos	daríamos
vosotros	daréis	daríais
ellos	darán	darían
IMPERFECT SUBJUNCTIVE	FORM 1	FORM 2
yo	diera	diese
tú	dieras	dieses
él	diera	diese
nosotros	diéramos	diésemos
vosotros	dierais	dieseis
ellos	dieran	diesen
	COMMAND	PRESENT PARTICIPLE
(tú)	da	dando
	no des	
(Ud.)	dé	
(nosotros)	demos	Past Participle
(vosotros)	dad	dado
	no deis	
(Uds.)	den	

Decir (to say)

Irregular –IR verb

	PRESENT	SUBJUNCTIVE
yo	digo	diga
tú	dices	digas
él	dice	diga
nosotros	decimos	digamos
vosotros	decís	digáis
ellos	dicen	digan
	PRETERITE	IMPERFECT
yo	dije	decía
tú	dijiste	decías
él	dijo	decía
nosotros	dijimos	decíamos
vosotros	dijisteis	decíais
ellos	dijeron	decían
	FUTURE	CONDITIONAL
yo	diré	diría
tú	dirás	dirías
él	dirá	diría
nosotros	diremos	diríamos
vosotros	diréis	diríais
ellos	dirán	dirían
IMPERFECT SUBJUNCTIVE	FORM 1	FORM 2
yo	dijera	dijese
tú	dijeras	dijeses
él	dijera	dijese
nosotros	dijéramos	dijésemos
vosotros	dijerais	dijeseis
ellos	dijeran	dijesen

	COMMAND	PRESENT PARTICIPLE
(tú)	di	diciendo
	no digas	
(Ud.)	diga	
(nosotros)	digamos	Past Participle
(vosotros)	decid	dicho
	no digáis	
(Uds.)	digan	

Dormir (to sleep)

Stem-changing (O > UE) –IR verb

	PRESENT	SUBJUNCTIVE
yo	duermo	duerma
tú	duermes	duermas
él	duerme	duerma
nosotros	dormimos	durmamos
vosotros	dormís	durmáis
ellos	duermen	duerman

	PRETERITE	IMPERFECT
yo	dormí	dormía
tú	dormiste	dormías
él	durmió	dormía
nosotros	dormimos	dormíamos
vosotros	dormisteis	dormíais
ellos	durmieron	dormían

	FUTURE	CONDITIONAL
yo	dormiré	dormiría
tú	dormirás	dormirías
él	dormirá	dormiría
nosotros	dormiremos	dormiríamos
vosotros	dormiréis	dormiríais
ellos	dormirán	dormirían

IMPERFECT SUBJUNCTIVE	FORM 1	FORM 2
yo	durmiera	durmiese
tú	durmieras	durmieses
él	durmiera	durmiese
nosotros	durmiéramos	durmiésemos
vosotros	durmierais	durmieseis
ellos	durmieran	durmiesen

	COMMAND	PRESENT PARTICIPLE
(tú)	duerme	durmiendo
	no duermas	
(Ud.)	duerma	
(nosotros)	durmamos	Past Participle
(vosotros)	dormid	dormido
	no durmáis	
(Uds.)	duerman	

Enviar (to send)

Regular –AR verb with irregular accentuation

	PRESENT	SUBJUNCTIVE
yo	envío	envíe
tú	envías	envíes
él	envía	envíe
nosotros	enviamos	enviemos
vosotros	enviáis	enviéis
ellos	envían	envíen

	PRETERITE	IMPERFECT
yo	envié	enviaba
tú	enviaste	enviabas
él	envió	enviaba
nosotros	enviamos	enviábamos
vosotros	enviasteis	enviabais
ellos	enviaron	enviaban

	FUTURE	CONDITIONAL
yo	enviaré	enviaría
tú	enviarás	enviarías
él	enviará	enviaría
nosotros	enviaremos	enviaríamos
vosotros	enviaréis	enviaríais
ellos	enviarán	enviarían

IMPERFECT SUBJUNCTIVE	FORM 1	FORM 2
yo	enviara	enviase
tú	enviaras	enviases
él	enviara	enviase
nosotros	enviáramos	enviásemos
vosotros	enviarais	enviaseis
ellos	enviaran	enviasen

	COMMAND	PRESENT PARTICIPLE
(tú)	envía	enviando
	no envíes	
(Ud.)	envíe	
(nosotros)	enviemos	Past Participle
(vosotros)	enviad	enviado
	no enviéis	
(Uds.)	envíen	

Estar (to be)

Irregular –AR verb

	PRESENT	SUBJUNCTIVE
yo	estoy	esté
tú	estás	estés
él	está	esté
nosotros	estamos	estemos
vosotros	estáis	estéis
ellos	están	estén

	PRETERITE	IMPERFECT
yo	estuve	estaba
tú	estuviste	estabas
él	estuvo	estaba
nosotros	estuvimos	estábamos
vosotros	estuvisteis	estabais
ellos	estuvieron	estaban

	FUTURE	CONDITIONAL
yo	estaré	estaría
tú	estarás	estarías
él	estará	estaría
nosotros	estaremos	estaríamos
vosotros	estaréis	estaríais
ellos	estarán	estarían

IMPERFECT SUBJUNCTIVE	FORM 1	FORM 2
yo	estuviera	estuviese
tú	estuvieras	estuvieses
él	estuviera	estuviese
nosotros	estuviéramos	estuviésemos

vosotros	estuvierais	estuvieseis
ellos	estuvieran	estuviesen
	COMMAND	PRESENT PARTICIPLE
(tú)	está	estando
	no estés	
(Ud.)	esté	
(nosotros)	estemos	Past Participle
(vosotros)	estad	estado
	no estéis	
(Uds.)	estén	

Hacer (to do, to make)
Irregular –ER verb

	PRESENT	SUBJUNCTIVE
yo	hago	haga
tú	haces	hagas
él	hace	haga
nosotros	hacemos	hagamos
vosotros	hacéis	hagáis
ellos	hacen	hagan
	PRETERITE	IMPERFECT
yo	hice	hacía
tú	hiciste	hacías
él	hizo	hacía
nosotros	hicimos	hacíamos
vosotros	hicisteis	hacíais
ellos	hicieron	hacían
	FUTURE	CONDITIONAL
yo	haré	haría
tú	harás	harías
él	hará	haría
nosotros	haremos	haríamos
vosotros	haréis	haríais
ellos	harán	harían
IMPERFECT SUBJUNCTIVE	FORM 1	FORM 2
yo	hiciera	hiciese
tú	hicieras	hicieses
él	hiciera	hiciese
nosotros	hiciéramos	hiciésemos
vosotros	hicierais	hicieseis
ellos	hicieran	hiciesen
	COMMAND	PRESENT PARTICIPLE
(tú)	haz	haciendo
	no hagas	
(Ud.)	haga	
(nosotros)	hagamos	Past Participle
(vosotros)	haced	hecho
	no hagáis	
(Uds.)	hagan	

Ir (to go)
Irregular –IR verb

	PRESENT	SUBJUNCTIVE
yo	voy	vaya
tú	vas	vayas
él	va	vaya
nosotros	vamos	vayamos
vosotros	vais	vayáis
ellos	van	vayan
	PRETERITE	IMPERFECT
yo	fui	iba
tú	fuiste	ibas
él	fue	iba
nosotros	fuimos	íbamos
vosotros	fuisteis	ibais
ellos	fueron	iban
	FUTURE	CONDITIONAL
yo	iré	iría
tú	irás	irías
él	irá	iría
nosotros	iremos	iríamos
vosotros	iréis	iríais
ellos	irán	irían
IMPERFECT SUBJUNCTIVE	FORM 1	FORM 2
yo	fuera	fuese
tú	fueras	fueses
él	fuera	fuese
nosotros	fuéramos	fuésemos
vosotros	fuerais	fueseis
ellos	fueran	fuesen
	COMMAND	PRESENT PARTICIPLE
(tú)	ve	yendo
	no vayas	
(Ud.)	vaya	
(nosotros)	vamos	Past Participle
	no vayamos	ido
(vosotros)	id	
	no vayáis	
(Uds.)	vayan	

Oír (to hear)
Irregular –IR verb

	PRESENT	SUBJUNCTIVE
yo	oigo	oiga
tú	oyes	oigas
él	oye	oiga
nosotros	oímos	oigamos
vosotros	oís	oigáis
ellos	oyen	oigan
	PRETERITE	IMPERFECT
yo	oí	oía
tú	oíste	oías
él	oyó	oía
nosotros	oímos	oíamos
vosotros	oísteis	oíais
ellos	oyeron	oían

	FUTURE	CONDITIONAL
yo	oiré	oiría
tú	oirás	oirías
él	oirá	oiría
nosotros	oiremos	oiríamos
vosotros	oiréis	oiríais
ellos	oirán	oirían
IMPERFECT SUBJUNCTIVE	**FORM 1**	**FORM 2**
yo	oyera	oyese
tú	oyeras	oyeses
él	oyera	oyese
nosotros	oyéramos	oyésemos
vosotros	oyerais	oyeseis
ellos	oyeran	oyesen
	COMMAND	**PRESENT PARTICIPLE**
(tú)	oye	oyendo
	no oigas	
(Ud.)	oiga	
(nosotros)	oigamos	*Past Participle*
(vosotros)	oíd	oído
	no oigáis	
(Uds.)	oigan	

Oler (to smell)
Irregular stem-changing (O > UE) –ER verb

	PRESENT	SUBJUNCTIVE
yo	huelo	huela
tú	hueles	huelas
él	huele	huela
nosotros	olemos	olamos
vosotros	oléis	oláis
ellos	huelen	huelan
	PRETERITE	**IMPERFECT**
yo	olí	olía
tú	oliste	olías
él	olió	olía
nosotros	olimos	olíamos
vosotros	olisteis	olíais
ellos	olieron	olían
	FUTURE	**CONDITIONAL**
yo	oleré	olería
tú	olerás	olerías
él	olerá	olería
nosotros	oleremos	oleríamos
vosotros	oleréis	oleríais
ellos	olerán	olerían
IMPERFECT SUBJUNCTIVE	**FORM 1**	**FORM 2**
yo	oliera	oliese
tú	olieras	olieses
él	oliera	oliese
nosotros	oliéramos	oliésemos
vosotros	olierais	olieseis
ellos	olieran	oliesen

	COMMAND	PRESENT PARTICIPLE
(tú)	huele	oliendo
	no huelas	
(Ud.)	huela	
(nosotros)	olamos	*Past Participle*
(vosotros)	oled	olido
	no oláis	
(Uds.)	huelan	

Reír (to laugh)
Irregular –IR verb

	PRESENT	SUBJUNCTIVE
yo	río ría	
tú	ríes	rías
él	ríe	ría
nosotros	reímos	riamos
vosotros	reís	riáis
ellos	ríen	rían
	PRETERITE	**IMPERFECT**
yo	reí	reía
tú	reíste	reías
él	rió	reía
nosotros	reímos	reíamos
vosotros	reísteis	reíais
ellos	rieron	reían
	FUTURE	**CONDITIONAL**
yo	reiré	reiría
tú	reirás	reirías
él	reirá	reiría
nosotros	reiremos	reiríamos
vosotros	reiréis	reiríais
ellos	reirán	reirían
IMPERFECT SUBJUNCTIVE	**FORM 1**	**FORM 2**
yo	riera	riese
tú	rieras	rieses
él	riera	riese
nosotros	riéramos	riésemos
vosotros	rierais	rieseis
ellos	rieran	riesen
	COMMAND	**PRESENT PARTICIPLE**
(tú)	ríe	riendo
	no rías	
(Ud.)	ría	
(nosotros)	riamos	*Past Participle*
(vosotros)	reíd	reído
	no riáis	
(Uds.)	rían	

Saber (to know)
Irregular –ER verb

	PRESENT	SUBJUNCTIVE
yo	sé sepa	
tú	sabes	sepas
él	sabe	sepa
nosotros	sabemos	sepamos
vosotros	sabéis	sepáis
ellos	saben	sepan

	PRETERITE	IMPERFECT
yo	supe	sabía
tú	supiste	sabías
él	supo	sabía
nosotros	supimos	sabíamos
vosotros	supisteis	sabíais
ellos	supieron	sabían
	FUTURE	CONDITIONAL
yo	sabré	sabría
tú	sabrás	sabrías
él	sabrá	sabría
nosotros	sabremos	sabríamos
vosotros	sabréis	sabríais
ellos	sabrán	sabrían
IMPERFECT SUBJUNCTIVE	FORM 1	FORM 2
yo	supiera	supiese
tú	supieras	supieses
él	supiera	supiese
nosotros	supiéramos	supiésemos
vosotros	supierais	supieseis
ellos	supieran	supiesen
	COMMAND	PRESENT PARTICIPLE
(tú)	sabe	sabiendo
	no sepas	
(Ud.)	sepa	
(nosotros)	sepamos	Past Participle
(vosotros)	sabed	sabido
	no sepáis	
(Uds.)	sepan	

Seguir (to follow, to continue)
Stem-changing (E > I) and spelling-change (GU > G) –IR verb

	PRESENT	SUBJUNCTIVE
yo	sigo	siga
tú	sigues	sigas
él	sigue	siga
nosotros	seguimos	sigamos
vosotros	seguís	sigáis
ellos	siguen	sigan
	PRETERITE	IMPERFECT
yo	seguí	seguía
tú	seguiste	seguías
él	siguió	seguía
nosotros	seguimos	seguíamos
vosotros	seguisteis	seguíais
ellos	siguieron	seguían
	FUTURE	CONDITIONAL
yo	seguiré	seguiría
tú	seguirás	seguirías
él	seguirá	seguiría
nosotros	seguiremos	seguiríamos
vosotros	seguiréis	seguiríais
ellos	seguirán	seguirían

IMPERFECT SUBJUNCTIVE	FORM 1	FORM 2
yo	siguiera	siguiese
tú	siguieras	siguieses
él	siguiera	siguiese
nosotros	siguiéramos	siguiésemos
vosotros	siguierais	siguieseis
ellos	siguieran	siguiesen
	COMMAND	PRESENT PARTICIPLE
(tú)	sigue	siguiendo
	no sigas	
(Ud.)	siga	
(nosotros)	sigamos	Past Participle
(vosotros)	seguid	seguido
	no sigáis	
(Uds.)	sigan	

Ser (to be)
Irregular –ER verb

	PRESENT	SUBJUNCTIVE
yo	soy	sea
tú	eres	seas
él	es	sea
nosotros	somos	seamos
vosotros	sois	seáis
ellos	son	sean
	PRETERITE	IMPERFECT
yo	fui	era
tú	fuiste	eras
él	fue	era
nosotros	fuimos	éramos
vosotros	fuisteis	erais
ellos	fueron	eran
	FUTURE	CONDITIONAL
yo	seré	sería
tú	serás	serías
él	será	sería
nosotros	seremos	seríamos
vosotros	seréis	seríais
ellos	serán	serían
IMPERFECT SUBJUNCTIVE	FORM 1	FORM 2
yo	fuera	fuese
tú	fueras	fueses
él	fuera	fuese
nosotros	fuéramos	fuésemos
vosotros	fuerais	fueseis
ellos	fueran	fuesen
	COMMAND	PRESENT PARTICIPLE
(tú)	sé	siendo
	no seas	
(Ud.)	sea	
(nosotros)	seamos	Past Participle
(vosotros)	sed	sido
	no seáis	
(Uds.)	sean	

Tener (to have)

Irregular –ER verb

	PRESENT	SUBJUNCTIVE
yo	tengo	tenga
tú	tienes	tengas
él	tiene	tenga
nosotros	tenemos	tengamos
vosotros	tenéis	tengáis
ellos	tienen	tengan
	PRETERITE	IMPERFECT
yo	tuve	tenía
tú	tuviste	tenías
él	tuvo	tenía
nosotros	tuvimos	teníamos
vosotros	tuvisteis	teníais
ellos	tuvieron	tenían
	FUTURE	CONDITIONAL
yo	tendré	tendría
tú	tendrás	tendrías
él	tendrá	tendría
nosotros	tendremos	tendríamos
vosotros	tendréis	tendríais
ellos	tendrán	tendrían
IMPERFECT SUBJUNCTIVE	FORM 1	FORM 2
yo	tuviera	tuviese
tú	tuvieras	tuvieses
él	tuviera	tuviese
nosotros	tuviéramos	tuviésemos
vosotros	tuvierais	tuvieseis
ellos	tuvieran	tuviesen
	COMMAND	PRESENT PARTICIPLE
(tú)	ten	teniendo
	no tengas	
(Ud.)	tenga	
(nosotros)	tengamos	Past Participle
(vosotros)	tened	tenido
	no tengáis	
(Uds.)	tengan	

Venir (to come)

Irregular stem-changing (E > IE) –IR verb

	PRESENT	SUBJUNCTIVE
yo	vengo	venga
tú	vienes	vengas
él	viene	venga
nosotros	venimos	vengamos
vosotros	venís	vengáis
ellos	vienen	vengan
	PRETERITE	IMPERFECT
yo	vine	venía
tú	viniste	venías
él	vino	venía
nosotros	vinimos	veníamos
vosotros	vinisteis	veníais
ellos	vinieron	venían
	FUTURE	CONDITIONAL
yo	vendré	vendría
tú	vendrás	vendrías
él	vendrá	vendría
nosotros	vendremos	vendríamos
vosotros	vendréis	vendríais
ellos	vendrán	vendrían
IMPERFECT SUBJUNCTIVE	FORM 1	FORM 2
yo	viniera	viniese
tú	vinieras	vinieses
él	viniera	viniese
nosotros	viniéramos	viniésemos
vosotros	vinierais	vinieseis
ellos	vinieran	viniesen
	COMMAND	PRESENT PARTICIPLE
(tú)	ven	viniendo
	no vengas	
(Ud.)	venga	
(nosotros)	vengamos	Past Participle
(vosotros)	venid	venido
	no vengáis	
(Uds.)	vengan	

Ver (to see)

Irregular –ER verb

	PRESENT	SUBJUNCTIVE
yo	veo	vea
tú	ves	veas
él	ve	vea
nosotros	vemos	veamos
vosotros	veis	veáis
ellos	ven	vean
	PRETERITE	IMPERFECT
yo	vi	veía
tú	viste	veías
él	vio	veía
nosotros	vimos	veíamos
vosotros	visteis	veíais
ellos	vieron	veían
	FUTURE	CONDITIONAL
yo	veré	vería
tú	verás	verías
él	verá	vería
nosotros	veremos	veríamos
vosotros	veréis	veríais
ellos	verán	verían
IMPERFECT SUBJUNCTIVE	FORM 1	FORM 2
yo	viera	viese
tú	vieras	vieses
él	viera	viese
nosotros	viéramos	viésemos
vosotros	vierais	vieseis
ellos	vieran	viesen
	COMMAND	PRESENT PARTICIPLE
(tú)	ve	viendo
	no veas	
(Ud.)	vea	
(nosotros)	veamos	Past Participle
(vosotros)	ved	visto
	no veáis	
(Uds.)	vean	

Appendix B

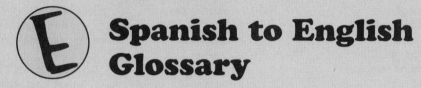

Spanish to English Glossary

A	
SPANISH	**ENGLISH**
abandonar	to abandon
la abeja	bee
abierto	open
el abogado	lawyer
abolir	to abolish
el abrazo	hug
el abrigo	overcoat
abril	April
abrir	to open
la abuela	grandmother
el abuelo	grandfather
aburrido	boring, bored
aburrir	to bore
aburrirse	to be bored
acá	around here
acabar	to finish
el accidente	accident
el aceite	oil
la aceituna	olive
aceptar	to accept
acercar	to move something closer
acercarse	to approach
acogedor	cozy
aconsejar	to advise
acordarse	to remember
acostar	to put to bed
acostarse	to go to bed
acostumbrarse	to get used to
la actitud	attitude
el actor	actor
la actriz	actress
actual	current
actualmente	at present
actuar	to act
acuchillar	to cut up (with a knife)
el acusador	accuser, accusing
adaptar	to adapt
adentro	inside
el adjetivo	adjective
admitir	to accept
adónde	to where
adoptar	to adopt
el adverbio	adverb
advertir	to warn
el aeropuerto	airport
afeitar(se)	to shave
el aficionado	fan
a fin de que	in order that
afligir	to afflict
agosto	August
agradecer	to thank
el agua	water
el agua mineral	mineral water
el aguacate	avocado
el águila	the eagle

ahogar	to choke, to drown
ahora	now
el ajedrez	chess
el ajo	garlic
la alabanza	praise
al final	at the end
al fondo	at the end
al lado de	next to
alegrarse	to be happy
la alegría	joy, happiness
alemán	German
Alemania	Germany
la alfombra	carpet
algo	something
alguien	someone, somebody
algún	some
algunas veces	sometimes
alguna vez	once, sometime
el alivio	relief
al ajillo	in garlic sauce
allí	there
el almacén	grocery store
la almohada	pillow
almorzar	to have lunch
alquilar	to rent
alrededor	around
alto	high, tall
el alumno	student
amable	nice
amar	to love
amarillo	yellow
el ambiente	environment
ambos, ambas	both
a menos que	unless
a menudo	often
americano, estadounidense	American
el amigo	friend
la amistad	friendship
el amor	love
la anarquía	anarchy
andar	to walk
andén	platform
anteayer	day before yesterday
el antebrazo	forearm
antemano	beforehand
los anteojos	glasses
antes	before
antiguo	old
antinatural	unnatural
la antipatía	antipathy
el antisudoral	antiperspirant
el antojito	appetizer
anunciar	to announce
el anuncio de trabajo	help-wanted ad
añadir	to join, to increase
el año	year
apagar	to turn off

aparecer	to appear
el apartamento	apartment
el apellido	last name
apenas	barely
a pesar de	despite
el apetito	appetite
a pie	on foot
aplaudir	to applaud
el aplauso	applause
aprender	to learn, to study
el aprendizaje	apprenticeship
apresurarse a	to hurry
apretar	to grip
aquél	that one
aquel	that
aquí	here
a quien corresponda	to whom it may concern
el árbol	tree
el archivo	filing cabinet
la arena	sand
la arepa	corn pancake
Argelia	Algeria
argelino	Algerian
argentino	Argentinean
el armario	dresser
arreglar	to fix, settle, arrange
arreglarse	to get ready
el arreglo	compromise
arriba	upstairs, above
el arroz	rice
el arroz con frijoles	rice and beans
el arroz con leche	rice pudding
el arte	art
el artículo	article
ascender	to go up
así	like that, so
el asiento	seat
asistir	to attend
asumir	to assume
el asunto	matter
el ateísmo	atheism
la atención	attention
atender	to serve
atentamente	sincerely
atento	attentive, sincere
atestado	full, packed
a tiempo	on time
a todos partes	everywhere
atravesar	to cross
atreverse	to dare to
atribuir	to attribute
el atún	tuna
el audífono	hearing aid
aumentar	to increase
aún	even
aunque	although
australiano	Australian

austríaco	Austrian
la autobiografía	autobiography
el autobús	bus
la autodefensa	self-defense
la autopista	highway
el autor	author
la autorización	authorization
la avaricia	avarice
el ave	poultry
a veces	sometimes
la avenida	avenue
avergonzado	embarrassed
el avión	plane
avisar	to tell
ayer	yesterday
ayudar	to help
el azúcar	sugar
azul	blue

B

SPANISH	ENGLISH
el bacalao	cod
bailar	to dance
bajar	to get off
bajo	short
el bancario	banker
el banco	bank, bench
bañar	to bathe
bañarse	to take a bath
barato	cheap, inexpensive
la barra de pan	loaf of bread
barrer	to sweep
bastante	rather
la basura	trash
la batería (tocar)	drums (to play)
el batido	milk shake
el bebé	baby
beber	to drink
la bebida	drink
beige	beige
belga	Belgian
Bélgica	Belgium
bello	beautiful, lovely
la berenjena	eggplant
besar	to kiss
la biblioteca	library
el bibliotecario	librarian
bien	well
bienvenidos	welcome
el bigote	moustache
el billete	ticket
billetera	wallet
el billón	trillion
el bistec	(beef) steak
blanco	white
blando	soft

Spanish	English
la blusa	blouse
la boca	mouth
el bocadillo	a little sandwich, snack
la boda	wedding
el boleto	ticket
el bolígrafo	pen
boliviano	Bolivian
la bolsa	handbag
el bolsillo	pocket
bonito	pretty
el borrador	board eraser
botas	boots
el bote	boat
el botón	key
el Brasil	Brazil
brasileño	Brazilian
brillante	shiny
la brisa	breeze
la bronquitis	bronchitis
bueno	good
la bufanda	scarf
el buñuelo	fritter
buscar	to look for
el buzón	mailbox

C

Spanish	English
el cabello	hair
caber	to fit
cada	each
caer	to fall
café	brown
el café	coffee
la cafetería	coffee shop
la caja	box, cash register
cajón	drawer
la calabaza	pumpkin
el calamar	squid, calamari
el calambre	cramp
el calcetín	sock
la calidad	quality
cálido	hot
caliente	hot
la calificación	grades
callarse	to be quiet, to shut up
la calle	street
el calor	heat
la cama	bed
la camarera	waitress
el camarero	waiter
el camarón	shrimp
cambiar	to change
caminar	to walk
el camino	road, way
el camión	truck
la camisa	shirt
la camiseta	t-shirt

Spanish	English
el campamento	camp
el campanario	bell tower
el campo	field, countryside
el Canadá	Canada
canadiense	Canadian
la canción	song
la canción de cuna	lullaby
cansado	tired
cantar	to sing
la capa	top
el capítulo	chapter
el capricho	caprice
la cara	face
cargar	to load
cariñoso	affectionate
la carne	meat
la carne de cerdo	pork
la carne de res	beef
caro	expensive
la carpeta	folder
la carta	menu, letter
la carta de acompañamiento	cover letter
el cartel	poster
la casa	house, home
casado	married
casar(se)	to marry (each other)
casi	almost
el caso	case
castaño	chestnut-colored
castellano	Spanish (the language)
la catedral	cathedral
el catedrático	professor
el catolicismo	Catholicism
católico	Catholic
catorce	fourteen
la cazadora	sports jacket
la cebolla	onion
la cena	dinner
el centro	downtown
cepillar(se)	to brush (teeth, hair)
la cerámica	ceramic pottery
cerca (de)	close by, near
cero	zero
cerrado	closed
cerrar	to close
la certidumbre	certainty
la cerveza	beer
el césped	lawn
la cesta	wastebasket
el ceviche	fish or seafood cured in lemon juice
el champiñón	mushroom
el champú	shampoo
la chaqueta	jacket
la charla	lecture
charlar	to chat
charlatán	talkative, boasting

la chica	girl	cómo	how
el chicle	chewing gum	como	as, like
el chico	boy	cómodo	comfortable
chileno	Chilean	compadecer	to sympathize with
los chiles rellenos	stuffed peppers	la compañía	company
chino	Chinese	el compás	compass
el chisme	gossip	complejo	complex
chismorrear	to gossip	comportarse bien	to be well behaved
el chiste	joke	comprar	to buy
el chivo	goat	comprender	to understand
chocar	to crash	comprobar	to check
el chocolate	chocolate	compromiso	obligation, commitment
el chorizo	pork sausage	la computadora	computer
la chuleta	rib, chop	común	common
la cicatriz	scar	la comunidad	community
el cielo	sky	comunista	communist
cien	hundred	con	with
cierto	some, true, certain	conceder	to concede, to grant, to award
cinco	five	concluir	to end, to conclude
cincuenta	fifty	conducir	to drive
el cine	movies	el conejo	rabbit
circular	circular	la conferencia	lecture
la cita	date	confiar	to confide
la ciudad	city	confundir	to confuse, to confound
claramente	clearly	con gas	carbonated
claro	bright, clear	la conjunción	conjunction
la clase	class	conjugar	to conjugate
el cliente	client	conmigo	with me
la clínica	clinic, hospital	conmover	to move, to touch
la cosa	thing	conocer	to know
cobrizo	coppery	con permiso	excuse me
la Coca Cola	Coke	consagrar	to consecrate
el coche	car	la consecuencia	consequence
el coche-restaurante	dining car	conseguir	to get, to achieve
la cocina	kitchen	el conservador	preservative
cocinar	to cook	consistir	to consist
el cocinero, la cocinera	cook, chef	el consorte	consort, accomplice
la cocineta	kitchenette	constiparse	to catch a cold
coger	to grab	consumir	to consume
la cola	waiting line, tail	contar	to tell, to count
el colchón	mattress	la contemplación	contemplation
el colegio	high school	contestar	to answer
el coliflor	cauliflower	contigo	with you
el collar	necklace	continuar	to continue
colocar	to put	con todo	despite, as
colocarse	to get a job, to find one's place	contra	against
colombiano	Colombian	la contracubierta	back cover
el color	color	el contragolpe	counter-blow
color de avellana	hazel	contrapelo	against the grain
la coma	comma	la contraseña	password
combatir	to fight, to combat	contribuir a	to contribute to
el comedor	dining room	convenir(le)	to suit
comenzar a	to begin to	convivir	to live together, to coexist
comer	to eat	la corbata	tie
cometer	to commit	el cordero	lamb
el cómico	comedian	coreano	Korean
las comillas	quotation marks	la corona	crown

la corpulencia	stoutness	deber	must
corpulento	fat	débil	weak
los correos	post office	la década	decade
el correo electrónico	e-mail	decaer	to decline
correr	to run	la decepción	disappointment
el cortado	coffee with a small amount of milk	decidir	to decide
corte de pelo	haircut	décimo	tenth
cortés	polite	decir	to say
la cortina	curtain	dedicarse a	to devote oneself to
corto	short	el dedo	finger
coser	to sew	deducir	to deduce
el/la cosmopolita	cosmopolitan	defender	to defend
costar	to cost	definir	to define
costarricense	Costa Rican	dejar	to leave
crecer	to grow	delante de	in front of
creer	to believe	el deleite	delight
la crema	cream	deletrear	to spell
la croqueta	croquette	delgado	thin
cruzar	to cross	el delito	crime
el cuadro	picture, painting	demandar, exigir	to demand
el cuaderno	notebook	de manera que	so that
cuál	which?	demasiado	too (adverb modifying an adjective)
cual	which	demás	the rest
cualquier	whichever	el/la dentista	dentist
cuándo	when?	de nada	you're welcome
cuando	when, then	dentro de	inside
cuánto	how much, how many?	la denuncia	denunciation
cuanto	as much, as many	el dependiente	shop assistant
cuarenta	forty	el deporte	sport
cuarto	fourth	el depósito	tank
el cuarto	room, bedroom	deprimir	to depress
cuatro	four	derecha	right
cuatrocientos	four hundred	derecho	straight, right
cubano	Cuban	derivar	to derive from
cubrir	to cover	desabrochar	to undo
la cuchara	spoon	el desayuno	breakfast
la cucharita	teaspoon	descansar	rest
el cuchillo	knife	descender	to descend
la cuenta	bill	describir	to describe
la cuerda	rope	descubrir	to discover
cuerdo	sane	desde	from, since
el cuerpo	body	descolorido	discolored
la cuestión	matter, question	deseable	desirable
el cuidado	care	descortés	rude
la culminación	culmination, end result	desembarcar	to disembark
culto	educated	el desempleo (paro)	unemployment
el cumpleaños	birthday	la desgracia	misfortune
cumplir	to complete, to finish	desgraciadamente	unfortunately
el curriculum profesional	resume	la deshonra	disgrace
		despacio	slowly
		despedir	to fire

D	
SPANISH	**ENGLISH**
danés	Danish
dar	to give
darse cuenta	to realize
de acuerdo	in agreement
debajo	under

despedirse	to say goodbye
después de	after
el destino	destination
destruir	to destroy
detener	to bring to a halt
detrás	behind

detenerse	to come to a halt
devolver	to return, to give back
el día	day
el dibujo	drawing
el diccionario	dictionary
diciembre	December
el diente	tooth
diez	ten
diecinueve	nineteen
dieciocho	eighteen
dieciséis	sixteen
diecisiete	seventeen
la dieta	diet
diferente(s)	various, different
difícil	difficult
dignificar	to dignify
Dinamarca	Denmark
el dinero	money
Dios	God
la dirección	address
dirigir	to direct
la discordia	disagreement
discutir	to discuss
disuadir	to dissuade
la diversión	fun, a hobby
divertido	fun
divertirse	to have fun
dividir	to divide
divorciado	divorced
doblar	to turn
doce	twelve
la docena	dozen
doler	to hurt
el domingo	Sunday
dominicano	Dominican
dónde	where?
donde	where, there
dormir	to sleep
dormirse	to go to sleep
dos	two
doscientos	two hundred
dosificar	to measure out (dose)
dos puntos	colon
la ducha	shower
dudar	to doubt
dudoso	doubtful
(el) dulce	candy, sweet
el dúo	duet
la duquesa	duchess
durante	during

E	
SPANISH	**ENGLISH**
echar	to put
echarse a	to start to
ecuatoriano	Ecuadorian
la edad	age

el edificio	building
educado	well-mannered, polite
efectivamente	really
egipcio	Egyptian
Egipto	Egypt
el ejemplo	example
el ejercicio	exercise
el/la electricista	electrician
el embarazo	pregnancy
el embarque	boarding
emitir	to emit
emocional	emotional
emocionante	thrilling, moving
la empanada	savory stuffed pastry, usually with meat
empezar (a)	to begin (to)
el empleado	employee
el empleo	job
en	in, on
encantar(le)	to enchant, delight
en caso de que	in case
encender	to light
encima	over
encoger	to shrink
encontrar	to find
en cuanto	as soon as
encubridor	concealing
la energía	energy
enero	January
enfadado	angry
enfadarse	to get angry
la enfermera	nurse
enfermo	sick
enfrente a	facing, across from
el engaño	deception
enlazar	to link
en línea	online
enmicar	to cover in plastic
enojarse	to get angry
la ensalada	salad
el ensayo	essay
la enseñanza	education
enseñar a	to teach how to
en seguida	immediately
entender	to understand
enterar(se)	to find out
la entrada	entrance, way in
entrar	to come in, to enter
entre	between
entrever	to glimpse
la entrevista	interview
entusiasta	enthusiastic
enviar	to send
envolver	to wrap
el equipaje	luggage
el equipo	team
equivocado	wrong

errar	to stray, to wander, to err
el error	mistake
escocés	Scottish
Escocia	Scotland
escolar	school (adj.)
escolástico	academic, scholarly
esconder	to hide
escribir	to write
el escritorio	desk
la escritura	writing
escuchar	to listen
la escuela	school
la escuela universitaria	college
la escultura	sculpture
escupir	to spit
ése	that one
ese	that
la esfera	sphere
España	Spain
español	Spanish (from Spain)
especial	special
la especie	species
esperar	to hope
espiar	to spy
la espinaca	spinach
la esposa	wife, spouse
el esposo	husband, spouse
esquiar	to ski
la esquina	corner
establecer	to establish
la estación	station
los Estados Unidos	United States
estadounidense	American
el estante	shelf
estar	to be (located)
estar estreñido	to be constipated
estatura	height
ésta	this
éste	this one
este	this
estimado	dear, esteemed
el estómago	stomach
la estrella	star
el/la estudiante	student
estudiar	to study
el estudio	study
estupendamente	stupendously
¡Estupendo!	Wonderful!
el euro	euro
el examen	test
exceder	to exceed
excepcional	rare
excepto	except
exhibir	to exhibit
exigir	to beg, to demand
el exilio	exile
existir	to exist

el éxito	success
expansivo	expansive
explicar	to explain
expresar	to express
extinguir	to extinguish
extraer	extract, draw
extrafino	superfine
el extranjero	foreigner, abroad
extraño	strange

F

SPANISH	ENGLISH
la fábrica	factory
fácil	easy
la falda	skirt
faltar(le)	to lack
la familia	the family
la farmacia	pharmacy
fascinar(le)	to fascinate
fastidioso	annoying
fatigoso	fatiguing
la fe	faith
febrero	February
la fecha	date
feliz	happy
feo	ugly
fiarse de	to trust
la fiebre	fever
la fiesta	party
el fin de semana	weekend
fingir	to pretend
finlandés	Finnish
la firma	signature
firmar	to sign
flaco	thin
el flan	custard
el flexivo	ending
flojo	loose
la flor	flower
la florería	florist's shop
la foto	photo
la frambuesa	raspberry
francés	French
Francia	France
frase	sentence
frente a	facing, across from
la fresa	strawberry
fresco	fresh
los frijoles	beans
frío	cold
la fruta	fruit
frutería	fruit store
la fuente	fountain
fuera	outside
fuera de línea	offline
fuerte	strong
fumador	smoker, smoking section

Spanish	English
fumar	to smoke
el fútbol	soccer
el futuro	future

G	
Spanish	English
las gafas	eyeglasses
las gafas de sol	sunglasses
el galán	handsome young man
el galardón	prize
galés	Welsh
la galleta	cookie
gamba	shrimp
ganar	to win, earn
la ganga	bargain
la garganta	throat
el gasóleo	diesel fuel
la gasolina	gasoline, petrol
gastar	to spend, to waste
el gasto	expense
el gato	cat
el gemelo	twin
gemir	to moan
generalmente	generally
la gente	people
el/la gerente	manager
el gimnasio	gym
el girasol	sunflower
gobernar	to govern
la goma de borrar	pencil eraser
gordo	fat
la gorra	hat
el gorrión	sparrow
grabar	to record
gracias	thank you
gracioso	funny, amusing
la gramática	grammar
el gramo	gram
gran(de)	large, great
el grano	pimple, grain
Grecia	Greece
griego	Greek
gris	gray
gruñir	to grunt, to growl
el grupo	group
el guante	glove
guapo	cute
guatemalteco	Guatemalan
la guerra	war
el/la guía	guide
guiar	to guide
el guión	dash, hyphen
gustar(le)	to like

H	
Spanish	English
haber	to have
la habilidad	ability, skill
hablar	to speak
hacer	to make, to do
hacerse	to become
haitiano	Haitian
el hambre	hunger
la hamburguesa	hamburger
la harina	flour
harto de	sick of
hasta	up to, until
hasta luego	see you later
hasta mañana	see you tomorrow
el helado	ice cream
la hermana	sister
la hermandad	brotherhood
el hermano	brother
la herramienta	tool
el hígado	liver
la hija	daughter
el hijo	son
el himno	hymn
hindú	Hindu
la historia	history, story
el hogar	home
la hoja	leaf, page
hola	hello
holandés	Dutch
holgazán	lazy
el hombre	man
el homicidio	homicide
hondureño	Honduran
la hora	hour
el horario	schedule
el hospital	hospital
la hosquedad	gloominess
el hotel	hotel
hoy	today
el huevo	egg
huir	to flee
húmedo	humid, damp
húngaro	Hungarian
Hungría	Hungary

I	
Spanish	English
ida	one way
ida y vuelta	round trip
el idioma	language
la iglesia	church
igual	equal
iletrado, analfabeto	illiterate, uneducated
imaginarse	to expect
impedir	to prevent
importar(le)	to be important

Spanish	English
la impresora	printer
imprimir	to print
la inacción	inaction
incluir	to include
increíble	incredible
incurrir	to incur
influir	to influence
la información	information
la informática	computing
el informe	report
el ingeniero	engineer
Inglaterra	England
inglés	English
el insecticida	insecticide
inscribir	to inscribe, to enroll
insistir	to insist
el intento	attempt
interactivo	interactive
interesado	interested
interesante	interesting
interesar	to interest
la interjección	interjection
la interpretación	interpretation
internacional	international, among nations
interrumpir	to interrupt
inútil	useless
invadir	to invade
invierno	winter
el invitado	guest
invitar a	to invite to
ir	to go
iraní	Iranian
iraquí	Iraqi
Irlanda	Ireland
irlandés	Irish
israelí	Israeli
italiano	Italian
izquierdo	left

J

Spanish	English
el jabón	soap
jamás	never
el jamón	ham
el jamón serrano	Spanish cured ham
el Japón	Japan
japonés	Japanese
el jardín	garden
el jarrón	vase, pitcher
la jerarquía	hierarchy
el jerez	sherry
joven	young
el/la joven	youth
las joyas	jewelry
el judaísmo	Judaism
judío	Jewish
el jueves	Thursday

Spanish	English
el jugador	player
jugar	to play
el jugo	juice
jugoso	juicy
el juguete	toy
el juicio	justice
julio	July
junio	June
juntos	together
justo	just, fair

K

Spanish	English
el kilómetro	kilometer
el kiosco	kiosk

L

Spanish	English
los labios	lips
el lado	side
el ladrón, la ladrona	thief
la lámpara	lamp
la lana	wool
la langosta	lobster
el lápiz	pencil
largo	long
la lástima	pity
lastimar	to hurt
lastimarse	to bother oneself
la lata	can
la latitud	latitude
la lavandería	Laundromat
lavar(se)	to wash
la lealtad	loyalty
la lección	lesson
la leche	milk
la lechuga	lettuce
el lector	reader
la lectura	reading
leer	to read
lejos	far
la lenteja	lentil
lento	slow
letra	letter
el letrero	sign
levantar	to raise, pick up
levantarse	to wake up, to get up
libanés	Lebanese
Líbano	Lebanon
la libertad	liberty
libre	free
la librería	bookstore
el libro	book
licenciado	graduate
el líder	leader
el liderazgo	leadership
el limón	lemon

los limpiaparabrisas	windshield wipers
limpiar(se)	to clean
lindo	nice, lovely
la línea	line
liso	straight
listo	ready
la literatura no novelesca	nonfiction
el litro	liter
llamar	to call, to name
la llave	key
llegar	to arrive
llegar a	to succeed in
lleno de	full of
llevar	to take
llover	to rain
la llovizna	rainfall
lo menos	at least
el lobo	wolf
el lomo de cerdo	pork loin
lo siento	I'm sorry
la lotería	lottery
lucir	to shine
el lugar	place
el lunes	Monday
la luz	light

M

SPANISH	ENGLISH
la madre	mother
madrileño	from Madrid
la madrina	godmother
la madrugada	early morning
los maduros	sweet (ripe) fried plantains
el maestro, la maestra	elementary school teacher
el maíz	corn
mal(o)	bad
la maldad	wickedness
el malecón	pier, seafront
el maletero	station porter
la mancha	stain
mandar	to send
manejable	manageable
la mano	hand
mantener	to support
la mantequilla	butter
la manzana	apple
la mañana	morning
mañana	tomorrow
el mapa	map
maquillarse	to put on makeup
la máquina de escribir	typewriter
el maratón	marathon
el mar	sea
maravilloso	wonderful
la marca	brand, make
marchar	to walk

marchitar(se)	to wither, to wilt
el marido	husband
la mariposa	butterfly
los mariscos	seafood
marrón	dark brown
marroquí	Moroccan
Marruecos	Morocco
el martes	Tuesday
marzo	March
más	more
mas	but
más bien	rather
la mascota	pet
las matemáticas	math
el matón	killer
la matrícula	registration
mayo	May
mayor	older
el mécanico	mechanic
mediano	medium
medianoche	midnight
las medias	socks
el médico	doctor
medio	half, average
mediodía	midday
medir	to measure
el mejillón	mussel
mejor	best
melancólico	melancholy
el melon	melon
mencionar	to mention
menor	younger
menos	less
mentir	to lie
la mermelada	marmelade
la mesa	table
el mercado	market
la merced	mercy
merecer	to deserve
meter	to put in
el metro	subway
mexicano	Mexican
México	Mexico
mi	my
el microondas	microwave
mientras	while
el miércoles	Wednesday
mil	thousand
el millón	million
el millonario	millionaire
los mil millones	billion
la minifalda	miniskirt
la mirada	look
mirar	to look
mismo	same, himself, itself
la mochila	backpack
moderno	modern

Spanish	English
el modismo	idiom
el mofongo	mashed plantains, often with seafood
mojado	wet
el mole	meat in chile sauce
molestar	to annoy, to bother
molestarse	to get annoyed
moquear	to have a runny nose
el mostrador	counter
la monarquía	monarchy
la moneda	coin
la montaña	mountain
montar	to climb
moreno	dark brown, dark-haired
morir	to die
la mosca	fly
mostrar	to show
la moto	motorcycle
la motocicleta	motorcycle
el motor	engine
muchas veces	often
mucho	many, a lot
mudar(se)	to move, change residence
mugriento	filthy
la mujer	wife, woman
la multa	fine
el mundo	world
la muñeca	doll
el museo	museum
la música	music
muy	very
muy bien	very good, very well

N	
SPANISH	ENGLISH
nacer	to be born
el nacimiento	birth
la nacionalidad	nationality
nada	nothing
nadar	to swim
nadie	no one
la naranja	orange
la nariz	nose
la navidad	Christmas
necesitar	to need
negarse a	to deny, to refuse
negro	black
neocelandés	New Zealander
neoyorquino	New Yorker
nevar	to snow
nicaragüense	Nicaraguan
la nieta	granddaughter
el nieto	grandson
ninguna vez	never once
ninguno	none
ni . . . ni	neither . . . nor
la niña	girl, child
la niñez	childhood

Spanish	English
el niño	boy, child
el nivel	level
no	no
la noche	night
el nombre	name
no obstante	regardless
el norte	north
norteamericano	North American
Noruega	Norway
noruego	Norwegian
nosotros	we
la nota	note, grade
las noticias	news
novecientos	nine hundred
noveno	ninth
noventa	ninety
la novia	girlfriend, fiancée
noviembre	November
el novio	boyfriend, fiancé
nublado	cloudy
la nuera	daughter-in-law
Nueva York	New York
Nueva Zelanda	New Zealand
nueve	nine
nuevo	new
la nuez	nut
el número	number
nunca	never

O	
SPANISH	ENGLISH
obedecer	to obey
obligar a	to force
la obra	play, work
el obrero	worker
el obstáculo	obstacle
obviamente	obviously
ochenta	eighty
ocho	eight
ochocientos	eight hundred
octavo	eighth
octubre	October
ocurrir	to occur
la oficina	office
ofrecer	to offer
oír	to hear
ojalá que	it's hoped that, I hope that
el ojo	eye
oler	to smell
olvidar	to forget
omitir	to omit
once	eleven
o . . . o	either . . . or
la opinión	opinion
optimista	optimistic
la orilla	shore
el oro	gold

oscuro	dark
el otoño	autumn
otorgar	to award
otra vez	again
otro	other, another
la oveja	sheep

P

SPANISH	ENGLISH
el padre	father
los padres	parents
el padrino	godfather
la paella	a saffron rice dish, usually prepared with seafood
el paciente	patient
pagar	to pay
pagar en efectivo	to pay in cash
la página	page
la página Web	Web page
la página principal	home page
el país	country
el pájaro	bird
pajizo	made of straw
la palabra	word
las palomitas de maíz	popcorn
el pan	bread
la panadería	bakery
Panamá	Panama
panameño	Panamanian
el panecillo	bread roll
los pantalones	pants
el pañuelo	handkerchief
las papas	potatoes
el papel	paper
la papelería	stationary store
el paquete	packet
el par	pair
para	for, to
el parabrisas	windshield
la parada	stop
la paradoja	paradox
parafrasear	to paraphrase
el paraguas	umbrella
paraguayo	Paraguayan
el paraíso	paradise
para que	so that
parar	to stop
parasitario	parasitic
pardo	brown
parecer	to seem
parecerse	to resemble
la pared	wall
la pareja	pair
los parientes	relatives
parisiense	Parisian
parpadear	to blink
el parque	park

partir	to divide, to split
el pasaporte	passport
pasar	to happen
pasear	to stroll, to walk (a dog)
el paseo	boulevard
el pasillo	hall, walkway
el pastel	cake, pie
la pastilla	pill
el pasto	grass
la patata	potato (in Spain)
el pato	duck
el patio de recreo	playground
el pavo	turkey
el pedazo	piece
pedir	to ask
la película	movie
peligroso	dangerous
pelirrojo	red
el pelo, el cabello	hair
pena	pity
el pensamiento	thought
pensar	to think
penúltimo	second to last
peor	worse, worst
el pepino	cucumber
pequeño	small
la pera	pear
percibir	to perceive
perder	to lose
el perdón	forgiveness
perdone	sorry, excuse me
perfectamente	perfectly
el perfume	perfume
el periódico	newspaper
perjurar	to perjure
permanecer	to remain
permitir	to permit, to allow
pero	but
el perro	dog
persistir	to persist
persuadir	to persuade
pertenecer	to belong
la pertinencia	relevance
peruano	Peruvian
pervivir	to survive
pesar	to weigh
el pescado	fish
el pez	fish
el/la pianista	pianist
la pierna	leg
el pimiento	pepper
la piña	pineapple
pintado de	painted
el pintor, la pintora	painter
el piso	floor
la pizarra	board
el planeta	planet

Spanish	English
el plano	map
plantar	to plant
la plata	silver, money
plátanos	banana
el plato	plate
la playa	beach
la plaza	square
la pluma	pen, feather
el pluscuamperfecto	past perfect
pobre	poor, unlucky
poco	a little
poco común	rare
poco	few
poder	to be able to
la poesía	poetry
la poetisa	poetess
polaco	Polish
la política	politics
el pollo	chicken
Polonia	Poland
el pomelo	grapefruit
poner	to put
ponerse a	to start to
por	by
por favor	please
por qué	why
porque	because
portugués	Portuguese
poseer	to own, to possess, to hold
posiblemente	possibly
la postal	postcard
el postre	dessert, pastry
el pozole	hominy stew
el precio	price
precisamente	precisely
precocinado	precooked
preferir	to prefer
el prefijo	prefix
la pregunta	question
preguntar	to ask (a question)
el premio	prize
prender	to catch, to turn on
prepararse a	to prepare to
la preposición	preposition
la presentación	presentation
presente	present
el preservativo	condom
el/la presidente	president
presidir	to preside
presumir	to presume
prestar	to lend, to pay attention
pretender	to try, to hope to achieve
el pretexto	pretext
prever	to forecast
prevenido	cautious
la previsión	foresight
previsto	due

Spanish	English
primavera	spring
primero	first
el primo	cousin
probablemente	probably
el problema	problem
probar	to try
procedente de…	arriving from…
proceder	to proceed
proclamar	to proclaim
producir	to produce
el profesor, la profesora	professor, teacher
la profesión	profession
prohibir	to prohibit, to forbid
el prólogo	prologue
prometer	to promise
el pronombre	pronoun
pronto	soon
propio	own
proponer	to propose
propulsar	to drive, propel
proteger	to protect
próximo	next
la prueba	quiz, test
público	public
pudrir	to rot, to decay
el pueblo	town
la puerta	door, gate
puertorriqueño	Puerto Rican
pues…	well…
pulir	to polish, to finish
el punto	period
el punto y coma	semicolon
la pureza	purity
puro	nothing but, just, pure

Q	
Spanish	**English**
qué	what?
que	what, that
quebrar	to break (something)
quebrarse	to break (a bone)
quedar	to leave
quedar(se)	to remain
quejarse	to complain
quemar	to burn
quemarse	to get burned
querer	to want
querido	dear
el queso	cheese
quién	who?
quien	who, that
quienquiera	whoever
la quietud	quiet, calmness
quince	fifteen
quinientos	five hundred
quinto	fifth
quiosco	newsstand

quitar(se)	to remove, take off
quizá, quizás	maybe

R	
SPANISH	**ENGLISH**
la radio	radio
rápido	fast
raro	rare, strange
un rato	a while
el ratón	mouse
rayas, a rayas	stripes, striped
la razón	reason
razonable	sensible
real	royal
realizar	to actualize
la rebaja	sale
rebajado	reduced (in price)
recapacitar	to reconsider
recargar	to refill
recibir	to receive
el recibo	receipt
recocido	overcooked
recoger	to gather
la recomendación	recommendation
recomendar	to recommend
recomenzar	to start again, to recommence
recordar	to remember
rechazar	to refuse
la red	network
reducido	reduced
reeligir	to re-elect
el refresco	soft drink
regalar	to give as a gift
el regalo	present
regar	to water
la región	region
regresar	to return
rehusar	to refuse
Reino Unido	United Kingdom
reír	to laugh
la religión	religion
el reloj	clock, watch
repaso	review
repetir	to repeat
la representación	performance (theater)
reproducir	to reproduce
la República Dominicana	Dominican Republic
reservar	to reserve
responder	to answer, respond
la respuesta	answer
el restaurante	restaurant
el retraso	delay
reunir	to join
reunirse	to gather, to get together
la revista	magazine
rezar	to pray
rezongar	to grumble

rico	rich
el río	river
la riqueza	riches, wealth
rizado	curly
la rodilla	knee
rogar	to beg
rojizo	reddish
rojo	red
el rollo	roll of film
romance	Romance (language)
romper(se)	to break
la ropa	clothes
rosa	pink
rubio	blond
la rueda	wheel
el ruido	noise
las ruinas	ruins
ruso	Russian

S	
SPANISH	**ENGLISH**
el sábado	Saturday
saber	to know
la sabiduría	wisdom
sacar	to take out
sacar (billete)	to buy (a ticket)
el sacerdote	priest
la sal	salt
la sala	livingroom
el salario	wages (often hourly)
la salchicha	sausage
la salchichón	salami
la salida	exit
salir	to go out, to leave
el salmón	salmon
el salpicón	cold non-vegetable salad (usually with seafood)
el saludo	greeting
la salsa	sauce
salvadoreño	Salvadoran
salvo	except
la sandalia	sandal
la sandía	watermelon
la sardina	sardine
la sangría	a wine, juice, and brandy punch
sano	healthy
santo	saint
el secador	hair dryer
la sección	section, department
el secretario	secretary
el secreto	secret
seguir	to follow, to continue
según	according to
segundo	second
seis	six
seiscientos	six hundred
sesenta	sixty

Spanish	English
el sello	stamp
el semáforo	traffic light
la semana	week
sembrar	to sow
la semejanza	similarity
la semilla	seed
sensato	sensible
sensible	sensitive
sentar	to sit
sentir	to feel
señor, Sr.	Mr.
señora, Sra.	Mrs., Ms.
señorita, Srta.	Miss
septiembre	September
séptimo	seventh
ser	to be
la serie	series
la serpiente	snake
servir	to serve
setecientos	seven hundred
setenta	seventy
sexto	sixth
sí	yes
si	if
siempre	always
la siesta	nap
siete	seven
siga	continue
el siglo	century
significar	to mean
el signo de exclamación	exclamation mark
el signo de interrogación	question mark
la silla	chair
simpático	nice
simple	just, simply, simple
la simplicidad	simplicity
sin	without
sin duda	without a doubt
sin embargo	nevertheless
sin gas	noncarbonated
sino	but (following a negative statement)
sin que	without
el síntoma	symptom
el sitio	site
situarse	to be situated
sobre	on, on top of
sobrevivir	to survive
la sobrina	niece
el sobrino	nephew
el sofá	sofa
sofocar	to choke, to suffocate
el sol	sun
la soledad	solitude
soler	to be used to
sólo	only
solo	alone
soltero	single (unmarried)
la solución	solution, answer
el sombrero	hat
sonar	to ring
sonarse la nariz	to blow one's nose
la sonrisa	smile
la sopa	soup
la sopa de frijol negro	black bean soup
soportar	to put up with
sorprenderse	to be surprised
su	your (formal), his, hers
subarrendar	to sublet
el subempleo	underemployment
subir	to rise, to go up, to board (a bus, etc.)
subjuntivo	subjunctive
subterráneo	underground
suceder	to succeed, to happen
el suceso	event
sudanés	Sudanese
Suecia	Sweden
sueco	Swedish
la suegra	mother-in-law
el suegro	father-in-law
el sueldo	salary
la suerte	luck
el suéter	sweater
suficiente	enough
el sufijo	suffix
sufrir	to suffer
suicidarse	to commit suicide
el suicidio	suicide
la Suiza	Switzerland
suizo	Swiss
la superficie	surface
supermercado	supermarket
suspender	to fail, to suspend
el sustantivo	noun
sustituir	to substitute

T	
Spanish	**English**
el tacón	heel
tailandés	Thai
Tailandia	Thailand
taiwanés	Taiwanese
talentoso	talented
la talla	size
tal vez	maybe
los tamales	corn patties, usually with minced meat
el tamaño	size
también	too, also
tampoco	neither, either
tan … como	as … as
tanto	so much
tapar	to cover, put a lid on
las tapas	appetizer-sized dishes
tardar	to take time

Spanish	English
tarde	late
la tarde	afternoon
la tarea	chore, homework
el taxi	taxi
el/la taxista	cab driver
la taza	cup
el té	tea
el teatro	theater
el techo	roof
tejer	to crochet, weave, knit, braid
la tela	fabric
el teléfono	telephone (number)
la televisión	television
temer	to dread, to fear
el templo	temple
temprano	early
el tenedor	fork
tener	to have
la tentación	temptation
tercero	third
terminar	to finish
el término	term
la ternera	veal
la tesis	thesis
la tía	aunt
el tiempo	time, weather
la tienda	shop
la tienda de campaña	tent (camping)
la tinta	ink
el tío	uncle
típico	typical
el tipo	type
tirar	to throw
tirarse	to jump
la tiza	chalk
la toalla	towel
tocar	to touch, to play
tocar la batería	to play the drums
el tocino	salted pork
todavía	still
todo	everything, all
todo recto	straight ahead
todos	everybody
la tolerancia	tolerance
tomar	to take, to drink
el tomate	tomato
la torta	cake
la tortilla española	Spanish potato omelette
toser	to cough
los tostones	savory fried plantains
trabajador	worker, hardworking
trabajar	to work
el trabajo	work
la traducción	translation
traducir	to translate
traer	to bring
el tráfico	traffic
tragar	to swallow
el traicinero	traitor
el traje	suit
transcribir	to transcribe
transmitir	to transmit
transparente	clear
el tranvía	streetcar
trece	thirteen
treinta	thirty
el tren	train
tres	three
trescientos	three hundred
triste	sad
la tristeza	sadness
la trucha	trout
tu	your
tú	you (informal)
turco	Turkish
Turquía	Turkey
tutearse	to address with tú

U

Spanish	English
último	last
últimamente	lately
único	only, unique
unido	united
el uniforme	uniform
la universidad	college, university
unívoco	one to one
un	a, one
un momento	a moment
unas, unos	some
unir	to unite
uruguayo	Uruguayan
útil	useful
la uva	grape

V

Spanish	English
la vacación	vacation
la vainilla	vanilla
vale	OK
valer	to be worth, to cost
variar	to vary
varios, varias	various
el varón	male
el vaso	drinking glass
el vecindario	neighborhood
los vegetales	green vegetables
veinte	twenty
la vejez	old age
la vela	candle
vencer	to win, to overcome
vender	to sell
venezolano	Venezuelan

Spanish	English
la venganza	vengeance
venir	to come
el ventilador	fan
ver	to see
el verano	summer
veraz	correct
el verbo	verb
la verdad	truth
verdaderamente	really
la verdad es que	actually
verdadero	real
verde	green
la vergüenza	shame
el vestíbulo	hall, lobby
el vestido	dress
vestido de	dressed in
vestir	to dress
vestirse	to get dressed
el vestuario	costume
la vez	time
la vía	platform
viajar	to travel
el viaje	trip
viejo	old
el viento	wind
el viernes	Friday
vietnamita	Vietnamese
el vino	wine
la violencia	violence
el virus	virus
el vistazo	look, glance
el vinagre	vinegar
visitar	to visit
vivir	to live
vociferante	vociferous, loud
volar	to fly
la voluntad	will
volver	to return
vos	you, informal singular (in parts of Río de la Plata region)
el vuelo	flight
la vuelta	return

Y	
Spanish	English
y	and
ya	already, now
la yegua	mare
el yerno	son-in-law
la yucca	a root vegetable similar to a potato

Z	
Spanish	English
la zanahoria	carrot
la zapatería	shoe store
la zapatilla de tenis	sneaker
el zapato	shoe
el zócalo	town square

Appendix C

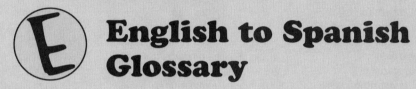

English to Spanish Glossary

A	
ENGLISH	SPANISH
a	un
to abandon	abandonar
ability	la habilidad
to abolish	abolir
above	arriba
to accept	aceptar, admitir
accident	el accidente
according to	según
accuser, accusing	el acusador
to achieve	conseguir
across from	enfrente a
to act	actuar
actor	el actor
actress	la actriz
to actualize	realizar
actually	la verdad es que
to adapt	adaptar
address	la dirección
adjective	el adjetivo
to adopt	adoptar
adverb	el adverbio
to advise	aconsejar
affectionate	cariñoso
to afflict	afligir
after	después de
afternoon	la tarde
again	otra vez
against	contra
age	la edad
airport	el aeropuerto
Algeria	Argelia
Algerian	argelino
all	todo
almost	casi
alone	solo
already	ya
although	aunque
always	siempre
American	americano, estadounidense
anarchy	la anarquía
and	y
angry	enfadado
to announce	anunciar
to annoy	molestar
annoying	fastidioso
to answer	contestar
answer	la respuesta
antipathy	la antipatía
antiperspirant	el antisudoral
apartment	el apartamento
to appear	aparecer
appetite	el apetito
appetizer	el antojito, la tapa
to applaud	aplaudir
applause	el aplauso

apple	la manzana
apprenticeship	el aprendizaje
to approach	acercarse
April	abril
Argentinean	argentino
around	alrededor
around here	acá
to arrive	llegar
arriving from…	procedente de…
art	el arte
article	el artículo
as	como
as…as	tan…como
to ask	pedir
to ask (a question)	preguntar
as much, as many	cuanto
as soon as	en cuanto
to assume	asumir
at least	lo menos
at present	actualmente
at the end	al final, al fondo
atheism	el ateísmo
attempt	el intento
to attend	asistir
attention	la atención
attentive	atento
attitude	la actitud
to attribute	atribuir
August	agosto
aunt	la tía
Australian	australiano
Austrian	austríaco
author	el autor
authorization	la autorización
autobiography	la autobiografía
autumn	otoño
avarice	la avaricia
avenue	la avenida
avocado	el aguacate
to award	otorgar

B	
ENGLISH	SPANISH
baby	el bebé
back cover	la contracubierta
backpack	la mochila
bad	mal(o)
bakery	la panadería
banana	plátanos
bank	el banco
banker	el bancario
barely	apenas
bargain	la ganga
to bathe	bañar
to be	ser
to be (located)	estar
to be able to	poder

English	Spanish
beach	la playa
beans	los frijoles
beautiful	bello
to be bored	aburrirse
to be born	nacer
because	porque
to become	hacerse
to be constipated	estar estreñido
bed	la cama
bee	la abeja
beef	la carne de res
(beef) steak	el bistec
beer	la cerveza
before	antes
beforehand	antemano
to beg	exigir, rogar
to begin (to)	empezar (a)
to begin to	comenzar a
to be happy	alegrarse
behind	detrás
beige	beige
to be important	importar(le)
to believe	creer
to belong	pertenecer
Belgian	belga
Belgium	Bélgica
bell tower	el campanario
to be quiet	callarse
best	mejor
to be surprised	sorprenderse
between	entre
to be used to	soler
to be worth	valer
bill	la cuenta
billion	los mil millones
bird	el pájaro
birth	el nacimiento
birthday	el cumpleaños
black	negro
black bean soup	la sopa de frijol negro
to blink	parpadear
blond	rubio
blouse	la blusa
blue	azul
to board (a bus, etc.)	subir
board	la pizarra
board eraser	el borrador
boarding	el embarque
boat	el bote
body	el cuerpo
Bolivian	boliviano
book	el libro
bookstore	la librería
boots	botas
to bore	aburrir
boring, bored	aburrido
boss	el jefe
both	ambos, ambas
to bother oneself	lastimarse
boulevard	el paseo
box	la caja
boy	el chico, el niño
boyfriend	el novio
brand (make)	la marca
Brazil	el Brasil
Brazilian	brasileño
bread	el pan
bread roll	el panecillo
to break	romper(se)
to break (a bone)	quebrarse
to break (something)	quebrar
breakfast	el desayuno
breeze	la brisa
bright	claro
to bring	traer
bronchitis	la bronquitis
brother	el hermano
brotherhood	la hermandad
brown	café
to brush (teeth, hair)	cepillar(se)
building	el edificio
to burn	quemar
bus	el autobús
but	pero
but (following a negative statement)	sino
butter	la mantequilla
butterfly	la mariposa
to buy	comprar
by	por

C	
English	Spanish
cab driver	el/la taxista
cake	la torta
cake	el pastel
camp	el campamento
can	la lata
Canada	el Canadá
Canadian	canadiense
candle	la vela
candy	dulce
caprice	el capricho
car	el coche
carbonated	con gas
care	el cuidado
carpet	la alfombra
carrot	la zanahoria
case	el caso
cat	el gato
cathedral	la catedral
Catholic	católico
Catholicism	el catolicismo
cauliflower	el coliflor

cautious	prevenido	common	común
century	el siglo	communist	comunista
ceramic pottery	la cerámica	community	la comunidad
certain	cierto	company	la companía
certainty	la certidumbre	compass	el compás
chair	la silla	to complain	quejarse
chalk	la tiza	to complete	cumplir
to change	cambiar	complex	complejo
chapter	el capítulo	compromise	el arreglo
to chat	charlar	computer	la computadora
cheap	barato	computing	la informática
to check	comprobar	concealing	encubridor
cheese	el queso	to concede	conceder
chess	el ajedrez	to conclude	concluir
chestnut-colored	castaño	condom	el preservativo
chewing gum	el chicle	to confide	confiar
chicken	el pollo	to confuse	confundir
childhood	la niñez	to conjugate	conjugar
Chilean	chileno	conjunction	la conjunción
Chinese	chino	to consecrate	consagrar
chocolate	el chocolate	consequence	la consecuencia
to choke	ahogar	to consist	consistir
chore	la tarea	consort	el consorte
Christmas	la navidad	to consume	consumir
church	la iglesia	contemplation	la contemplación
circular	circular	to continue	continuar, seguir
city	la ciudad	continue	siga
class	la clase	to contribute to	contribuir a
to clean	limpiar(se)	to cook	cocinar
clear	claro, transparente	cook	el cocinero, la cocinera
clearly	claramente	cookie	la galleta
client	el cliente	coppery	cobrizo
to climb	montar	corn	el maíz
clinic	la clínica	corner	la esquina
clock	el reloj	correct	veraz
to close	cerrar	cosmopolitan	el/la cosmopolita
close by	cerca	to cost	costar
closed	cerrado	Costa Rican	costarricense
clothes	la ropa	costume	el vestuario
cloudy	nublado	to cough	toser
cod	el bacalao	to count	contar
coffee	el café	counter	el mostrador
coffee shop	la cafetería	counter-blow	el contragolpe
coin	la moneda	country	el país
Coke	la Coca Cola	cousin	el primo
cold	frío	to cover	cubrir, tapar
college	la universidad	cover letter	la carta de acompañamiento
Colombian	colombiano	cozy	acogedor
colon	dos puntos	cramp	el calambre
color	el color	to crash	chocar
to combat	combatir	cream	la crema
comedian	el cómico	crime	el delito
to come	venir	croquette	la croqueta
comfortable	cómodo	to cross	atravesar, cruzar
comma	la coma	crown	la corona
to commit	cometer	Cuban	cubano
to commit suicide	suicidarse	cucumber	el pepino

English	Spanish
culmination	la culminación
cup	la taza
curly	rizado
current	actual
curtain	la cortina
custard	el flan
cute	guapo
to cut up (with a knife)	acuchillar

D

English	Spanish
to dance	bailar
dangerous	peligroso
Danish	danés
to dare to	atreverse
dark	oscuro
dark brown	marrón
dark haired	moreno
dash (hyphen)	el guión
date (appointment)	la cita
date	la fecha
daughter	la hija
daughter-in-law	la nuera
day	el día
day before yesterday	anteayer
dear	querido
dear	estimado
decade	década
December	diciembre
deception	el engaño
to decide	decidir
to decline	decaer
to deduce	deducir
to defend	defender
to define	definir
delay	el retraso
delight	el deleite
to demand	demandar, exigir
Denmark	Dinamarca
dentist	el/la dentista
denunciation	el denuncio
to deny	negarse a
to depress	deprimir
to derive from	derivar
to descend	descender
to describe	describir
to deserve	merecer
desirable	deseable
desk	el escritorio
despite	a pesar de
dessert	el pastel
destination	el destino
to destroy	destruir
to devote oneself to	dedicarse a
dictionary	el diccionario
to die	morir
diesel fuel	el gasóleo

English	Spanish
diet	la dieta
different	diferente
difficult	difícil
to dignify	dignificar
dining car	el coche-restaurante
dining room	el comedor
dinner	la cena
to direct	dirigir
disagreement	la discordia
disappointment	la decepción
discolored	decolorado
to discover	descubrir
to discuss	discutir
to disembark	desembarcar
disgrace	la deshonra
to dissuade	disuadir
to divide	dividir, partir
divorced	divorciado
to do	hacer
doctor	el médico
dog	el perro
doll	la muñeca
Dominican	dominicano
Dominican Republic	la República Dominicana
door	la puerta
to doubt	dudar
doubtful	dudoso
downtown	el centro
dozen	la docena
drawer	cajón
drawing	el dibujo
to dread	temer
to dress	vestir
dress	el vestido
dressed in	vestido de
dresser	el armario
to drink	beber, tomar
drink	la bebida
drinking glass	el vaso
to drive	conducir, propulsar
drums (to play)	la batería (tocar)
duchess	la duquesa
duck	el pato
due	previsto
duet	el dúo
during	durante
Dutch	holandés

E

English	Spanish
each	cada
early	temprano
early morning	la madrugada
to earn	ganar
easy	fácil
Ecuadorian	ecuatoriano
educated	culto

English	Spanish
education	la enseñanza
egg	el huevo
eggplant	la berenjena
Egypt	Egipto
Egyptian	egipcio
eight	ocho
eight hundred	ochocientos
eighteen	dieciocho
eighth	octavo
eighty	ochenta
either	tampoco
either . . . or	o . . . o
electrician	el/la electricista
eleven	once
email	el correo electrónico
embarrassed	avergonzado
to eat	comer
to emit	emitir
emotional	emocional
employee	el empleado
to enchant	encantar(le)
to end	concluir
ending	el flexivo
energy	la energía
engine	el motor
engineer	el ingeniero
England	Inglaterra
English	inglés
enough	suficiente
to enter	entrar
enthusiastic	entusiasta
entrance	la entrada
environment	el ambiente
equal	igual
to err	errar
essay	el ensayo
to establish	establecer
euro	el euro
even	aún
event	el suceso
everybody	todos
everything	todo
every	a todos partes
example	el ejemplo
to exceed	exceder
except	excepto, salvo
exclamation mark	el signo de exclamación
excuse me	con permiso, perdone
exercise	el ejercicio
to exhibit	exhibir
exile	el exilio
to exist	existir
exit	la salida
expansive	expansivo
to expect	imaginarse
expense	el gasto
expensive	caro

English	Spanish
to explain	explicar
to express	expresar
to extinguish	extinguir
extract	extraer
eye	el ojo
eyeglasses	las gafas

F

English	Spanish
fabric	la tela
face	la cara
facing	enfrente a
factory	la fábrica
faith	la fe
to fall	caer
family	la familia
fan (of something)	el aficionado
fan	el ventilador
far	lejos
to fascinate	fascinar(le)
fast	rápido
fat	corpulento, gordo
father	el padre
father-in-law	el suegro
to fear	temer
feather	la pluma
February	febrero
to feel	sentir
fever	la fiebre
few	poco
fiancé	el novio
fiancée	la novia
field	el campo
fifteen	quince
fifth	quinto
fifty	cincuenta
to fight	combatir
filing cabinet	el archivo
to find	encontrar
to find out	enterar(se)
fine	la multa
finger	el dedo
to finish	acabar, terminar
Finnish	finlandés
to fire	despedir
fire station	la estación de bomberos
first	primero
fish	el pescado (cooked), el pez
to fit	caber
five	cinco
five hundred	quinientos
to flee	huir
flight	el vuelo
floor	el piso
florist's shop	la florería
flour	harina
flower	el flor

English	Spanish
to fly	volar
fly	la mosca
folder	la carpeta
to follow	seguir
for	para
to force	obligar a
forearm	el antebrazo
to forecast	prever
foreigner	el extranjero
foresight	la previsión
to forget	olvidar
forgiveness	el perdón
fork	el tenedor
forty	cuarenta
fountain	la fuente
four	cuatro
four hundred	cuatrocientos
fourteen	catorce
fourth	cuarto
France	Francia
free	libre
French	francés
fresh	fresco
Friday	el viernes
friend	el amigo
friendship	la amistad
fritter	el buñuelo
from Madrid	madrileño
from	desde
fruit	la fruta
fruit store	frutería
full of	lleno de
fun	divertido
funny	gracioso
future	el futuro

G	
English	**Spanish**
garden	el jardín
garlic	el ajo
gasoline	la gasolina
to gather	recoger
generally	generalmente
German	alemán
Germany	Alemania
girl	la chica
girlfriend	la novia
to give	dar
glasses	los anteojos
to glimpse	entrever
gloominess	la hosquedad
glove	el guante
goat	el chivo
to go	ir
to go up	subir
God	dios
godfather	el padrino

English	Spanish
godmother	la madrina
gold	el oro
good	bueno
gossip	el chisme
to go to bed	acostarse
to go to sleep	dormirse
to go up	ascender
to govern	gobernar
to grab	coger
grades	la calificación
graduate	licenciado
gram	el gramo
grammar	la gramática
granddaughter	la nieta
grandfather	el abuelo
grandmother	la abuela
grandson	el nieto
grape	la uva
grapefruit	el pomelo
gray	gris
great	gran(de)
Greece	Grecia
Greek	griego
green	verde
greeting	el saludo
to grip	apretar
grocery store	el almacén
group	el grupo
to grow	crecer
to growl	gruñir
to grumble	rezongar
Guatemalan	guatemalteco
guest	el invitado
to guide	guiar
guide	el guía
gym	el gimnasio

H	
English	**Spanish**
hair	el cabello, el pelo
hair dryer	el secador
haircut	corte de pelo
Haitian	haitiano
half	medio
hall	el pasillo, el vestíbulo
ham	el jamón
hamburger	la hamburguesa
hand	la mano
handbag	la bolsa
handkerchief	el pañuelo
to happen	pasar
happy	feliz
hat	la gorra, el sombrero
to have	tener, haber
to have lunch	almorzar
hazel	color de avellana
healthy	sano

to hear	oír
hearing aid	el audífono
heat	el calor
heel	el tacón
height	estatura
hello	hola
to help	ayudar
help-wanted ad	el anuncio de trabajo
here	aquí
to hide	esconder
hierarchy	la jerarquía
high school	el colegio
high school teacher	el profesor, la profesora
high	alto
highway	la autopista
history	la historia
home	el hogar
home page	la página principal
homicide	el homicidio
Honduran	hondureño
to hope	esperar
hospital	el hospital, la clínica
hot	caliente, cálido
hotel	el hotel
hour	la hora
house	la casa
how?	cómo
how much?	cuánto
how many?	cuántos
hug	el abrazo
humid	húmedo
hundred	cien
Hungarian	húngaro
Hungary	Hungría
hunger	el hambre
to hurry	apresurarse a
to hurt	doler, lastimar
husband	el marido
husband	el esposo

I	
ENGLISH	SPANISH
ice cream	el helado
idiom	el modismo
if	si
illiterate	iletrado, analfabeto
I'm sorry	lo siento
immediately	en seguida
in agreement	de acuerdo
in case	en caso de que
in front of	delante de
in order that	a fin de que
in	en
inaction	la inacción
to include	incluir
to increase	aumentar
incredible	increíble

to incur	incurrir
Indian	indio, natural de la India
to influence	influir
information	la información
ink	la tinta
to inscribe	inscribir
insecticide	el insecticida
inside	adentro, dentro de
to insist	insistir
interactive	interactivo
to interest	interesar
interested	interesado
interesting	interesante
interjection	la interjección
international	internacional
interpretation	la interpretación
to interrupt	interrumpir
interview	la entrevista
to invade	invadir
to invite to	invitar a
Iranian	iraní
Iraqi	iraquí
Ireland	Irlanda
Irish	irlandés
Israeli	israelí
Italian	italiano

J	
ENGLISH	SPANISH
jacket	la chaqueta
January	enero
Japan	el Japón
Japanese	japonés
jewelry	las joyas
Jewish	judío
job	el empleo
to join	reunir, añadir
joke	el chiste
joy	la alegría
Judaism	el judaísmo
juice	el jugo
juicy	jugoso
July	julio
to jump	tirarse
June	junio
just (fair)	justo
just	simple
justice	el juicio

K	
ENGLISH	SPANISH
key	la llave
killer	el matón
kilometer	el kilómetro
kiosk	el kiosco
to kiss	besar
kitchen	la cocina

English	Spanish
kitchenette	la cocineta
knee	la rodilla
knife	cuchillo
to knit	tejer
to know	conocer, saber
Korean	coreano

L	
ENGLISH	**SPANISH**
to lack	faltar(le)
lamb	el cordero
lamp	lámpara
language	el idioma
large	gran(de)
last	último
last name	el apellido
late	tarde
lately	últimamente
latitude	la latitud
to laugh	reír
Laundromat	la lavandería
lawn	el césped
lawyer	el abogado, la abogada
lazy	holgazán
leader	el líder
leadership	el liderazgo
leaf	la hoja
to learn	aprender
to leave	dejar, quedar, salir
Lebanese	libanés
Lebanon	Líbano
lecture	la charla
lecture	la conferencia
left	izquierdo
leg	la pierna
lemon	el limón
lentil	la lenteja
less	menos
lesson	la lección
letter	letra, carta
lettuce	la lechuga
level	el nivel
liberty	la libertad
librarian	el bibliotecario
library	la biblioteca
to lie	mentir
to light	encender
light	la luz
to like	gustar(le)
like	como
like that	así
line	la línea
to link	enlazar
lips	los labios
to listen	escuchar
liter	el litro
little	poco

English	Spanish
to live	vivir
liver	el hígado
to live together	convivir
livingroom	la sala
to load	cargar
loaf of bread	la barra de pan
lobster	la langosta
long	largo
to look	mirar
to look for	buscar
loose	flojo
to lose	perder
lottery	la lotería
to love	amar
love	el amor
loyalty	la lealtad
luck	la suerte
luggage	el equipaje
lullaby	la canción de cuna

M	
ENGLISH	**SPANISH**
magazine	la revista
mailbox	el buzón
to make	hacer
male	el varón
man	el hombre
manageable	manejable
manager	el/la gerente
many	mucho
map	el mapa, el plano
marathon	el maratón
March	marzo
market	el mercado
marmelade	la mermelada
married	casado
to marry (each other)	casar(se)
math	las matemáticas
matter	el asunto
mattress	el colchón
May	mayo
maybe	quizá, quizás
to mean	significar
to measure	medir
to measure out (dose)	dosificar
meat	la carne
mechanic	el mécanico
medium	mediano
melon	el melón
to mention	mencionar
menu	la carta
mercy	la merced
Mexican	mexicano
Mexico	México
microwave	el microondas
midday	mediodía
midnight	medianoche

milk	la leche	New York	Nueva York
milk shake	el batido	New Yorker	neoyorquino
million	el millón	New Zealand	Nueva Zelanda
millionaire	el millonario	New Zealander	neocelandés
mineral water	el agua mineral	news	las noticias
miniskirt	la minifalda	newspaper	el periódico
misfortune	la desgracia	newsstand	quiosco
Miss	señorita, Srta.	next	próximo
mistake	el error	next to	al lado de
to moan	gemir	Nicaraguan	nicaragüense
modern	moderno	nice	amable, simpático
a moment	un momento	niece	la sobrina
monarchy	la monarquía	night	la noche
Monday	el lunes	nine	nueve
money	el dinero	nine hundred	novecientos
more	más	nineteen	diecinueve
morning	la mañana	ninety	noventa
Moroccan	marroquí	ninth	noveno
Morocco	Marruecos	no	no
mother	la madre	no one	nadie
mother-in-law	la suegra	noise	el ruido
motorcycle	la moto	noncarbonated	sin gas
motorcycle	la motocicleta	none	ninguno
mountain	la montaña	nonfiction	la literatura no novelesca
mouse	el ratón	north	el norte
moustache	el bigote	Norway	Noruega
mouth	la boca	Norwegian	noruego
to move (change residence)	mudar(se)	nose	la nariz
movie	la película	note	la nota
Mr.	señor, Sr.	notebook	el cuaderno
Mrs., Ms.	señora, Sra.	nothing	nada
museum	el museo	noun	el sustantivo
mushroom	el champiñón	November	noviembre
music	la música	now	ahora, ya
mussel	el mejillón	number	el número
must	deber	nurse	el enfermero / la enfermera
my	mi	nut	la nuez

N	
ENGLISH	SPANISH
to name	llamar
name	el nombre
nap	la siesta
nationality	la nacionalidad
near	cerca de
necklace	el collar
to need	necesitar
neighborhood	el vecindario
neither . . . nor	ni . . . ni
neither	tampoco
nephew	el sobrino
network	la red
never	jamás
never	nunca
never once	ninguna vez
nevertheless	sin embargo
new	nuevo

O	
ENGLISH	SPANISH
to obey	obedecer
obligation	compromiso
obstacle	el obstáculo
obviously	obviamente
to occur	ocurrir
October	octubre
to offer	ofrecer
office	la oficina
offline	fuera de línea
often	a menudo
oil	el aceite
OK	vale
old	antiguo, viejo
old age	la vejez
older	mayor
olive	la aceituna
to omit	omitir

English	Spanish
to open	abrir
on	en, sobre
one	un
once	alguna vez
one way	ida
on foot	a pie
onion	la cebolla
online	en línea
only	sólo
on time	a tiempo
on top of	sobre
open	abierto
opinion	la opinión
optimistic	optimista
orange	la naranja
other	otro
our	nuestro/nuestra/nuestros/nuestras
outside	fuera
over	encima
overcoat	el abrigo
overcooked	recocido
to own	poseer
own	propio

P

English	Spanish
packed	atestado
packet	el paquete
page	la página
painted	pintado de
painter	el pintor, la pintora
pair	el par, la pareja
Panama	el Panamá
Panamanian	panameño
pants	los pantalones
paper	el papel
paradise	el paraíso
paradox	la paradoja
Paraguayan	paraguayo
to paraphrase	parafrasear
parasitic	parasitario
parents	los padres
Parisian	parisiense
park	el parque
party	la fiesta
passport	el pasaporte
password	la contraseña
past perfect	el pluscuamperfecto
pastry	el postre
pasture	el pasto
patient	el paciente
to pay	pagar
pear	la pera
pen	el bolígrafo
pen	la pluma
pencil	el lápiz
pencil eraser	la goma de borrar

English	Spanish
people	la gente
pepper	el pimiento
to perceive	percibir
perfectly	perfectamente
performance (theater)	la representación
perfume	el perfume
period	el punto
to perjure	perjurar
to permit	permitir
to persist	persistir
to persuade	persuadir
Peruvian	peruano
pet	la mascota
pharmacy	la farmacia
photo	la foto
pianist	el/la pianista
picture	el cuadro
piece	el pedazo
pier	el malecón
pill	la pastilla
pillow	la almohada
pimple	el grano
pineapple	la piña
pink	rosa
pitcher	el jarrón
pity	la lástima, pena
place	el lugar
plane	el avión
planet	el planeta
to plant	plantar
plate	el plato
platform	el andén,
to play	jugar
play	la obra
player	el jugador
playground	el patio de recreo
please	por favor
pocket	el bolsillo
poetess	la poetisa
poetry	la poesía
Poland	Polonia
to polish	pulir
Polish	polaco
polite	cortés
politics	la política
poor	pobre
popcorn	las palomitas de maíz
pork	la carne de cerdo
pork loin	el lomo de cerdo
pork sausage	el chorizo
Portuguese	portugués
to possess	poseer
possibly	posiblemente
post office	los correos
postcard	la postal
poster	el cartel
potato (in Spain)	la patata

potatoes	las papas	quiz	la prueba
poultry	la ave	quotation marks	las comillas
praise	la alabanza		
to pray	rezar		

precisely	precisamente		**R**	
precooked	precocinado	**ENGLISH**		**SPANISH**
to prefer	preferir	rabbit		el conejo
prefix	el prefijo	radio		la radio
pregnancy	el embarazo	to rain		llover
to prepare to	prepararse a	rainfall		la llovizna
preposition	la preposición	to raise (pick up)		levantar
present	presente	rare		excepcional, raro
present	el regalo	raspberry		la frambuesa
presentation	la presentación	rather		bastante
preservative	el conservador	to read		leer
to preside	presidir	reader		el lector
president	el/la presidente	reading		la lectura
to presume	presumir	ready		listo
to pretend	fingir	real		verdadero
pretext	el pretexto	to realize		darse cuenta
pretty	bonito	really		efectivamente
to prevent	impedir	really		verdaderamente
price	el precio	reason		la razón
priest	el sacerdote	receipt		el recibo
to print	imprimir	to receive		recibir
printer	la impresora	to recommend		recomendar
prize	el premio, el galardón	recommendation		la recomendación
probably	probablemente	to reconsider		recapacitar
problem	el problema	to record		grabar
to proceed	proceder	red		pelirrojo, rojo
to proclaim	proclamar	reddish		rojizo
to produce	producir	reduced		reducido
profession	la profesión	reduced (in price)		rebajado
professor	el catedrático	to re-elect		reeligir
to prohibit	prohibir	to refill		recargar
prologue	el prólogo	to refuse		rechazar, rehusar
to promise	prometer	regardless		no obstante
pronoun	el pronombre	region		la región
to propose	proponer	registration		la matrícula
to protect	proteger	relatives		los parientes
public	público	relevance		la pertinencia
Puerto Rican	puertorriqueño	relief		el alivio
pumpkin	la calabaza	religion		la religión
pure	puro	to remain		quedar(se)
purity	la pureza	to remember		acordarse, recordar
to put	poner	to remove		quitar(se)
to put in	meter	to reproduce		reproducir
to put on makeup	maquillarse	to rent		alquilar
to put to bed	acostar	to repeat		repetir
to put up with	soportar	report		el informe
		to respond		responder
		to resemble		parecerse
	Q		to reserve	reservar
ENGLISH		**SPANISH**	the rest	demás
quality	la calidad	rest		descansar
question	la pregunta	restaurant		el restaurante
question mark	el signo de interrogación	resume		el curriculum profesional
quiet	la quietud	to return		volver

English	Spanish
rhythm	el compás
to ring	sonar
return	la vuelta
review	repaso
rib	la chuleta
rice	el arroz
rich	rico
right	derecha
to rise	subir
river	el río
road	el camino
roll of film	el rollo
Romance (language)	romance
roof	el techo
room	el cuarto
rope	la cuerda
to rot	pudrir
round trip	ida y vuelta
royal	real
rude	descortés
ruins	las ruinas
to run	correr
Russian	ruso

S

English	Spanish
sad	triste
sadness	la tristeza
saint	santo
salad	la ensalada
salami	el salchichón
salary	el sueldo
sale	la rebaja
salmon	el salmón
salt	la sal
salted pork	el tocino
Salvadoran	salvadoreño
same	mismo
sand	la arena
sandal	la sandalia
sane	cuerdo
sardine	la sardina
Saturday	el sábado
sauce	la salsa
sausage	la salchicha
to say	decir
to say goodbye	despedirse
scar	la cicatriz
scarcely	apenas
scarf	la bufanda
schedule	el horario
school	la escuela
Scotland	Escocia
Scottish	escocés
sculpture	la escultura
sea	el mar
seafood	los mariscos

English	Spanish
seat	el asiento
second	segundo
second to last	penúltimo
secret	el secreto
secretary	el secretario
section	la sección
to see	ver
seed	la semilla
to seem	parecer
self-defense	la autodefensa
to sell	vender
semicolon	el punto y coma
to send	enviar, mandar
sensible	razonable, sensato
sensitive	sensible
sentence	frase
September	septiembre
series	la serie
to serve	servir
seven	siete
seven hundred	setecientos
seventeen	diecisiete
seventh	séptimo
seventy	setenta
to sew	coser
shame	la vergüenza
shampoo	el champú
to shave	afeitar(se)
sheep	la oveja
shelf	el estante
sherry	el jerez
to shine	lucir
shiny	brillante
shirt	la camisa
shoe	el zapato
shoe store	la zapatería
shop	la tienda
shop assistant	el dependiente
short	bajo, corto
to show	mostrar
shower	la ducha
shrimp	el camarón, la gamba
to shrink	encoger
sick	enfermo
sick of	harto de
side	el lado
sign	el letrero
to sign	firmar
signature	la firma
silver	la plata
similarity	la semejanza
simplicity	la simplicidad
since	desde
sincerely	atentamente
to sing	cantar
single (unmarried)	soltero
sister	la hermana

to sit	sentar	sports jacket	la cazadora
site	el sitio	spouse	el esposo
six	seis	spring	primavera
six hundred	seiscientos	to spy	espiar
sixteen	dieciséis	square	la plaza
sixth	sexto	squid	el calamar
sixty	sesenta	stain	la mancha
size	la talla, el tamaño	stamp	el sello
to ski	esquiar	star	la estrella
skirt	la falda	station	la estación
sky	el cielo	stationary store	la papelería
to sleep	dormir	still	todavía
slow	lento/a	stomach	el estómago
slowly	despacio	to stop	parar
small	pequeño	stop	la parada
to smell	oler	stoutness	la corpulencia
smile	la sonrisa	straight	liso
to smoke	fumar	straight ahead	todo recto
smoking section	fumador	strange	extraño
snake	la serpiente	strawberry	la fresa
sneaker	la zapatilla de tenis	to stray	errar
to snow	nevar	street	la calle
soap	el jabón	stripes, striped	rayas, a rayas
soccer	el fútbol	to stroll	pasear
sock	el calcetín	strong	fuerte
socks	las medias	student	el alumno
sofa	el sofá	student	el/la estudiante
soft	blando	to study	estudiar
soft drink	el refresco	study	el estudio
solitude	la soledad	stuffed peppers	los chiles rellenos
solution	la solución	stupendously	estupendamente
some	algún	subjunctive	subjuntivo
some	unas, unos	to sublet	subarrendar
someone, somebody	alguien	to substitute	sustituir
something	algo	subway	el metro
sometimes	a veces	to succeed	suceder
son	el hijo	success	el éxito
song	la canción	Sudanese	sudanés
son-in-law	el yerno	to suffer	sufrir
soon	pronto	suffix	el sufijo
sorry	perdone	sugar	el azúcar
soup	la sopa	suicide	el suicidio
to sow	sembrar	to suit	convenir(le)
Spain	España	suit	el traje
Spanish (the language)	castellano	summer	el verano
Spanish (from Spain)	español	sun	el sol
sparrow	el gorrión	Sunday	el domingo
to speak	hablar	sunflower	el girasol
special	especial	sunglasses	las gafas de sol
species	la especie	superfine	extrafino
to spell	deletrear	supermarket	supermercado
to spend	gastar	to support	mantener
sphere	la esfera	surface	la superficie
spinach	la espinaca	to survive	pervivir, sobrevivir
to spit	escupir	to suspend (from school)	suspender
spoon	cuchara	to swallow	tragar
sport	el deporte	sweater	el suéter

Sweden	Suecia
Swedish	sueco
to sweep	barrer
to swim	nadar
Swiss	suizo
Switzerland	la Suiza
to sympathize with	compadecer
symptom	la síntoma

T

ENGLISH	SPANISH
table	la mesa
Taiwanese	taiwanés
to take	llevar, tomar
to take out	sacar
to take time	tardar
talented	talentoso
talkative	charlatán
tall	alto
tank	el depósito
taxi	el taxi
tea	el té
to teach how to	enseñar a
team	el equipo
teaspoon	la cucharita
telephone (number)	el teléfono
television	la televisión
to tell	avisar
temple	el templo
ten	diez
tent (camping)	la tienda de campaña
tenth	décimo
term	el término
test	el examen
Thai	tailandés
Thailand	Tailandia
to thank	agradecer
thank you	gracias
that	aquel, ese, que
that one	aquél, ése
theater	el teatro
there	allí
thesis	la tesis
thief	el ladrón, la ladrona
thin	delgado, flaco
thing	la cosa
to think	pensar
third	tercero
thirteen	trece
thirty	treinta
this	ésta
this one	éste
thought	el pensamiento
thousand	mil
three	tres
three hundred	trescientos
thrilling	emocionante

to throw	tirar
Thursday	el jueves
ticket	el billete
ticket	el boleto
tie	la corbata
time	la vez
time	el tiempo
tired	cansado
today	hoy
together	juntos
tolerance	la tolerancia
tomato	el tomate
tomorrow	mañana
too (adverb modifying an adjective)	demasiado
too	también
tool	la herramienta
tooth	el diente
top	la capa
to touch	tocar
towel	la toalla
town	el pueblo
toy	el juguete
traffic	el tráfico
traffic light	el semáforo
train	el tren
traitor	traicionero
to transcribe	transcribir
to translate	traducir
translation	la traducción
to transmit	transmitir
trash	la basura
to travel	viajar
tree	el árbol
trillion	el billón
trip	el viaje
trolley	el tranvía
trout	la trucha
truck	el camión
trunk	el baúl, el cofre
to trust	fiarse de
truth	la verdad
to try	probar
t-shirt	la camiseta
Tuesday	el martes
tuna	el atún
turkey	el pavo
Turkey	Turquía
Turkish	turco
to turn	doblar
to turn off	apagar
twelve	doce
twenty	veinte
twin	el gemelo
two	dos
two hundred	doscientos
type	el tipo

| typewriter | la máquina de escribir |
| typical | típico |

U	
ENGLISH	SPANISH
ugly	feo
umbrella	el paraguas
uncle	el tío
under	debajo
underemployment	el subempleo
underground	subterráneo
to understand	comprender, entender
to undo	desabrochar
unemployment	el desempleo (paro)
unfortunately	desgraciadamente
uniform	el uniforme
to unite	unir
united	unido
United Kingdom	Reino Unido
United States	los Estados Unidos
university	la universidad
unless	a menos que
unnatural	antinatural
until	hasta
upstairs	arriba
up to	hasta
Uruguayan	uruguayo
useful	útil
useless	inútil

V	
ENGLISH	SPANISH
vacation	la vacación
vanilla	la vainilla
various	varios, varias
various	diferente(s)
to vary	variar
vase	el jarrón
veal	la ternera
Venezuelan	venezolano
vengeance	la venganza
verb	el verbo
very	muy
Vietnamese	vietnamita
vinegar	el vinagre
violence	la violencia
virus	el virus
to visit	visitar

W	
ENGLISH	SPANISH
wages (often hourly)	el salario
waiter	el camarero
waitress	la camarera
to wake up	levantarse
to walk	andar, caminar, marchar
walkway	el pasillo

wall	la pared
wallet	billetera
to wander	errar
to want	querer
war	la guerra
to warn	advertir
to wash	lavar(se)
wastebasket	la cesta
watch	el reloj
to water	regar
water	el agua
watermelon	la sandía
wave	la orilla
we	nosotros
weak	débil
Web page	la página Web
wedding	la boda
Wednesday	el miércoles
week	la semana
weekend	el fin de semana
welcome	bienvenidos
well	bien
well…	pues…
Welsh	galés
what	que
what?	qué
wheel	la rueda
to weigh	pesar
wet	mojado
when	cuando
when?	cuándo
where	donde
where?	dónde
to where	adónde
which	cual
which?	cuál
whichever	cualquier
while (a while)	mientras (un rato)
white	blanco
who	quien
who?	quién
whoever	quienquiera
why	por qué
wife	la esposa
wife	la mujer
will	la voluntad
to win	ganar
wind	el viento
windshield	el parabrisas
windshield wipers	los limpiaparabrisas
wine	el vino
winter	invierno
wisdom	la sabiduría
with	con
with me	conmigo
with you	contigo
without	sin

without	*sin que*
without a doubt	*sin duda*
wolf	*el lobo*
woman	*la mujer*
wonderful	*maravilloso*
Wonderful!	*¡Estupendo!*
wool	*la lana*
word	*la palabra*
to work	*trabajar*
work	*el trabajo*
worker	*el obrero*
worker	*trabajador*
world	*el mundo*
worse	*peor*
to wrap	*envolver*
to write	*escribir*
writing	*la escritura*
wrong	*equivocado*

Y

ENGLISH	SPANISH
year	*el año*
yellow	*amarillo*
yes	*sí*
yesterday	*ayer*
you (informal)	*tú*
you're welcome	*de nada*
young	*joven*
younger	*menor*
your	*tu*
your (formal), his, hers	*su*
youth	*el/la joven*

Z

ENGLISH	SPANISH
zero	*cero*

E Appendix D
Answer Key

Part 1: Nouns and Articles
Exercise 1: Name a Noun

1. Tengo dos **billetes**.
2. Soy de los **Estados Unidos**.
3. A los **guatemaltecos** les gusta comer la **comida** guatemalteca.
4. El **gato** come el **pescado**.
5. El **río** se llama **Río Grande**.
6. Tanta **libertad** es una **tentación**.
7. La **natación** es un **deporte** que exige **talento**.
8. Todos los **miembros** del **equipo** han llegado.

Exercise 2: At Home

1. el dormitorio
2. el salón
3. el comedor
4. el cuarto de baño
5. el pasillo
6. el piso
7. el techo
8. el colchón
9. el estante
10. el sofá
11. el espejo
12. el televisor
13. el refrigerador
14. el lavaplatos
15. el horno

Exercise 3: Check the Ending

1. El Señor Escobar tiene una <u>hija</u>. feminine
2. El <u>perro</u> no ladra mucho. masculine
3. Acabo de comprar un <u>carro</u> nuevo. masculine
4. La <u>fiesta</u> estuvo muy divertida. feminine
5. Es la <u>hora</u> de celebrar nuestra victoria. feminine
6. ¿Prefieres la <u>falda</u> gris o los pantalones negros? feminine
7. Vamos a empezar nuestros estudios el próximo <u>año</u>. masculine
8. Es mejor cocinar con <u>aceite</u> de maíz. masculine

Exercise 4: Feminine Nouns Camouflaged

serie	nariz	**ciudad**	**organización**
papel	varón	**tesis**	**vacación**
televisión	**crisis**	árbol	**verdad**
cicatriz	**quietud**	virus	**luz**
universidad	**niñez**	amor	calambre
comedor	*interpretación*	*amistad*	compás

Exercise 5: It's a Profession

1. La doctora cura enfermedades.
2. El conductor conduce coches.

3. La pastora cuida a sus ovejas.
4. El profesor enseña a los estudiantes.
5. La escultora crea esculturas.
6. La enfermera cuida a los pacientes.
7. El pintor pinta.
8. El cocinero prepara comidas.

Exercise 6: En Route

1. El español es un **idioma**.
2. Este pequeño pueblo no está en el **mapa**.
3. ¿Cuándo es el **día** de tu cumpleaños?
4. La carta no fue escrita con máquina de escribir, sino a **mano**.
5. Para el desayuno, me gustaría un vaso de **leche**.
6. Tomé una **foto** del Coliseo la última vez que viajaba por Roma.
7. Cuando nos mudamos, transportamos todas las cosas por el **camión**.
8. Aquí en la región del Mediterráneo, el **clima** es templado.

Exercise 7: Tricky Endings

1. No entiendo el <u>mapa</u>. masculine
2. Ya tenemos <u>hambre</u>. feminine
3. ¿Qué llevas en la <u>mano</u>? feminine
4. No he oído esta canción por la <u>radio</u>. feminine
5. No hay muchas variaciones en el <u>clima</u> de Puerto Rico. masculine
6. Vivimos en el <u>planeta</u> llamado Tierra. masculine
7. Es muy fácil llegar allá en <u>tranvía</u>. masculine
8. Cuando era joven, soñaba con tener mi propia <u>moto</u>. feminine

Exercise 8: One or More?

1. fundadores (founders)
2. martes (Tuesday)
3. nueces (walnuts)
4. día (day)
5. observaciones (observations)
6. español (Spaniard)
7. inglés (Englishman)
8. campos (fields)
9. limpiaparabrisas (windshield wipers)
10. hijas (daughters)

Exercise 9: The Right Indefinite

1. un gato
2. una falda
3. unos billetes
4. una chica
5. un mapa
6. unas ciudades
7. unos libros

8. unos idiomas
9. un doctor
10. una persona

Exercise 10: Get It Right

1. Quiero el plato con quesos y **una** cerveza, por favor.
2. Busco **un** restaurante donde sirven tacos auténticos.
3. Mis amigos son **unas** personas muy inteligentes.
4. Ésta no es **una** actitud muy útil.
5. Ella es **una** vendedora de postres.
6. Necesito unos sellos para mandar **una** postal.
7. La calle Marín está en **uno** de estos mapas.
8. Saquen **unos** papeles y un bolígrafo, por favor.

Exercise 11: The Right Definite

1. el gato
2. la falda
3. los billetes
4. la chica
5. el mapa
6. las ciudades
7. los libros
8. los idiomas
9. el doctor
10. la persona

Exercise 12: To and From

1. Ya no voy **al** cine.
2. El banco está en la calle **de la** Flecha.
3. Ama **a** los seres humanos.
4. Patricio regresará **del** viaje mañana.
5. El mensajero entrega los paquetes **a la** hora y en el lugar que usted designe.
6. El espectáculo empezará **a las** ocho.
7. Es la corona **del** rey.
8. Primero, hay que leer la introducción **a los** ensayos.
9. Los estudiantes van a elegir **al** representante de su clase.
10. Hoy es la primera presentación **del** programa.

Exercise 13: Merry Old England

1. Londres es una ciudad grande.
2. El sistema subterráneo de trenes de Londres.
3. El gran reloj que está en Londres.
4. La reina de Inglaterra se llama Isabel Segunda.
5. Una de las tiendas más grandes del mundo es Harrod's.
6. Esta tienda está en la calle Brompton.
7. Se puede probar comida india en unos de los restaurantes de la calle Drummond.
8. Algunos consideran el pollo tikka marsala como el plato nacional de los británicos.
9. El fútbol es el deporte más popular de Inglaterra.
10. David Beckham es un jugador de fútbol muy exitoso.

Exercise 14: Land of the Free

1. El país norteamericano donde viven los estadounidenses: los Estados Unidos
2. La capital de este país: Washington D.C.
3. El vecino al norte de este país: el Canadá
4. El primer presidente de este país: George Washington
5. El hogar del presidente de este país: la Casa Blanca
6. La avenida donde está este hogar: la avenida Pennsylvania
7. El océano al este de este país: el océano Atlántico
8. El autor del himno de este país: Francis Scott Key
9. Palomitas de maíz populares en este país, particularmente cuando se asiste a los partidos de béisbol: Cracker Jack
10. Una organización política internacional: las Naciones Unidas

Exercise 15: Checking In

Q: Receptionist: Good day, sir. How are you?
A: Sr. Ibáñez: Okay, thanks. I have a reservation at this hotel.

Q: Receptionist: What is your last name?
A: Sr. Ibáñez: Ibáñez.

Q: Receptionist: What is your first name?
A: Sr. Ibáñez: Enrique.

Q: Receptionist: Very well. What is your address?
A: Sr. Ibáñez: 12 Ochoa Avenue, Barcelona, Spain.

Q: Receptionist: What is your telephone number?
A: Sr. Ibáñez: 55-555-1234.

Q: Receptionist: How many days do you plan to spend at our hotel?
A: Sr. Ibáñez: Four days.

Q: Receptionist: Very well. Welcome!
A: Sr. Ibáñez: Thanks.

Exercise 16: The Correct Choice

1. Hay **un** vaso de vino en la mesa.
2. Aquellos chicos son **los** hijos de la Señora Martín.
3. Carlos es el **sobrino** de Ramón.
4. Mi madre está llena **de** caridad.
5. Cuando hace sol, me gusta ir **a la** playa.
6. Las **intenciones** de ella son buenas.
7. Es verdaderamente **una** buena idea.
8. Nunca vamos **al** cine.
9. Es **la** tercera vez que pierdes el camino a casa.
10. Yo la visité muchas **veces**.

Exercise 17: In (Dis)agreement

1. las revistas, profesoras, **gatos**, chicas
1. una maldad, **interés**, criatura, ciencia
2. el sentido, tomate, **serie**, encubridor
3. el **culminación**, fin, cabo, pan
4. la mañana, impresión, vejez, **aceite**
5. el mundo, **acción**, margen, cantante
6. un centro, amor, **actriz**, flor
7. unas **curas**, barbaridades, maridos, pesadumbres
8. los cuentos, amaneceres, seres, **simpatías**
9. unos bolsillos, **ideas**, tranvías, espíritus
10. la mano, quietud, lealdad, **problema**

Exercise 18: Dr. Domínguez

1. Se llama Paco Domínguez.
2. El Señor Domínguez es un médico.
3. El Señor Domínguez trabaja en el hospital San Juan de Dios en Bogotá, Colombia.
4. Sus pacientes son los niños.
5. Sí, le gusta porque es muy gratificante.
6. Es de un pequeño pueblo colombiano llamado Sonsón.
7. Él vive con su familia.
8. Capitán es el perrito de la familia Domínguez.
9. Su dirección es Avenida 127, No. 21-20, Bogotá, Colombia.
10. Su número de teléfono es 57-1-1234555.

Part 2: Pronouns
Exercise 1: Personal Appearances

1. **Él** (he) es un chico muy guapo.
2. **Ella** (she) es alta y flaca.
3. **Nosotros** (we) somos morenos.
4. Señor Morales, **usted** (you) es muy elegante.
5. **Tú** (you) eres bajo y joven.
6. Charlie y Alberto no son morenos; **ellos** (they) son rubios.
7. **Yo** (I) soy pesado y de altura media.
8. **Nosotras** (we) somos feas.

Exercise 2: You, You, You

1. el hermano: tú
2. los abuelos: ustedes
3. el grupo de gente: ustedes
4. el colaborador del trabajo: usted (until using *tú* is mutually agreed)
5. los jóvenes estudiantes: ustedes (*vosotros* in Spain)
6. el policía: usted
7. el mejor amigo: tú
8. los médicos: ustedes

Exercise 3: Make It Direct

1. Tú **me** amas.
   You love me.

2. Yo tengo los boletos. Yo **los** tengo.
   I have the tickets. I have them.
3. María **te** ve.
   Maria sees you (singular, informal).
4. Ella escribirá las cartas. Ella **las** escribirá.
   She will write the letters. She will write them.
5. Jose tiene el libro. Él **lo** tiene.
   Jose has a book. He has it.
6. María golpeó a José. María **lo** golpeó.
   Maria hit Jose. Maria hit him.
7. La profesora **os** ayudará.
   The teacher will help you (plural, informal).
8. Él **nos** lleva al trabajo.
   He takes us to work.

Exercise 4: In School

1. Todos los estudiantes los conocen.
2. El estudiante tiene que leerlo para la clase.
3. Mis amigos me encontraron en la biblioteca.
4. El profesor lo contó a la clase.
5. La profesora de matemáticas te designó para explicar el problema a la clase.
6. Las voy a obtener./Voy a obtenerlas.
7. Ernesto la buscó para invitarla al baile escolar.
8. No la veo desde la última fila de escritorios.
9. El director de la escuela nos rezongó por no asistir a las clases.
10. Señora Rodríguez, no la vi entrar.

Exercise 5: Indirectly Said

1. **Me** contó toda la historia.
2. **Te** lo ruego, déjame en paz.
3. Espero que **le** sea útil.
4. Felipe, **nos** canta una canción.
5. **Les** hablo a los otros estudiantes.
6. **Le** responderé más tarde.
7. Cualquier duda que tenga **se** la podremos solucionar.
8. La madre **nos** prepara el desayuno cada mañana.

Exercise 6: Give and Take

1. El camarero **les** da el menú. (los esposos)
2. ¿Por qué no **le** das el dulce? (el chico)
3. **Se** los daré la próxima clase. (las estudiantes)
4. ¿Quién **te** dio este CD? (tú)
5. Voy a dar**le** una copa de agua. (usted)
6. Mi tía **les** da muchos regalos por su cumpleaños. (mis primos)
7. Los empleados del supermercado **os** darán muestras gratis. (vosotros)
8. **Se** lo daré en un momento. (ustedes)

Exercise 7: The Daily Grind

1. Él **se** despierta tarde.
2. Tú **te** lavas el pelo con el champú especial.
3. Ustedes **se** van a la casa de prisa.
4. Vosotros **os** sentís bien después de descansar.
5. Usted **se** viste de moda.
6. El señor Molina **se** pone el traje para ir a la oficina.
7. Elisa y yo **nos** dormimos a las once de la noche.
8. Yo **me** llamo Julia.

Exercise 8: Reflexive or Not?

1. Él **se** da cuenta. (reflexive pronoun)
2. **Lo** bailas muy bien. (direct object pronoun)
3. **Tú te** imaginas qué pasará allí. (subject pronoun, reflexive pronoun)
4. **Ustedes** no entienden la situación. (subject pronoun)
5. A Alina **le** gustan las flores. (indirect object pronoun)
6. **Se lo** prepara para las dos. (indirect object pronoun, direct object pronoun)
7. **Me** manda la carta lo más pronto posible. (indirect object pronoun)
8. Es que **vosotros** estáis listos. (subject pronoun)

Exercise 9: For Each Other

1. María y José **se** aman.
2. Tú y yo **nos** entendemos.
3. Pedro y su socio **se** necesitan mucho.
4. Los amigos **se** miran en sorpresa.
5. Nosotros **nos** queremos mucho.
6. ¿Vosotros todavía no **os** habláis?
7. Los amantes **se** besaban bajo la luna.
8. Angelina y yo **nos** llamamos todos los días.

Exercise 10: Whose Is It, Anyway?

1. Son sus problemas.
2. Es mi colchón.
3. Es tu corbata.
4. Son mis ideas.
5. Es su cuento.
6. Son vuestros libros.
7. Es nuestra bicicleta.
8. Son tus zapatos.

Exercise 11: Yours and Mine

1. Julio trabaja con **sus** padres.
2. María y yo vamos a la casa de **nuestros** amigos.
3. Yo estoy buscando **mis** nuevos guantes de lana.
4. El estudiante no tiene **su** mochila.
5. Tú nunca olvides **tu** trabajo.
6. Ustedes no tienen **sus** boletos.
7. Tú no conoces a **tus** nietos.
8. Yo sé que es **mi** responsabilidad.

Exercise 12: In Possession

1. mis amigos	los amigos míos	los míos
2. **su coche**	el coche suyo	**el suyo**
3. nuestra casa	**la casa nuestra**	**la nuestra**
4. **tu libro**	el libro tuyo	el tuyo (libro)
5. sus revistas	**las revistas suyas**	**las suyas**
6. **su hermana**	**la hermana suya**	la suya (hermana)
7. nuestros gritos	**los gritos nuestros**	**los nuestros**
8. **tus manzanas**	las manzanas tuyas	**las tuyas**

Exercise 13: In Our Class

1. **Ése** es el chico más inteligente. (eso)
2. **Aquél** es el profesor de arte. (aquello)
3. **Esto** es imposible. (esto)
4. **Éstas** son las estudiantes más jóvenes. (esto)
5. **Aquéllas** son las profesoras menos simpáticas. (aquello)
6. Nunca he visto **aquello**. (aquello)
7. **Ésta** es la planta para la clase. (esto)
8. **Ésas** no son las plantas para la clase. (eso)

Exercise 14: Something Indefinite

1. alguien (someone)
2. nada (nothing)
3. algo (something)
4. quienquiera (whoever)
5. alguna (someone, a certain one)
6. ningunos (no one, nobody, pl.)
7. cada uno (each one)
8. tanto (so much)
9. cualquiera (anyone, whoever)
11. todo (everything)

Exercise 15: Which Is Indefinite?

1. **Algunos** de los estudiantes están retrasados. Some of the students are late.
2. **Ambos** son culpables. Both are guilty.
3. La **otra** es la mía. It's the other that's mine.
4. Estas cosas son **todo** lo que vamos a repasar. These things are everything we're going to review.
5. Es **algo** que no puedo explicar. It's something I can't explain.
6. **Muchas** todavía no saben conducir. Many still don't know how to drive.
7. Es lo **poco** que tengo. It's the little I have.
8. **Nadie** sabe la verdad. No one knows the truth.
9. Es como **cualquiera**. It's just like any other.
10. **Unos** que no saben nada de ese tema. Some who know nothing of that theme.

Exercise 16: A Little of That

1. María, **quien** es de España, vive en México.
2. **Lo que** quiero es un helado.
3. Lo mejor es **que** pudiéramos descansar muy pronto.

4. Lola quiere **que** Elena la acompañe.
5. Son muchas las razones por las **cuales** deben ayudarme.
6. Son profesionales de los negocios, **quienes** han tenido mucho éxito en sus esfuerzos.
7. Esto no es **lo que** estoy buscando.
8. Vivimos en una época en la **cual** es posible ser libre.

Exercise 17: In Combination

1. Tengo muchos amigos, quienes son muy simpáticos.
2. Nosotros miramos la película, que era muy buena.
3. Juego al fútbol, que es el mejor deporte.
4. José es mi amigo con el cual voy a viajar.
5. Los libros son muy interesantes. He leído muchos libros que son muy interesantes.
6. Trabajo mucho, que es muy fatigoso.
7. Mi coche, que es muy viejo, funciona bien.
8. No veo lo que está pasando.

Exercise 18: In the Apartment Building

1. **¿Quién** es él? Es Julio, el inquilino del apartamento en el segundo piso.
2. **¿Qué** es esto? Es la puerta al apartamento.
3. **¿Cuáles** son los responsabilidades de los inquilinos? Cuidar las áreas comunes y pagar la renta.
4. **¿Quiénes** son los inquilinos? Son generalmente estudiantes o la gente que trabaja en la universidad.
5. **¿Cuál** es el mejor inquilino? El Señor López, porque siempre paga su renta a tiempo.

Exercise 19: Full of Exclamations

1. ¡Qué pena! What a pity!
2. ¡Qué día! What a day!
3. ¡Quién lo diría! Who would say that!
4. ¡Qué divertido! What fun!
5. ¡Cómo cantan! How they sing!
6. ¡Cuán interesante! How interesting!
7. ¡Quién sabe! Who knows!
8. ¡Qué cosa más rara! What a strange thing!

Exercise 20: Identification, Please

1. Serena ya **lo** sabe. (direct object pronoun)
2. **La** encuentro muy bella. (direct object pronoun)
3. El hombre **que** trabajaba aquí ya se jubiló. (relative pronoun, reflexive pronoun)
4. Ellos **se** quieren mucho. (reciprocal pronoun)
5. Susana **le** compró un regalo. (indirect object pronoun)
6. **Su** novio es italiano. (possessive adjective)
7. **¿Quiénes** son ellos? (interrogative pronoun)
8. Yo **me** alegro **que** no pasó **nada** malo. (reflexive pronoun, relative pronoun, indefinite pronoun)
9. **Nadie** dijo **nada**. (indefinite pronouns)
10. Estas cartas son las **suyas**. (possessive pronoun)

Exercise 21: A Pronoun Pro

1. Nadie me contó la verdad. nadie, me
2. Éste es el tipo de música que me gusta escuchar. éste, me
3. Explícamelo, porque yo no lo entiendo. me, yo, lo
4. ¿Cuál es su coche? cuál, su
5. Ana te visitará mañana. te
6. No es mi culpa que no estés contento. mi
7. El dueño de esta casa soy yo. yo
8. Este regalo es para ti. ti
9. Te lo voy a mostrar más tarde. te lo
10. Cuando Teresa estaba enferma, su madre le dio pastillas. su, le
11. Ellos son novios y se van a casar pronto. ellos, se
12. No les pido nada a ustedes. les, ustedes
13. Alguna de estas bicicletas es la mía. alguna, mía
14. ¡Cuidado, no te caigas! te
15. No tengo las respuestas para usted. usted
16. Nuestras vidas no son fáciles. nuestras
17. Es la razón por la cual estamos aquí. cual
18. Antes de comer, me lavo las manos. me
19. ¿Quién sabe cocinar comida puertorriqueña? quién
20. Vosotros sois estudiantes del primer grado, ¿verdad? vosotros

Exercise 22: Another Way of Saying It

1. Ella es una chica muy buena.
2. Voy a decírselo.
3. ¿Quién tiene tus libros?
4. Se la contamos.
5. Es nuestra casa.
6. La veo caminando por la calle.
7. Nosotros somos muy buenos amigos.
8. ¿Dónde está el suyo?

Exercise 23: Before or After?

1. It must be verified. (direct object pronoun)
2. The problem isn't interesting him. (indirect object pronoun)
3. Go to sleep! (reflexive pronoun)
4. She's going to sing me a lullaby. (indirect object pronoun)
5. Invite her to the party! (direct object pronoun)

Exercise 24: At Work

Answers may vary.

Part 3: Adjectives and Adverbs
Exercise 1: The Right Form

1. unos edificios **altos** (alto)
2. una mujer **bonita** (bonito)
3. las naranjas **deliciosas** (delicioso)

4. un idioma **difícil** (difícil)
5. mis zapatos **nuevos** (nuevo)
6. las playas **soleadas** (soleado)
7. el helado **frío** (frío)
8. la mesa **roja** (rojo)
9. la ciudad **grande** (grande)
10. el vino **blanco** (blanco)

Exercise 2: In Your Opinion

Answers may vary.
1. equivocada, correcta, interesante
2. gordos, anaranjados, amistosos
3. grandes, pequeñas, acogedoras
4. deliciosa, mal preparada, salada
5. inteligente, perezoso, trabajador
6. malhumorado, simpático, difícil
7. largas, interesantes, incomprensibles
8. estúpida, compartida, eterna
9. diligentes, poderosos, cansados
10. difícil, nueva, diferente

Exercise 3: At the Marketplace

1. Los mercados al aire libre están llenos de gente.
2. Se esfuerzan por atraer clientes a sus propios puestos.
3. Estos vendedores son vociferantes.
4. Se venden frutas y vegetales de estación.
5. Las manzanas pueden ser rojas, amarillas o verdes.
6. Se venden todos los tipos de calabazas, pequeñas y grandes, de varios colores.
7. El aire fresco huele a la dulce fragancia de la sidra y las hojas caídas.
8. Se venden productos dulces de panadería: pasteles, galletas y tortas.
9. Se venden quesos campesinos.
10. Los girasoles son amarillos.

Exercise 4: A Gender Switch

1. la chica charlatana
2. los empleados organizadores
3. la ayudante personal
4. la profesora superior
5. la asesina encubridora
6. las hermanas inteligentes
7. el científico optimista
8. la señora galana
9. las mujeres acusadoras
10. la hija cortés

Exercise 5: The Right Word for the Occasion

1. Yo soy una mujer demasiado **cosmopolita** para vivir en el campo.
2. Estamos muy **felices** y contentos.

3. Él es una persona **optimista**: siempre espera lo mejor.
4. Vuestra casa es un lugar **acogedor**; es un placer quedarse allá.
5. Ella es una chica muy **habladora**: siempre tiene algo que decir.
6. Eso es muy **interesante**, cuéntamelo otra vez.
7. Caperucita **roja** fue a visitar a su abuela y fue comida por el lobo.
8. Estas joyas no son **bonitas**, sino feas.
9. Tengo mucha energía e interés: soy un hombre **entusiasta**.
10. Los estudiantes de nuestra escuela son gente muy **trabajadora** y hacen todas sus tareas a tiempo.

Exercise 6: The Right Color

1. El cielo no es rojo, sino **azul**.
2. El chocolate no es azul, sino **café**.
3. Las plantas no son negras, sino **verdes**.
4. El letrero PARE no es azul, sino **rojo**.
5. La combinación de rojo y amarillo no es morado, sino **anaranjado**.
6. Los nubes no son blancas, sino **grises**.
7. La nieve no es azul, sino **blanca**.
8. Las uvas no son amarillas, sino **moradas**.
9. El sol no es rojo, sino **amarillo**.
10. La tinta no es azul, sino **negra**.

Exercise 7: A Pretty Picture

*Tamara es una estudiante **universitaria**. Su clase **favorita** es el arte. Hoy, ella pinta una pintura muy **bonita** de un campo. El campo está lleno de flores **lindas**. En el cielo **azul** hay unas pocas nubes **blancas**. En la parte **baja** de la pintura, hay un perrito **alegre**. Ésta es la pintura **favorita** de Tamara. Para terminar, ella espera ganar una buena nota por su trabajo.*

Exercise 8: According to the Calendar

1. Domingo es el **primer** día de la semana.
2. Marzo es el **tercer** mes del año.
3. Jueves es el **quinto** día de la semana.
4. Septiembre es el **noveno** mes del año.
5. Viernes es el **sexto** día de la semana.
6. Sábado es el **séptimo** día de la semana.
7. Octubre es el **décimo** mes del año.
8. Febrero es el **segundo** mes del año.
9. Abril es el **cuarto** mes del año.
10. Agosto es el **octavo** mes del año.

Exercise 9: A Quantity of Things

1. **Ambas** chicas quieren tener un perrito. Both girls want to have a doggie.
2. Hay **siete** días en la semana. There are seven days in the week.
3. Tengo **algún** dinero, pero no es bastante para comprarlo. I have some money, but it's not enough to buy it.

4. Tengo **treinta** y **tres** años. I am thirty-three years old.
5. No tenemos **tanta** prisa. We're not in such a hurry.
6. Ella tiene **varias** razones. She has various reasons.
7. Nos quedábamos aquí **todo** el tiempo. We were here the whole time.
8. Yo sé **muchas** cosas. I know a lot of things.
9. No creo que tengas **suficiente** valor. I don't think you have enough courage.
10. Algún día, vamos a vivir en **esta** ciudad. One day, we'll live in this city.

Exercise 10: This or That

Daniel: *Sofía, ¿Ves* **aquellas** *cajas con dulces allá en* **aquella** *balda?*
Sofia: *Sí. Voy a cogerlas. Y tú, coge* **esas** *galletas cerca de ti, ¿bien?*
Daniel: *Pues, no me gustan* **estas** *galletas. Prefiero las otras, cerca de ti. ¿Te parece que compremos* **esas** *galletas?*
Sofia: ***Éstas*** *no me gustan mucho. Vamos a ver. ¿Te gustan* **aquellas** *galletas, allá, en las cajitas verdes?*
Daniel: *Sí.* **Aquellas** *galletas en las cajitas verdes me gustan tanto como* ***ésas***.

Exercise 11: Compare and Contrast

1. México tiene más habitantes que Honduras.
2. Este gato es tan mono como aquél.
3. Alma es menos linda que Hortensia.
4. El señor Flores es tan inteligente como el señor Fermoso.
5. Mi hijo es más joven que el tuyo.
6. Nuestro presidente es más famoso que el de Ecuador.
7. Estas noticias no son tan interesantes como las de ayer.
8. Mi idea es mejor que la suya.
9. Roberto es menos alto que Valentino.
10. Su maleta no es más grande que la mía.

Exercise 12: Who's It Gonna Be?

1. Mi abuelo es mayor que mi abuela.
2. Carla es más inteligente que José.
3. Mi prima Jacinta es menos linda que mi otra prima Yazmín.
4. Los elefantes son animales más grandes que las ratas.
5. El sol es tan amarillo como las flores.
6. Yo soy menor que mi hermana.
7. Jaime es más rico que Juana.
8. Paco es peor que Javier.
9. Enrique es menos pesado que Patricio.
10. Los estudiantes son tan trabajadores como los obreros.

Exercise 13: The Best and the Brightest

1. Es la ciudad más grande en el país.
2. Es el pueblo más pequeño en la región.
3. Es la escritora más inteligente en la asociación de los escritores.

4. Es el libro más interesante de todos los que leí este año.
5. Es la torta más deliciosa de todas las que he probado.
6. Es la enfermera más simpática en el hospital.
7. Es el ejercicio más difícil en el libro.
8. Es la razón más extraña de las que me han dicho.
9. Es la canción más linda en la recopilación.
10. Es el hombre más guapo de la oficina.

Exercise 14: From Adjective to Adverb

1. rápidamente
2. efectivamente
3. claramente
4. actualmente
5. obviamente
6. felizmente
7. atentamente
8. difícilmente
9. tristemente
10. lentamente

Exercise 15: The Right Adverb

1. Juan es un buen conductor. Conduce **bien**.
2. El coche no es rápido. Se mueve **lentamente**.
3. Camila está contenta. Se ríe **alegremente**.
4. Los estudiantes están muy interesados. Están escuchando **atentamente**.
5. No quiero despertar a mamá. Paso por su cuarto **silenciosamente**.
6. No puedo encontrar mis gafas. Veo mucho **peor**.
7. Ellos visitan el parque no más que una vez cada año. Ellos visitan el parque **raramente**.
8. Yo no canto muy bien. Eduardo canta **mejor**.
9. Nosotros nos vemos casi todos los días. Nosotros no vemos **frecuentemente**.
10. A Tomás, le duele la cabeza. Él se siente **mal**.

Exercise 16: In Place

1. Siempre comen el desayuno **aquí.** They always eat breakfast here.
2. ¿Qué es esto? What is this?
3. El restaurante está muy **lejos**. The restaurant is very far.
4. Estamos **cerca** de la ciudad. We are near the city.
5. El gorrión está **allá**, en el árbol. The sparrow is over there, on the tree.
6. El regalo está **dentro** de la caja sobre la mesa. The present is inside the box on the table.
7. Los sombreros están **arriba**, sobre el armario. The hats are up above, over the cabinet.
8. El teatro se sitúa **detrás** de la estación de trenes. The theater is situated behind the train station.
9. ¿Quién está **adentro**? Who is inside?
10. Es cierto que los libros necesarios están **ahí**. It's certain that the necessary books are there.

Exercise 17: A Timely Matter

1. Me gustaría ir a casa **pronto** (pronto, ayer, nunca).
2. El autobús se fue **tarde** (mañana, tarde, todavía).
3. Es domingo. Nosotros tenemos que trabajar **mañana** (siempre, ayer, mañana).
4. No tomé el desayuno **ayer** (siempre, ayer, mañana).
5. No he comido el almuerzo **todavía** (todavía, pronto, siempre).
6. Voy a terminar el libro **luego** (nunca, luego, aún), después de la cena.
7. No lo he probado **nunca** (siempre, temprano, nunca).
8. Es demasiado **temprano** (temprano, ya, tarde) para dormirse—son solamente las nueve de la noche.
9. Ya habrá mejorado **aún** (después, luego, aún) más.
10. Es mejor terminar los ejercicios **ahora** (temprano, ahora, aún) y no demorar.

Exercise 18: Language Skills

*Pedro tiene trece años pero **ya** habla tres idiomas. Tuvo su clase de francés **ayer** y **mañana** tendrá su clase de inglés. Su profesora de francés, la Señora Duprés, normalmente llega **tarde**, pero **ayer** ella llegó allá **temprano** para el repaso antes del examen. Pedro estaba muy sorprendido. Ella **nunca** lo había hecho **antes**.*

Exercise 19: Not Too Little and Not Too Much

1. Me duele mucho la cabeza. mucho
2. Hay tan harto trabajo para hacer. tan
3. Puedo correr más lejos que tú. más
4. Hace demasiado frío aquí en el invierno. demasiado
5. La amistad es algo difícil de encontrar. algo
6. La excursión a la montaña fue bastante dura. bastante
7. Espero que la fiesta sea muy divertida. muy
8. El proceso de cómo funciona el cerebro es poco entendido. poco
9. Apenas tuve tiempo para vestirme y salir de casa. apenas
10. Temo que tú me extrañes menos de lo que yo te extraño a ti. menos
11. Esta canción no es tan bella como la anterior. tan
12. Es casi cierto que yo voy a ganar. casi

Exercise 20: One or the Other

1. María es **bonita**. adjective
2. **Ambos** lugares son muy bellos. adjective
3. No me importa **ya**. adverb
4. Nada es **peor** que encontrarse completamente solo. adjective
5. Las muñequitas **pequeñas** son las mejores. adjective
6. La película resultó **tan** impresionante. adverb
7. Son mis **primeros** pasos después del accidente. adjective
8. La música se toca **lentamente**. adverb
9. Esto es **poco** interesante. adverb

10. Ya estamos muy **lejos**. adverb

Exercise 21: A Game of Translation

1. No hay nada que ver.
2. Tengo dos pedazos de torta.
3. Es el último día de las vacaciones.
4. Las manzanas son mis frutas favoritas.
5. Es mejor quedarse tranquilo.
6. Es la cuarta vez que yo he visto esto.
7. Es un jugador entusiasta.
8. Ellos viven en una casa grande.

Exercise 22: A Typical Day at a Typical College

Adjectives: *linda, norte, mucha, pequeño, inteligentes, interesantes, española, nuevos, todos, divertido, atestado.*

Adverbs: *mucho, aquí, muy, tantas, muchos, juntos, luego, frecuentemente, a menudo, muy*

Part 4: Prepositions, Conjunctions, and More
Exercise 1: On and Away

1. Vamos en tren.
2. Duermen siete horas por día.
3. Soy de Londres.
4. Vamos a la casa de Marco.
5. No soy nada sin usted.
6. Bebo café con leche.
7. Está en la ducha.
8. La chica comienza a llorar.
9. Vamos a Argentina.
10. Sé muy poco de mi familia.

Exercise 2: A, De, En, or Sin

1. Se reunieron **en** la casa de Pedro.
2. **A** veces yo no la comprendo.
3. Es el collar **de** oro.
4. Ella a menudo anda **sin** zapatos.
5. Ayudo **a** cargar el camión de mudanza.
6. Dame un pedazo **de** pan, por favor.
7. El perro duerme **en** el piso.
8. Es posible vivir bien **sin** dinero.
9. Ellos no ven **a** la profesora.
10. Déjame **en** paz.

Exercise 3: By and By

1. Los niños corren **por** la casa.
2. En Francia, María tomó el tren **para** Alemania.
3. Gracias **por** la comida.
4. La casa es bella **por** fuera y **por** dentro.
5. Caminamos **por** toda la ciudad.
6. Estamos aquí **para** visitar a nuestros abuelos.
7. Estábamos en Granada **por** motivo de las fiestas.

8. Este regalo es **para** mi esposa.
9. Se venden las piñas **por** cuatro dólares cada una.
10. La novela fue escrita **por** el famoso autor.

Exercise 4: Make It Spanish

1. Ella va a la oficina de correos para comprar sellos.
2. Ella es muy educada para ser una americana.
3. Caminamos por todas partes.
4. Los platos nuevos son para las celebraciones especiales.
5. Él pagó veinte dólares por su nueva camisa.
6. Vamos para la casa de nuestra abuelita.
7. Yo lo/la compré para ti.
8. Lo toman por idiota.
9. Gracias por toda tu/su ayuda.
10. Necesito el informe para la próxima semana.

Exercise 5: Over and Under

1. El cuaderno está **sobre** la mesa.
2. Javier trabaja **al lado de** Félix en la tienda de deportes.
3. El restaurante está **cerca de** las tiendas.
4. La luna está **encima de** la ciudad.
5. En el centro, el parque está a la izquierda y el almacén está **a la derecha**.
6. El túnel corre **debajo del** río.
7. Voy a esconderme **detrás de** los árboles.
8. El cine está **entre** la tienda de zapatos y un restaurante tailandés.
9. La ciudad de México está **lejos de** Nueva York.
10. En el coche, la silla del conductor está **a la izquierda**.

Exercise 6: Where Is It?

1. La escuela está cerca de la estación de bomberos.
2. Ella está detrás de Miguel.
3. Los árboles están delante de las ventanas.
4. La lavandería está contra la panadería.
5. Mis amigos están lejos de aquí.
6. El circo está al lado del río.
7. El hospital está enfrente de los dormitorios.
8. Los zapatos están debajo de la cama.
9. La escuela está a la derecha del patio de recreo.
10. El teatro está entre el museo y el zoológico.

Exercise 7: In a Timely Fashion

1. Junio llega **después de** mayo.
2. Nosotros nos lavamos las manos **antes de** comer.
3. No estaremos listos **hasta** las ocho.
4. **Después del** cine, generalmente vamos al café.
5. Tome precauciones **antes que** sea tarde.
6. Emilio siempre reza **antes de** dormir.
7. Voy a esperar **hasta** que mis hijos lleguen a casa.
8. Ellos limpian la cocina **después de** cocinar la cena.
9. ¡**Hasta** luego!

10. Los jardineros terminan todas sus tareas afuera de la casa **antes que** anochezca.

Exercise 8: Choose the Right Phrase

1. Trabajamos **en la cafetería**.
2. Caminamos **al supermercado**.
3. Es el coche **de él**; es su coche.
4. Nadie **por aquí** sabe jugar al tenis.
5. Trabajo aquí **desde enero**.
6. ¿Conoces **a Raúl**?
7. No oí nada **de esto**.
8. Este año voy a asistir a muchas fiestas **de Navidad**.
9. Voy a completar el proyecto **sin ningún problema**.
10. Es el mejor juguete **para los niños**.

Exercise 9: Where's That Prepositional Phrase?

1. a la tienda, en lugar, de Miguel
2. de nuestros amigos
3. dentro del coche.
4. hasta las once
5. en esta pequeña ciudad
6. con el menú, del día, sobre la mesa
7. sin ellos
8. con tu ayuda
9. para nosotros
10. por eso

Exercise 10: In Conjunction

1. Me siento cansada **e** irritable.
2. Busco alguna comida **o** por lo menos algo que beber.
3. No me gusta, **pero** estoy feliz.
4. ¿Es este niño rebelde **u** obediente?
5. Yo no estoy contenta, **sino** enfadada.
6. Hay muchos jóvenes **y** niños aquí.

Exercise 11: And, Or, What?

1. ¿Es extraño **u** ordinario que no haya nadie en las calles de este pueblo?
2. Es muy tarde **y** vamos a acostarnos.
3. Las manzanas son rojas **y** dulces.
4. Esta película es poco interesante **pero** no es tan aburrida.
5. ¿Vamos al teatro **o** al museo?
6. No tengo interés en la música rock, **sino** en la salsa.
7. En octubre todavía está templado, **pero** llueve mucho.
8. Yo hablo español **e** inglés.

Exercise 12: Either-Or, Neither-Nor

(answers may vary)
1. Me gustaría comer o manzanas o peras.
2. Puedo o coser o tejer.
3. Él conduce o el coche o el camión.
4. Voy a preparar o carne de res o tocino.

5. Para llegar allá, no es posible ni caminar ni ir en bicicleta.
6. Ella no toca ni la guitarra ni el violín.
7. No puedo ni cocinar ni comer la carne.
8. Sus ojos no son ni azules ni verdes.

Exercise 13: In Subordination

1. **Si** quisiera hacer algo, lo haría.
2. Estamos bien **a pesar de** la situación.
3. Estoy muy cansado; **sin embargo**, continúo caminando.
4. Abro la puerta **para que** ellos puedan entrar.
5. Vamos a la playa, **a menos que** llueva.
6. Busco a Elena **porque** ella me debe dinero.
7. Es una persona inteligente, **aunque** compleja.
8. Podemos empezar **cuando** quieras.
9. Nada es imposible, **salvo** vivir para siempre.
10. Ella está muy mal **con todo** lo que pasó.

Exercise 14: The Correct Conjunction

1. No entiendo **cómo** instalarlo.
2. Pienso **que** ellos tienen la razón.
3. Ella lo quiere **a pesar de** todo.
4. Yo se lo daría a ustedes **si** lo necesitaran.
5. Necesito comer **porque** tengo mucha hambre.
6. Hay que terminar este proyecto **aunque** trabajemos toda la noche.
7. Es importante ganar, **no obstante** el obstáculo.
8. Tengo todo, **excepto** el honor.
9. No hay mucha gente, **salvo** los turistas.
10. **Cuando** terminó la película, todos sintieron mucho alivio.

Exercise 15: One, Two, Three . . .

You will hear the following numbers: 1, 2, 3, 4, 5, 6, 7, 8, 9, 10, 11, 12, 13, 14, 15, 16, 17, 18, 19, 20, 21, 30, 40, 50, 60, 70, 80, 90, 100, 123, 200, 1000

Exercise 16: In Digits

1. 18
2. 22
3. 54
4. 93
5. 114
6. 269
7. 562
8. 735
9. 899
10. 2.352.613

Exercise 17: Spell It Out

1. diecisiete
2. ochenta y ocho

3. doscientos veintiséis
4. trescientos cincuenta y cinco
5. mil quinientos doce
6. tres millones cuatrocientos ochenta y dos mil cuatrocientos quince

Exercise 18: What's First?

1. Marzo es el **primer** mes de la primavera.
2. Agosto es el **tercer** mes del verano.
3. La medalla de plata es galardonada por el **segundo** lugar.
4. El último día de febrero es generalmente el día **veintiocho**.
5. El sentido adicional a los cinco sentidos se llama el **sexto** sentido.
6. El niño tiene nueve años; tendrá su **décimo** cumpleaños en dos semanas.
7. Mayo es el **quinto** mes del año.
8. El último día de los doce días de Navidad es el día **duodécimo**.

Exercise 19: Spell It Out

1. mariposa
2. aquí
3. interesante
4. zócalo
5. llegado
6. tristeza
7. carretera
8. jabón
9. mañana
10. gigante
11. taxi
12. video
13. horario
14. convivir
15. yegua

Exercise 20: Spelling Bee

1. decir
2. jardín
3. ir
4. amarillo
5. novio
6. mañana
7. mexicano
8. perro
9. falda
10. común

Exercise 21: Make It Cute

1. abuelita
2. momentito
3. hermanita
4. pobrecito
5. pedacito

Exercise 22: Toughen Things Up

1. animalote
2. grandote
3. buenazo
4. solterón
5. perronas

Exercise 23: The Very Best

1. facilísimo
2. agradabilísimo
3. gordísimo
4. altísima
5. rapidísimo
6. larguísimas
7. riquísimo
8. trabajadorísimos

Exercise 24: Preposition Practice

1. Él habla antes de escuchar.
2. Hay dos minutos hasta la medianoche.
3. Bebo el té con limón.
4. Ella está detrás de usted.
5. Nosotros estamos cerca de nuestros padres.
6. Está en el centro de la ciudad.
7. El museo está a la derecha del parque.
8. Para mí, nada es muy importante.

Exercise 25: In Relation to a Pronoun

1. Prefiero comer la sopa **con** el pan.
2. No conozco **a** Paulina.
3. Su novio vive **en** Canadá.
4. Toma las pastillas cuatro veces **al** día.
5. Viajamos **por** avión.
6. Ella es la hermana **de** Dimitrio.
7. Estudiamos **en** la universidad.
8. Busco a Emilio **para** decirle algo importante.

Exercise 26: Which Conjunction?

1. Voy a Inglaterra **pero** no tengo mucho dinero. (coordinating)
2. Yo me pregunto **si** me ama. (subordinating)
3. Me gustaría **o** el rojo **o** el azul. (correlative)
4. Era tarde **cuando** regresamos a casa. (subordinating)
5. Aprender idiomas es algo difícil **e** interesante. (coordinating)
6. Es mejor **que** ella nos vea. (subordinating)

7. Yo soy **ni** bella **ni** fea. (correlative)
8. Me siento feliz **a pesar de** haber perdido el juego. (subordinating)

Exercise 27: An Interview

(answers may vary)

1. Hay dos libros, un cuaderno, y una pluma.
2. Afuera me gusta jugar al fútbol y a las escondidas.
3. Con menos de cincuenta centavos, puedo comprar un paquete de chicle.
4. No. Ni Sevilla ni Barcelona es la capital de España.
5. Sí, Alemania e Inglaterra son miembros de la Unión Europea.
6. No, no puedo limpiarla si estoy enfermo.
7. No. Decir la verdad sí es sabio.
8. En Turquía se habla turco.
9. En la década de 1980, yo era un estudiante de la universidad de San Juan.
10. Me gusta más viajar por coche porque es una manera menos cara de viajar.
11. Tengo veinte años.
12. Cerca de mi casa hay un banco y una biblioteca.
13. Yo prefiero el té.
14. Voy a estudiar hasta las seis.
15. Después de estudiar voy a tomar una siesta.

Part 5: Verbs 101 and the Present Tense
Exercise 1: Look at the Ending

1. *comer* ER verb
2. *amar* AR verb
3. *beber* ER verb
4. *asistir* IR verb
5. *hablar* AR verb
6. *poner* ER verb
7. *tutear* AR verb
8. *distribuir* IR verb
9. *oír* IR verb
10. *perder* ER verb

Exercise 2: A Verb or a Noun?

1. Beber es poco sano. Drinking is unhealthy.
2. Necesito comprar unos zapatos. I need to buy some shoes.
3. Es importante leer todo el libro. It's important to read the entire book.
4. Cantar es un verbo regular. "To sing" is a regular verb.
5. Cocinar es una habilidad muy útil. Cooking is a very useful skill.

Exercise 3: What It Means

1. miro (I look)
2. paga (he pays)
3. miramos (we look)

4. entráis (you enter)
5. viaja (she travels)
6. entran (you enter)
7. amo (I love)
8. hablas (you speak)
9. lava (you wash)
10. ganan (they win)

Exercise 4: The Right Form

1. Tú nunca me **ayudas**.
2. Nosotros **cantamos** muy bien.
3. Usted **nada** tan rápidamente.
4. Carlos **trabaja** en la universidad.
5. Yo **necesito** algo más.
6. Ella **compra** frutas en el mercado.
7. Elena **toma** el autobús al centro de la ciudad.
8. Nosotros **paramos** antes de la estatua.
9. Él **fuma** mucho cuando bebe vino.
10. Vosotras **lleváis** vestidos al baile.

Exercise 5: Depending on the Pronoun

1. metes (you put)
2. comemos (we eat)
3. tejen (they knit)
4. leo (I read)
5. corre (he runs)
6. aprendéis (you learn)
7. debe (you owe)
8. temen (they fear)
9. vendo (I sell)
10. prometes (you promise)

Exercise 6: The Right Ending

1. Ella no **bebe** la leche porque le duele el estómago.
2. Yo **coso** ropa para mi bebé.
3. La tierra está seca y **absorbe** el agua muy rápidamente.
4. Tú **barres** el suelo cada dos días.
5. Usted no **cree** en Dios.
6. Ellos **dependen** de nuestra ayuda.
7. Tú **corres** el riesgo de caer.
8. Ella **tose** mucho; está enferma.
9. Vosotros os **rompéis** vuestras cabezas por el problema.
10. Nosotros nunca **cometemos** semejantes errores.

Exercise 7: The Right Choice

1. vivimos (we live)
2. abro (I open)
3. escribe (you write)
4. subo (I go up)
5. dividís (you divide)
6. discutimos (we discuss)
7. admite (she accepts)

8. parten (they leave)
9. describe (you describe)
10. interrumpes (you interrupt)

Exercise 8: In Translation

1. Yo **recibo** regalos cada cumpleaños.
2. Ella **sube** las escaleras.
3. Ustedes **deciden** qué hacer juntos.
4. Vosotros **discutís** la solución.
5. Yo **sufro** el calor.
6. Esta película me **aburre**.
7. Nosotros **recibimos** los mensajes pronto.
8. Tú **percibes** el cambio en la temperatura.
9. Esto **ocurre** solo una vez en el siglo.
10. Ellos **viven** en el campo.

Exercise 9: Getting the Endings Down

hablar	beber	asistir
yo hablo	yo bebo	yo asisto
tú hablas	tú bebes	tú asistes
él, ella, usted habla	él, ella, usted bebe	él, ella, usted asiste
nosotros hablamos	nosotros bebemos	nosotros asistimos
vosotros habláis	vosotros bebéis	vosotros asistís
ellos, ellas, ustedes hablan	ellos, ellas, ustedes beben	ellos, ellas, ustedes asisten

Exercise 10: Choose Well

1. encojo (I shrink)
2. estableces (you establish)
3. espiamos (we spy)
4. concluyo (I conclude)
5. lucen (they shine)
6. afligimos (we afflict)
7. reproduce (he reproduces)
8. huyo (I flee)
9. deducís (you deduce)
10. pertenecen (you belong)

Exercise 11: Conjugation Conundrum

1. Yo **pertenezco** a este grupo también.
2. Tú no **obedeces** a tus padres.
3. Nosotros **enviamos** dinero a nuestros abuelos en el Perú.
4. Ellos no **merecen** este galardón.
5. Yo no **finjo** la enfermedad.
6. Vosotros **conducís** coches italianos.
7. Usted **continúa** aprendiendo español.
8. Marisa **evalúa** mi página de Internet.
9. Yo **destruyo** toda su confianza.
10. Ustedes probablemente los **conocen** a ellos.

Exercise 12: Up to You

1. almuerzan (they eat lunch)
2. siento (I feel)
3. quebramos (we break)
4. sigues (you follow)
5. contáis (we count)
6. gimes (you moan)
7. miente (she lies)
8. muero (I die)
9. medís (you measure)
10. muestra (you show)

Exercise 13: What It Means

1. Ella **pide** perdón por ofender a la profesora.
2. Tú **duermes** poco para un niño de tu edad.
3. Él raramente **prueba** nuevas cosas.
4. Nosotros **decimos** la verdad.
5. Ustedes **recomiendan** beber ocho vasos de agua por día.
6. Usted **piensa** que todo está bien.
7. Yo **sirvo** huevos y pan tostado para el desayuno.
8. Nosotros **volvemos** a casa muy tarde.
9. Tú **comienzas** escribir con talento.
10. ¿Vosotros **recordáis** a Teresa?

Exercise 14: One out of Three

1. doy (I give)
2. sabes (you know)
3. son (they are)
4. estoy (I am)
5. sonreís (you smile)
6. hueles (you smell)
7. hemos (we have)
8. sé (I know)
9. vas (you go)
10. oigo (I hear)

Exercise 15: The Right Version

1. Nosotros **somos** italianos.
2. **Hay** treinta personas aquí.
3. Ellos **van** al restaurante para cenar.
4. Usted **ve** este color.
5. Su energía **decae** lentamente.
6. Yo **rio** cuando empiezas a hacer chistes.
7. Tú **yerras** en tus cálculos.
8. Yo no **quepo** en esta pequeña silla.
9. Vosotros **estáis** demasiado lejos.
10. Yo no **quepo** en este cuartito.

Exercise 16: Yes and No

1. Nunca me despierto temprano.
2. No hablo español.
3. Nunca se viste bien.
4. No me gustaría ni café ni té.
5. No conozco a nadie aquí.
6. Ella no está en ningún sitio.
7. Los hermanos Martín no juegan afuera.
8. Su interés en el arte no es nada impresionante.
9. No estoy muy contento tampoco.
10. No voy a decírselo ninguna vez. Nunca voy a decírselo.

Exercise 17: The Answer Is "No"

1. No, los niños no tienen hambre.
2. No, no tenemos nada que decirte.
3. No, no conozco a nadie en esta fiesta.
4. No, los mariachis no están aquí.
5. No, no hay nadie en el coche.
6. No, no hay nada para beber.
7. No, no necesitamos nada.
8. No, tampoco voy con vosotros.
9. Nadie tiene ningunos dulces.
10. No voy con nadie.

Exercise 18: It's Either One or the Other

(answers may vary)
1. El restaurante chino no está en la calle Roja.
2. Pienso que ella no tiene razón.
3. María no es cubana.
4. El perro no come mucho.
5. No compramos carne o quesos en el mercado.
6. Los médicos no escuchan al regetón.
7. No viajas a México nunca.
8. No tenemos ningunas revistas.

Exercise 19: No Way, No How!

1. **No** quiero saber **nada** de eso.
2. **No** puedo encontrarla **por ninguna parte**.
3. **Nunca** me voy a someter a tu poder.
4. **No** es posible lograr los resultados esperados **de ninguna manera**.
5. A ella **no** le gusta bailar, y a mí **tampoco**.
6. **Jamás** oí algo tan descortés.
7. **No** he probado la comida japonesa **ninguna vez**.
8. **Nadie** sabe lo que pasó entre Julio y yo.
9. No me siento **ni** triste **ni** contento; me siento melancólico.
10. En las últimas tres horas, **no** he visto pasar a **ningún** hombre.

Exercise 20: Make It Passive

1. La chaqueta es comprada por Elena.
2. La comida para cocinar es vendida en el supermercado.
3. El coche es parado en la calle por mí.
4. La torre es vista por mí.
5. Esta idea es comprendida por nosotros.
6. Los sacrificios son hechos por los sacerdotes.

7. La música es escuchada por nosotros.
8. Nuestra seguridad es garantizada por los soldados.
9. Estos sentimientos no son sentidos nunca por mí.
10. La cerveza es bebida por ellos.

Exercise 21: In the Mood

1. I saw the movie yesterday. (indicative)
2. Let's go out to the movies. (imperative)
3. If I were the owner, I'd expand the menu. (subjunctive)
4. I would love it if she were my boss. (subjunctive)
5. We went yesterday. (indicative)
6. I insist that he leave. (subjunctive)
7. Turn down the volume. (imperative)
8. I need a new car. (indicative)
9. Please close the window. (imperative)
10. We recommended that he fill out the form. (subjunctive)

Exercise 22: To Be or Not to Be

1. No **es** verdad.
2. Esta semana nosotros **estamos** en Buenos Aires.
3. Yo **soy** francés.
4. Hoy **es** martes.
5. Mientras ellos **están** en la calle, no saben las nuevas noticias.
6. Jane **es** de Australia.
7. **Son** las cinco y media de la tarde.
8. Tú **estás** muy cansado.
9. Clara, tú **eres** la hermana de Enrique, ¿no es así?
10. La tienda **está** abierta hoy.

Exercise 23: The Right "Be"

1. Estoy en el tren, esperando la llegada.
2. Mi mamá y papá son abogados.
3. El banco está cerrado.
4. Estas cosas son las suyas.
5. Mi abuela es muy vieja.
6. El vestido de Rosa es verde y blanco.
7. Estamos muy confundidos.
8. Tú eres muy inteligente.
9. Los ojos de Carolina son azules.
10. Vosotros estáis tristes.

Exercise 24: Conjugation Practice

cantar (regular AR verb)

yo canto	nosotros cantamos
tú cantas	vosotros cantáis
él, ella, usted canta	ellos, ustedes cantan

vivir (regular IR verb)

yo vivo	nosotros vivimos
tú vives	vosotros vivís
él, ella, usted vive	ellos, ustedes viven

meter (regular ER verb)

yo meto	nosotros metemos
tú metes	vosotros metéis
él, ella, usted mete	ellos, ustedes meten

mostrar (stem-changing verb)

yo muestro	nosotros mostramos
tú muestras	vosotros mostráis
él, ella, usted muestra	ellos, ustedes muestran

coger (spelling-change verb)

yo cojo	nosotros cogemos
tú coges	vosotros cogéis
él, ella, usted coge	ellos, ustedes cogen

tener (stem changing, spelling-change verb)

yo tengo	nosotros tenemos
tú tienes	vosotros tenéis
él, ella, usted tiene	ellos, ustedes tienen

ser (irregular verb)

yo soy	nosotros somos
tú eres	vosotros sois
él, ella, usted es	ellos, ustedes son

Exercise 25: A Hard Day of Work

(answers may vary)

1. Soy abogado.
2. Está en una oficina en el centro de la ciudad.
3. Represento a personas acusadas de varios crímenes.
4. Suelo trabajar setenta o aún ochenta horas cada semana.
5. Empiezo a trabajar a las ocho de la mañana.
6. Lo que más me gusta es defender a los inocentes de las acusaciones falsas.
7. Lo que menos me gusta es la gran cantidad de tiempo que necesito trabajar.
8. No. Disfruto mi trabajo y no me gustaría hacer nada diferente.
9. Hay que asistir a la facultad de derecho y tomar el examen especial.
10. Viajo con mi esposa, leo novelas de misterio, y me relajo.

Exercise 26: Regular or Not?

1. Usted **encuentra** mucho en su vida.
2. Yo no **distingo** las cosas en la oscuridad sin mis gafas.
3. Ustedes no me **aman**.
4. Nosotros **rompemos** las barreras.
5. Él **acepta** su invitación.
6. Yo **la sigo** amando a pesar de todo.
7. Ella **empieza** sus estudios el próximo día.
8. Tú **cubres** nuestros gastos; eres muy generoso.

Exercise 27: Hear the Voice

1. La carta ya está escrita. (passive voice)
2. Ella es artista. (active voice)
3. Yo he escrito la carta. (active voice)
4. Toda la ciudad es vista. (passive voice)
5. Soy muy inteligente. (active voice)
6. Ellos son encerrados en la cárcel. (passive voice)
7. El libro es muy interesante. (active voice)
8. El libro es colocado aquí por el estudiante. (passive voice)

Part 6: Verbs and Objects
Exercise 1: The Object of This Lesson

1. Julia le escribe una carta. direct object
2. Yo se lo compro a ella. indirect object
3. Nunca me los dan. direct object
4. Voy a decirles la verdad. indirect object
5. Lo cantan en voz alta. direct object
6. Me ocurre algo interesante. direct object
7. Quiero dárselas. indirect object
8. Estoy aprendiéndolo. direct object

Exercise 2: Objectively Speaking

1. Ella canta **canciones** para los niños.
2. Yo visito **la tumba** de mi abuelita cada año.
3. Nosotros compramos **los muebles** para nuestra casa.
4. La mamá cocinó **el desayuno** para la familia.
5. Esta bailarina ganó **el premio** del baile flamenco.
6. Dígame **la verdad**.
7. Voy a contarles **toda la historia**.
8. Los chicos dibujaban **caras de animalitos** en la arena.
9. ¡Tírame **la pelota**!
10. No permito **el uso de diccionarios** durante la clase.

Exercise 3: Indirectly Necessary

1. Ella **me** habla en español. She speaks to me in Spanish.
2. María **les** compra dulces a sus niños. Maria buys her kids candy.
3. La compañía **le** ofrece el trabajo a usted. The company is offering you the job.
4. Su madre quiere traer**os** alguna comida. Your mother wants to bring you some food.
5. Él **se** las manda a ella. He sends them to her.
6. Yo **se** lo doy a ustedes. I give it to you.
7. Su novia no **le** contesta a él. His girlfriend doesn't answer him.
8. Tú **me** escribes cartas cada semana. You write me letters every week.

Exercise 4: Test Your Reflexes

1. Yo **me cepillo** los dientes todos los días.
2. En pocos días ellos **se mudan** a California.
3. Nosotros no **nos afeitamos** ya.

4. Vosotros **os enteráis** de la verdad.
5. Tú **te vistes** mal, con ropa sucia.
6. Ustedes no **se quedan** aquí.
7. Usted **se alegra** de que todo vaya bien.
8. ¿Yo no **me acuerdo** nada?

Exercise 5: Build Your Own Sentence

1. **María y su hermana mayor** se levantan a las seis de la mañana.
2. **Yo** me pongo la ropa.
3. **Elena y tú** os cansáis de mis quejas.
4. **La abuelita** se enferma mucho durante los inviernos.
5. **Tú** te cepillas los dientes.

Exercise 6: Passive Constructions

1. Fruits and vegetables are sold here.
2. It's said that truth always wins.
3. Beef isn't eaten in India.
4. A hair dryer can't be used inside the bathtub.
5. The elephants are seen at the zoo.

Exercise 7: The Big Date

1. Aquel día, me desperté temprano porque me acordé que tenía una cita importante.
2. Rápidamente, corrí al baño para bañarme.
3. Tampoco me olvidé de cepillarme los dientes.
4. Después de la ducha, me maquillé y me peiné el cabello.
5. Entonces, me pareció que estaba más presentable, pero todavía no había escogido la ropa para vestirme.
6. Primero, me puse una blusa blanca y una falda azul.
7. Desgraciadamente, algo me molestaba—quizás la blusa era demasiado ajustada.
8. Me quité la blusa y escogí otra, de color negro.
9. Finalmente acabé de vestirme y me miré en el espejo por última vez.
10. Ya no tenía más tiempo para quedarme en casa y me fui.

Exercise 8: In Transit

1. Tú corres el riesgo de perder todo. (Transitive)
2. En nuestra escuela, los estudiantes llevan uniformes. (Transitive)
3. Yo corro por el parque cada día. (Intransitive)
4. Ellos no comen dulces antes de la cena. (Transitive)
5. Yo vivo en Nueva York. (Intransitive)
6. Por eso ya no lo hago más. (Transitive)
7. Nosotros nunca caminamos. (Intransitive)
8. Usted no llegó temprano. (Intransitive)
9. Vosotros lleváis camisas blancas. (Transitive)
10. Cuando estamos contentos, cantamos. (Intransitive)

Exercise 9: Label That Verb

1. nadar (to swim) intransitive
2. tener (to have) transitive
3. salir (to leave) intransitive
4. correr (to run) both
5. oler both
6. tomar (to take, to play, to drink) transitive
7. ver (to see) both
8. viajar (to travel) intransitive

Exercise 10: Look for the Clues

(answers may vary)

1. Ella limpia **la casa**. direct object
2. Le voy a regalar las rosas **a Evita**. indirect object
3. Tomamos **el té** en el desayuno. direct object
4. Nosotros les escribimos mensajes **a nuestros amigos**. indirect object
5. No le metas miedo **al niño**. indirect object

Exercise 11: Reflexive Challenge

1. Patricio no **se siente** bien hoy.
2. Tú **levantas** las manos cuando hablas.
3. Ustedes **duermen** en la cama.
4. Nosotros no los **lastimamos** a ustedes, ¿verdad?
5. Yo **divierto** a los niños con chistes.
6. Mariana **coloca** los libros en el estante.
7. Vosotros **os sentáis** en el sofá.
8. Usted **se decide** demasiado rápido.
9. Los empleados **ponen** el dinero en el banco.
10. Yo **me ducho** al menos una vez al día.

Exercise 12: Translate It!

1. Miguel gets up.
2. I dress for the occasion.
3. We fall down into the snow.
4. She burned her arm.
5. You are trying on a shirt.
6. You are getting ready for the party.
7. They get engry when they don't understand the lesson.
8. You feel very well.

Exercise 13: Getting Up

Answers will vary.

Part 7

Past, Future, Conditional, and Perfect Tenses

Exercise 1: Memorizing Preterite Endings

hablar	*beber*	*asistir*
yo hablé	*yo bebí*	*yo asistí*
tú hablaste	*tú bebiste*	*tú asististe*
él, ella, usted habló	*él, ella, usted bebió*	*él, ella, usted asistió*
nosotros hablamos	*nosotros bebimos*	*nosotros asistimos*
vosotros hablasteis	*vosotros bebisteis*	*vosotros asististeis*
ellos, ellas, ustedes hablaron	*ellos, ellas, ustedes bebieron*	*ellos, ellas, ustedes asistieron*

Exercise 2: Choose or Lose

1. adaptaron (they adapted)
2. pidió (he asked for)
3. tuve (I had)
4. llevó (you wore)
5. escribió (he wrote)
6. fuiste (you went)
7. comisteis (you ate)
8. tomé (I took)
9. oímos (we heard)
10. durmieron (you slept)

Exercise 3: What's Done Is Done

1. Nosotros **miramos** la televisión. (mirar)
2. Ustedes **vendieron** sandías en el mercado. (vender)
3. Enrique **habló** con Elena ayer. (hablar)
4. Yo **di** las maletas al camarero. (dar)
5. Tú **insististe** en conducir el coche. (insistir)
6. El señor Ochoa y su esposa **creyeron** a su vecino. (creer)
7. Vosotros **sentisteis** que ella no estuvo muy contenta. (sentir)
8. Yo **entré** en la casa y cerré la puerta. (entrar)
9. Usted **omitió** admitir la verdad. (omitir)
10. Marina **dijo** que nunca volvería a aquel lugar. (decir)

Exercise 4: Complete Conjugations

hablar

hablaba	*hablábamos*
hablabas	*hablabais*
hablaba	*hablaban*

beber

bebía	*bebíamos*
bebías	*bebíais*
bebía	*bebían*

asistir

asistía	asistíamos
asistías	asistíais
asistía	asistían

Exercise 5: Imperfect Endings, Perfectly

1. fumaba (I smoked)
2. cometía (he committed)
3. iba (you went)
4. dormían (they slept)
5. vendía (you sold)
6. pagabais (you paid)
7. leías (you read)
8. veías (you saw)
9. traducía (she translated)
10. trabajábamos (we worked)

Exercise 6: It Used to Be . . .

1. **Eran** las dos cuando la clase terminó. (ser)
2. Ella siempre me **daba** miedo. (dar)
3. Nosotros nunca **teníamos** la oportunidad de hablar con él. (tener)
4. Yo **andaba** por el camino cada día. (andar)
5. Ustedes **prometían** pagar la renta. (prometer)
6. El hombre **moría** del aburrimiento. (morir)
7. Tú y yo **íbamos** a la discoteca los sábados por la noche. (ir)
8. Cuando era joven, usted **compraba** los dulces baratos. (comprar)
9. Vosotros **hacíais** todo lo posible para evitar la separación. (hacer)
10. En aquellos días, tú **aprendías** a bailar con la Señora Serrano. (aprender)

Exercise 7: Future Actions

1. Nosotras **viajaremos** a Europa en otoño. (viajar)
2. Yo **abriré** la puerta para ustedes. (abrir)
3. Ella **mirará** por la ventana en un momento. (mirar)
4. Vosotros **pondréis** los platos en la lavadora después de comer. (poner)
5. Usted **correrá** el riesgo de perder. (correr)
6. Tú me **darás** las notas a mí más tarde. (dar)
7. Ellos **serán** buenos padres para el bebé. (ser)
8. Yo **diré** la respuesta a todos ustedes. (decir)
9. Ellos **decidirán** lo que hacer sin usted. (decidir)
10. Él **oirá** mejor con el uso del audífono. (oír)

Exercise 8: Back to the Future

1. Los músicos podrán tocar sonatas.
2. ¿Querrá usted comer el desayuno?
3. Marilena estará en casa antes que yo.
4. Cuando te conozca, ya sabré bailar.
5. Tú no trabajarás mañana.

6. La torta consistirá en harina, huevos, y otros ingredientes.
7. La semana próxima, yo aprenderé los verbos irregulares.
8. Nosotros tendremos la oportunidad de conocer a una estrella del teatro.
9. Ustedes cantarán muy bien.
10. Vosotros dormiréis todo el día.

Exercise 9: In Twenty Years

(answers may vary)

1. Viviré en Nueva York.
2. Espero que todavía estaré casado.
3. Sí, creo que seré mucho más inteligente.
4. Habrá mucha más gente en el mundo.
5. Creo que sí, pero también habrá otras formas de transporte.
6. Creo que sí, vamos a tener los robots u otros tipos de máquinas para limpiar nuestras casas.
7. Es posible que sí, será más fácil aprender los idiomas extranjeros.
8. Puede ser que la naturaleza necesite de nuestra ayuda.
9. Sí, es probable que podamos viajar a otros planetas.
10. En veinte años, creo que vamos a depender más de las computadoras en nuestra vida diaria.

Exercise 10: Potentially Right

1. gustarían (they would like)
2. metería (you would put)
3. salía (I would leave)
4. comeríamos (we would eat)
5. decidíais (you would decide)
6. cabría (it would fit)
7. nadarías (you would swim)
8. bañarían (you would bathe)
9. vendría (I would come)
10. escribiríamos (we would write)

Exercise 11: A Tricky Condition

1. Si pudiera, yo **iría** adentro. (ir)
2. Ellas **repetirían** la pregunta otra vez. (repetir)
3. Él **haría** lo que le gusta. (hacer)
4. Usted **pediría** perdón si él lo hubiera hecho primero. (pedir)
5. Yo **cerraría** la puerta; no estoy segura. (cerrar)
6. Si salierais, vosotros **perderíais** vuestro lugar en la fila. (perder)
7. Si hiciera frío, tú **cubrirías** con la manta. (cubrir)
8. Usted **volvería** aquí y no a su propia casa. (volver)
9. Estos vestidos **valdrían** más con camisetas a juego. (valer)
10. En este lugar nosotros **almorzaríamos** más tarde. (almorzar)

Exercise 12: The Participle Form

1. pensado
2. decidido
3. hecho
4. ganado
5. abierto
6. comido
7. dicho
8. pagado
9. vendido
10. escribido

Exercise 13: A Perfect Conjugation

1. Yo **he abierto** la puerta. (abrir)
2. Usted **ha trabajado** mucho. (trabajar)
3. Vosotros **habéis leído** tantos libros. (leer)
4. Cristina **ha puesto** los zapatos afuera del dormitorio. (poner)
5. Tú **has subido** arriba antes. (subir)
6. Ustedes **han traído** el perro al veterinario. (traer)
7. Los camareros **han servido** a los clientes. (servir)
8. Nosotros ya **hemos cantado** esta canción. (cantar)
9. Yo **he pasado** tres años en Nueva York. (pasar)
10. Pedro **ha visto** esas cosas muchas veces. (ver)

Exercise 14: Past and Perfect

1. habían vuelto (they had returned)
2. habíais sorprendido (you had surprised)
3. había andado (I had walked)
4. habías ido (you had gone)
5. habíamos salido (we had left)
6. había escuchado (I had listened)
7. había enseñado (you had taught)
8. había dicho (I had said)
9. habías fumado (you had smoked)
10. habían mirado (you had watched)

Exercise 15: Had to Be Right

1. Yo me **había levantado** antes que ellos me llamaran. (levantar)
2. Ustedes **habían estado** allá. (estar)
3. Marco no **había creído** en Dios hasta el accidente. (creer)
4. Verónica les **había pedido** que la llevaran con ellos. (pedir)
5. Nosotros les **habíamos prohibido** a ellos organizar una fiesta en el apartamento. (prohibir)
6. Aquel día, vosotros **habíais entrado** en la casa por la ventana. (entrar)
7. Ellos no lo **habían aprendido** el año pasado. (aprender)
8. Tú no lo **habías dicho** a tiempo. (decir)
9. Las flores **habían tenido** mucha fragrancia. (tener)

10. Usted nos **había mostrado** cierto interés. (mostrar)

Exercise 16: In the Distant Past

1. hubimos viajado (we had traveled)
2. hubieron muerto (they had died)
3. hube resuelto (I had resolved)
4. hubiste ido (you had gone)
5. hubisteis escrito (you had written)
6. hubo demostrado (you had demonstrated)
7. hubieron impuesto (you had imposed)
8. hubo traído (he had brought)
9. hube concedido (I had conceded)
10. hubo amado (she had loved)

Exercise 17: In the Perfect Future

1. habrán terminado (they will have finished)
2. habrá ocurrido (it will have occurred)
3. habréis bañado (you will have bathed)
4. habremos descrito (we will have described)
5. habrás traído (you will have brought)
6. habré comprendido (I will have understood)
7. habrán esperado (you will have waited)
8. habré ido (I will have gone)
9. habrás barrido (you will have swept)
10. habrá pagado (you will have paid)

Exercise 18: Will and Will Have

1. Mañana Mauricio **habrá lavado** su ropa. (lavar)
2. Usted **habrá vuelto** a Madrid en marzo. (volver)
3. Yo **habré parado** en frente del café. (parar)
4. Vosotros **habréis oído** el sonido. (oír)
5. A ciento veinte millas por hora, el coche **habrá excedido** la velocidad máxima. (exceder)
6. Nosotros no lo **habremos permitido**. (permitir)
7. Los empleados nos **habrán enviado** las mercancías. (enviar)
8. A ti te **habrá gustado** correr después de mucha práctica. (gustar)
9. Yo lo **habré puesto** en el banco. (poner)
10. Ustedes **habrán insistido** en no cambiarlo. (insistir)

Exercise 19: The Perfect Condition

1. I wouldn't have answered her.
2. Pedro would have helped her anyway.
3. You would have opened all the windows.
4. You would have drunk all the juice.
5. Catalina wouldn't have met them here.
6. We wouldn't have taken the last piece.
7. You would have written the entire essay that night.
8. You would have sewn a lot of clothes.
9. I would have bathed beforehand.
10. The soldiers would have gone up on time.

Exercise 20: Answers, Unconditionally

1. habría tenido (I would have had)
2. habríamos impreso (we would have printed)
3. habría resuelto (he would have resolved)
4. habríais prometido (you would have promised)
5. habría rehecho (you would have remade)
6. habrías compensado (you would have compensated)
7. habríamos resuelto (we would have resolved)
8. habrían ganado (you would have won)
9. habrían perdido (they would have lost)
10. habría vuelto (I would have returned)

Exercise 21: Lost in Time, Lost in Thought

1. Después de que terminé el libro, no pensé más en él. (Preterite)
2. Y tú, ¿qué habrás pensado más tarde? (Future perfect)
3. Estamos pensando en algo muy interesante. (Present progressive)
4. Si pudiera, habría pensado más. (Conditional perfect)
5. Pienso hacer una visita a mis padres. (Present)
6. ¿Ha pensado usted en cómo empezar la presentación? (Present perfect)
7. Habíamos pensado que así sería mejor. (Pluperfect)
8. Pensaré en las consecuencias más tarde. (Future)
9. En esos días, pensaba que todo me quedaba bien. (Imperfect)
10. Si me dijeran la verdad, yo pensaría diferente. (Conditional)

Exercise 22: Two Pasts, One Answer

1. ¿(Usted) **descansó** (descansar) un rato?
2. Hace unos días que nosotros **regresamos** (regresar) de las vacaciones.
3. Yo nunca **terminaba** (terminar) de hacer preguntas.
4. Generalmente ustedes **caminaban** (caminar) a casa.
5. Ellos **pensaban** (pensar) encontrarla en el parque, pero Lisa no **llegó** (llegar) allá a la hora predeterminada.
6. Mientras mi padre **cortaba** (cortar) el césped, mi madre **cocinaba** (cocinar) los bistecs.
7. Ya vosotros le **contasteis** (contar) a su madre toda la historia.
8. La clase se **acabó** (acabar) a las dos.
10. Tú **estabas** (estar) escribiendo una carta cuando ella **llamó** (llamar) por teléfono.

Exercise 23: Lost in Time

1. comerán (future)
2. vivieron (preterite)
3. he hecho (present perfect)
4. podrá (future)
5. escribiríamos (conditional)
6. amaba (imperfect)
7. dio (preterite)

8. habíais pedido (pluperfect)
9. habría entrado (conditional perfect)
10. habrán vendido (future perfect)

Exercise 24: Haber Revisited

1. Present

he	hemos
has	habéis
ha	han

2. Past

había	habíamos
habías	habíais
había	habían

3. Preterite

hube	hubimos
hubiste	hubisteis
hubo	hubieron

4. Future

habré	habremos
habrás	habréis
habrá	habrán

5. Conditional

habría	habríamos
habrías	habríais
habría	habrían

Part 8: Subjunctive and Imperative Moods
Exercise 1: At the Root

1. compr–
2. describ–
3. promet–
4. concluy–
5. veng–
6. deb–
7. repit–
8. caig–

Exercise 2: A Subjunctive Matter

1. Le contaré la historia para que usted me **ayude** a lavar los platos. (ayudar)
2. Es necesario que vosotros **cojáis** a los culpables. (coger)
3. Espero que tú ya los **conozcas** a ellos. (conocer)
4. Ellos me aconsejan que yo **viva** con mis padres para ahorrar el dinero. (vivir)
5. Vosotros dudáis que nosotros **oigamos** el ruido. (oír)
6. Mis padres me exigen que yo **aprenda** italiano antes del viaje. (aprender)
7. Ustedes necesitan que ellos **entren** a la escuela por la puerta detrás de la cafetería. (entrar)
8. Tenemos dudas que las maletas **quepan** en el maletero del coche. (caber)

Exercise 3: Irregular Conjugations

1. tú saques (sacar)
2. nosotros vayamos (ir)
3. yo defienda (defender)
4. ella duerma (dormir)
5. usted esté (estar)
6. ellos quieran (querer)
7. él dé (dar)
8. vosotros costéis (costar)

Exercise 4: An Approximate Translation

1. I clean the house so that it is clean.
2. I make supper in case the kids get hungry.
3. It's probable that they don't know the truth.
4. It's doubtful that we can run so quickly.
5. I'm going to the movies, provided that they go with me.
6. They feel sad when you complain about your problems.
7. We are going to the beach unless it rains.
8. It's necessary that you return home on time.

Exercise 5: Right or Wrong?

The following answers are wrong (corrections are in bold):

1. Ella siempre escucha el disco que **repite** la misma canción.
4. Es cierto que ustedes no **duermen** suficiente.
8. Ella está en el restaurante donde **sirven** el mejor bistec.

Exercise 6: The Perfect Ending

1. Yo sé que este empleo no **paga** mucho. (pagar)
2. Es malo que nosotros no **estemos** listos. (estar)
3. Según este periódico, el presidente no **está** en la Casa Blanca, pero no lo creo. (estar)
4. Me gusta **vivir** en este vecindario. (vivir)
5. Los estudiantes piden que el director de la escuela **sustituya** al nuevo profesor por algún otro. (sustituir)
6. Yo dudo que **sea** posible entrar por esta puerta sin ningún ruido. (ser)
7. No hay duda que la película **empieza** en un momento. (empezar)
8. Es interesante que vosotros **paguéis** tanto dinero por estos boletos. (pagar)

Exercise 7: Perfect Subjunctives

1. Es dudoso que yo **haya caminado** por la casa mientras dormía. (andar)
2. Espero que vosotros ya lo **hayáis dicho**. (decir)
3. Es probable que él no **haya bebido** casi nada. (beber)
4. Es bueno que nosotros lo **hayamos puesto** en un lugar seguro. (poner)
5. Muchos se consideran bien educados sin que ellos **hayan ido** al teatro. (ir)

6. No es bueno nadar aquí, a menos que tú **hayas nadado** aquí en el pasado. (nadar)
7. Ojalá que usted ya **haya escrito** muchas novelas. (escribir)

Exercise 8: The Subjunctive Past

1. Fue desafortunado que ella **hubiera comido** algo mal cocido y se sintiera muy mal. (comer)
2. Ojalá que nosotros **hubiéramos abierto** una tienda para vender joyas. (abrir)
3. En aquellos tiempos, quiso que ustedes me **hubieran agradecido**. (agradecer)
4. No era cierto que tú la **hubieras visto** en la playa aquel día. (ver)
5. Si ellos me **hubieran pagado** por el collar, no los hubiera perseguido. (pagar)
6. Usted piensa que yo **hubiera vivido** en California. (vivir)
7. Prefirió que vosotros **hubierais hecho** lo que había pedido. (hacer)

Exercise 9: The English Version

1. I thought that you had felt something.
2. It was possible that I had been here before.
3. I am looking for a person who has had success with this diet.
4. They deny that we have come to an agreement.
5. I would have liked to be able to love you forever.
6. It's terrible that the programs has repeated two or three times.
7. If they could have spoken, they would have screamed.
8. It's possible that our love has gone.

Exercise 10: Seeing Double

hablar	
yo hablara	yo hablase
tú hablaras	tú hablases
él, ella, usted hablara	él, ella, usted hablase
nosotros habláramos	nosotros hablásemos
vosotros hablarais	vosotros hablaseis
ellos, ellas, ustedes hablaran	ellos, ellas, ustedes hablasen

beber	
yo bebiera	yo bebiese
tú bebieras	tú bebieses
él, ella, usted bebiera	él, ella, usted bebiese
nosotros bebiéramos	nosotros bebiésemos
vosotros bebierais	vosotros bebieseis
ellos, ellas, ustedes bebieran	ellos, ellas, ustedes bebiesen

asistir	
yo asistiera	yo asistiese
tú asistieras	tú asistieses
él, ella, usted asistiera	él, ella, usted asistiese
nosotros asistiéramos	nosotros asistiésemos
vosotros asistierais	vosotros asistieseis
ellos, ellas, ustedes asistieran	ellos, ellas, ustedes asistiesen

Exercise 11: Give Me a *Ra*!

1. Fernando habló en voz baja, como si se **hablara** a sí mismo. (hablar)
2. Quien **pensara** que ellos regresarían a este pueblo, estaba equivocado (pensar)
3. Nosotros **quisiéramos** que alguien nos **esperara** aquí. (querer, esperar)
4. Si ellos **vivieran**, tendrían ya veinte años. (vivir)
5. El alcalde sugirió que el pueblo **construyera** el nuevo ayuntamiento. (construir)
6. Si nosotros **supiéramos** la verdad, nunca consentiríamos a este proyecto. (saber)
7. Si yo **tuviera** quince años, podría conseguir tantas cosas. (tener)
8. Si usted **escribiera** una novela, ella me serviría como inspiración. (escribir)

Exercise 12: Give me a *Se*!

1. Fernando habló en voz baja, como si se **hablase** a sí mismo. (hablar)
2. Quien **pensase** que ellos regresarían a este pueblo, estaba equivocado (pensar)
3. Nosotros **quisiésemos** que alguien nos **esperase** aquí. (querer, esperar)
4. Si ellos **viviesen**, tendrían ya veinte años. (vivir)
5. El alcalde sugirió que el pueblo **construyese** el nuevo ayuntamiento. (construir)
6. Si nosotros **supiésemos** la verdad, nunca consentiríamos a este proyecto. (saber)
7. Si yo **tuviese** quince años, podría conseguir tantas cosas. (tener)
8. Si usted **escribiese** una novela, ella me serviría como inspiración. (escribir)

Exercise 13: It's a Command

1. Quedémonos.
2. No grites.
3. Abran sus cuadernos, por favor.
4. Comed vuestras galletas.
5. No me lo dé.

Exercise 14: Make It Positive

1. Ponlo allá.
2. Salid de aquí.
3. Mándeselos.
4. Hazlo.
5. Diles algo.

Exercise 15: A Suggestion, a Command

1. Tú, ¡cállate la boca! You, shut your mouth!
2. ¡Esperemos! ¡No nos vayamos de aquí ya! Let's wait! Let's not leave from here yet!

3. Señor Jiménez, ¡siéntese aquí, por favor! Mr. Jimenez, please sit here!
4. Invitados, ¡no se preocupen por la hora! No es demasiado temprano. Guests, don't worry about the time! It's not too early.
5. Estudiantes, ¡conducid con mucho cuidado! Students, drive very carefully!
6. Todos ustedes, ¡no olviden lo que voy a decirles! All of you, don't forget what I'm going to tell you.
7. Tú, ¡no pierdas más tiempo! You, don't waste more time!
8. ¡Quedémonos en casa un rato más! Let's stay at home a little longer!
9. Mis hijos, ¡no vayan al parque solos! My children, don't go to the park alone!
10. Profesor Márquez, ¡por favor, preste atención a mi pregunta! Mr. Marquez (teacher), please pay attention to my question!

Exercise 16: In Tense

1. preferamos: present subjunctive
2. hubiera olido: past perfect subjunctive
3. cerrad: imperative
4. sepáis: present subjunctive
5. describieran: imperfect subjunctive
6. ven: imperative
7. haya dicho: present perfect
8. mentid: imperative

Exercise 17: In the Mood

1. Si fuera rico, no trabajaría un día más. (Subjunctive)
2. Es cierto que no sabes nada de eso. (Indicative)
3. Mándenme mensajes electrónicos lo más pronto posible. (Imperative)
4. Es muy importante que tú te laves las manos antes de comer. (Subjunctive)
5. Vámonos al teatro o a lo mejor al cine. (Imperative)
6. No comas con la boca abierta. (Imperative)
7. Me alegro que no seas tonto. (Subjunctive)
8. Tú eres un verdadero imbécil. (Indicative)
9. Me gustaría tener una familia grande. (Indicative)
10. Es dudoso que todo esté bien. (Subjunctive)

Exercise 18: Your Wish Is My Command

1. Don't shout!
2. Let's not go to the beach.
3. Don't do it with such strength.
4. Shut up!
5. Close the doors right now.
6. Put them on.
7. Please don't lend her money.
8. Don't think about the consequences.

Exercise 19: If It's Any Indication

1. Es posible que ella no **esté** allá. (estar)
2. Ojalá que no **hayan** problemas con esto. (haber)
3. ¡No me **dejes** aquí! (dejar)
4. Yo **sé** que todo está bien. (saber)
5. Ellos no me **conocen**. (conocer)
6. Chico, no **seas** un imbécil. (ser)
7. Es cierto que ellos lo **tienen**. (tener)
8. Nosotros se las **escribimos**. (escribir)

Part 9: Verbal Constructions and More

Exercise 1: Assembling Participles

1. escribiendo
2. cantando
3. sirviendo
4. pensando
5. haciendo
6. creando
7. durmiendo
8. yendo

Exercise 2: This Very Second

1. Ella me **está mirando** a mí. (mirar)
2. Nosotros **estamos diciendo** algo muy importante. (decir)
3. Usted **está leyendo** el libro. (leer)
4. Yo **estoy abriendo** la ventana. (abrir)
5. Vosotros **estáis sintiendo** tantas cosas. (sentir)
6. Tú no **estás actuando**, eres sincero. (actuar)
7. Marco **está andando** por la calle. (andar)
8. Ustedes nos **están pidiendo** un gran favor. (pedir)

Exercise 3: Make It Right Now

1. Me estoy lavando las manos.
2. Usted está tomando el agua.
3. Elena está comprando un vestido y pantalones.
4. Los atletas están practicando natación.
5. Lo estamos escuchando a él.
6. Estoy yendo a la escuela.
7. Carlos está bailando en la discoteca.
8. Estáis cocinando paella.

Exercise 4: A Time of Imperfections

1. Las enfermeras **estaban ayudando** al médico. (ayudar)
2. Vosotros **estabais viendo** algo mover por la pantalla. (ver)
3. Yo **estaba viniendo** a la fiesta. (venir)
4. Nosotros **estábamos hablando** del arte. (hablar)
5. Usted **estaba pidiendo** perdón. (pedir)
6. Patricia **estaba almorzando** cuando su marido llegó a casa. (almorzar)
7. El autobús **estaba volviendo** a la estación. (volver)
8. Yo **estaba repitiendo** cada palabra. (repetir)

Exercise 5: Up to a Point

1. Tú **estuviste fumando** hasta que el cigarillo se extinguió. (fumar)
2. Vosotros **estuvisteis temiendo** algo incomprensible. (temer)
3. Yo **estuve comiendo** hasta que no pude comer más. (comer)
4. Enrique **estuvo pensando** en algo importante cuando oyó el grito. (pensar)
5. Nosotros **estuvimos durmiendo** cuando sonó el despertador. (dormir)

Exercise 6: There Is a Way

1. There is a market on Green Street.
2. There will be fruits and vegetables to buy.
3. There was a problem with the car.
4. In this case there would be something to do.
5. There was a reason for his/her/your refusal.
6. There was something for each person.
7. There is candy in the package.
8. There may have been errors in his leadership.

Exercise 7: Finish It Already

1. Tú vas a comprar jabón.
2. Yo voy a viajar por avión.
3. Ustedes van a trabajar en el salón de automóviles.
4. Vosotros vais a mirar el programa deportivo.
5. Ella va a comer una pera.

Exercise 8: What Are You Going to Do?

(answers may vary)
1. Tienes hambre. Voy a comer.
2. Hace mucho calor. Voy a quitarme la chaqueta.
3. Es el día de cumpleaños de tu amiga. Voy a comprarle un regalo.
4. No te gusta tu trabajo. Voy a buscar otro.
5. Estás enfermo. Voy a tomar medicinas.

Exercise 9: It Must Be Done

1. Vas a dormir ocho horas por la noche.
2. Él va a terminar sus tareas.
3. Vamos a aprender de memoria el vocabulario español.
4. Mis hermanas van a ayudar a mi madre a cocinar la gran cena.
5. Yo voy a cumplir mis promesas.
6. Ustedes van a regar las flores cada día.
7. Ella no va a hacer nada.
8. Vosotros vais a comportaros bien.
9. El Señor Blanco va a terminar la clase en cinco minutos.
10. Los chicos van a respetar a las chicas.

Exercise 10: Blast from the Recent Past

1. Usted acaba de leer la revista.
2. Acabo de ver la imagen.
3. Vosotros acabáis de fingir alegría.
4. La tienda acaba de cerrar.
5. El señor acaba de morir.

Exercise 11: What Did You Just Do?

(answers may vary)
1. Acabo de limpiar la casa.
2. Acabo de comer mucho.
3. Acabo de tocar música en el escenario.
4. Acabo de peinarme el cabello.
5. Acabo de recibir muchos regalos.

Exercise 12: What You Know, You Know

1. Elena sabe los nombres de todos los estudiantes en la clase. Elena knows the names of all the students in the class.
2. Cuando no podía encontrar a nadie, no supe qué hacer. When I couldn't find anybody, I didn't know what to do.
3. No conozco a ninguna persona en esta fiesta. I don't know anyone at this party.
4. Nunca sabré cómo coser mi propia ropa. I'll never know how to sew my own clothes.
5. No conozco Madrid, pero espero visitarla pronto. I don't know Madrid, but I hope to visit it soon.
6. Ustedes conocen a mi prima Felipa, ¿verdad? You know my cousin Felipa, right?
7. Estos niños ya saben caminar. These toddlers already know how to walk.
8. Espero conocer al nuevo empleado pronto. I hope I'll meet the new employee soon.
9. Ya no sé. No tengo ninguna idea. I don't know anymore. I don't have any idea.
10. ¿Conociste a David antes de conocerme a mí? Did you meet David before you met me?

Exercise 13: You Either Know It or Know It

1. Carmen **conoció** a David ayer en la escuela.
2. Hasta hoy, ellos no **sabían** los detalles de esta historia.
3. Cuando vea la respuesta, yo **sabré** si tenía la razón.
4. Yo **la conozco** a ella, es la novia de Felipe.
5. Es probable que vosotros no **conozcan** a aquel hombre.

Exercise 14: A Verb Unverbed

1. La casa tiene dos puertas **abiertas**. (abrir)
2. Ponte la chaqueta **comprada** en la tienda La Ropa de Marco. (comprar)
3. Son los libros más **vendidos** por la Red. (vender)
4. Ellos leyeron las palabras **escritas** en la pared. (escribir)
5. Por favor acepten nuestras más **sentidas** palabras. (sentir)
6. Es la carta **enviada** por Ramón. (enviar)
7. No es el ensayo **rehecho**, es la misma versión. (rehacer)
8. Ya veo el edificio **descrito** por los viajeros a este lugar. (describir)
9. El coche **parado** allá es el mío. (parar)
10. No me des los lápices **rotos**. (romper)

Exercise 15: The Weather Report

1. Va a nevar mañana.
2. ¿Está lloviendo?
3. Ayer hacía más frío que hoy.
4. Está nublado afuera.
5. Hace mal tiempo hoy.
6. En la playa hace sol.
7. ¿Cómo es el tiempo en tu/su país?
8. Tengo frío.

Exercise 16: What Time Is It?

1. Son las tres.
2. Son las once y cuarto.
3. Son las cuatro menos cuarto.
4. Es la una y cinco.
5. Son las ocho y veintidós.
6. Son las siete menos diez.
7. Son las cinco y media.
8. Son las dos y dos.
9. Son las seis de la mañana.
10. Son las nueve y treinta y tres de la noche.

Exercise 17: Many Blanks to Fill In

Present Indicative:

estoy	estamos
estás	estáis
está	están

Imperfect:

estaba	estábamos
estabas	estabais
estaba	estaban

Preterite:

estuve	estuvimos
estuviste	estuvisteis
estuvo	estuvieron

Exercise 18: Living in the Moment

1. Estoy pensando en algo muy interesante.
2. Si quisieran, ustedes estarían bailando.
3. Ella estuvo hablando de sus intereses.
4. Las aves están cantando con entusiasmo.
5. Tú estarás completando el proyecto mañana.

6. Ayer estábamos esperando al sol pero nunca llegó desde las nubes.
7. Si pudiera, estaría cantando en voz alta.
8. Estuvimos escuchando la radio hasta que la mamá la apagó.
9. Un día, te estarás sintiendo contento con esta decisión.
10. Cuando se sentía enfermo, no estaba durmiendo mucho.

Exercise 19: Playing with Time

1. El ave acaba de volar al techo de la casa. El ave va a volar al techo de la casa.
2. Mi hermana acaba de caminar a la escuela. Mi hermana va a caminar a la escuela.
3. Nosotros acabamos de leer el periódico. Nosotros vamos a leer el periódico.
4. Tú acabas de tomar el jugo de naranja para el desayuno. Tú vas a tomar el jugo de naranja para el desayuno.
5. Ustedes acaban de cerrar las ventanas. Ustedes van a cerrar las ventanas.

Exercise 20: Hope You Were Paying Attention

1. It just finished raining.
2. I am going to do it at 5:30.
3. You don't know her very well.
4. It was too cold last night.
5. I was walking to school when it started snowing.
6. The tired woman just finished her project.
7. It was sunny all last week.
8. I am going to sleep at 11:15 pm.

Part 10: The Final Exam
Exercise 1: Common Questions

1. Can you help me, please?
2. How are you?
3. How much does this thing cost?
4. How old are you?
5. Can you repeat that, please?
6. Can you write it down, please?
7. What time is it?
8. Where is the bathroom?

Exercise 2: Speak Up

1. Estoy muy bien.
2. Son las seis y media.
3. Voy a terminar mis estudios y luego visitar a mi amiga.
4. El café más cercano de aquí está en la calle Main, al lado de la panadería.
5. Empecé a aprender español porque es un idioma muy útil.
6. Nunca completaré el estudio. Pienso estudiar el español toda mi vida.

7. Es mi libro.
8. Cuando era niña, me gustaba jugar con las muñecas.
9. En la próxima Navidad, me gustaría recibir una computadora nueva.
10. Si tuviera una gran cantidad de dinero, viajaría por el mundo.

Exercise 3: At the Doctor's Office

1. El doctor y el paciente, Carlos.
2. Se siente muy mal. Está enfermo.
3. Le duele la cabeza. Le duele la garganta y no puede tragar. Moquea mucho. Tiene una tos. Y tiene fiebre.
4. Hace tres días, el lunes.
5. Empezó a sonarse la nariz el martes.
6. Ha tenido fiebre durante dos días.
7. El diagnóstico es que Carlos tiene bronquitis.
8. Carlos debe tomar medicinas.
9. Ambos hombres, el doctor y Carlos mismo, esperan que él se recupere pronto.

Exercise 4: The Articles

1. el banco
2. los coches
3. los días
4. la mano
5. las hijas
6. el paquete
7. las postales
8. el hotel
9. la naranja
10. los pepinos

Exercise 5: Hard Decisions

Answers may vary

El junio pasado, mi novia Carolina y yo pasamos nuestras vacaciones juntos. No fue fácil escoger un destino. A Carolina le gusta ir de compras, ver las obras de arte en los museos, y caminar por las estrechas calles de las viejas ciudades. Pero a mí me gusta más descansar en un lugar cálido, con la playa llena de arena y el mar con orillas de agua tibia. Un lugar lleno de sol y quietud.

Entonces, cuando Carolina sugirió visitar Londres, yo me imaginé un lugar oscuro y lluvioso. Por supuesto, rehusé esta opción y en cambio sugerí una de las islas del Caribe, como Aruba. A Carolina, Aruba le sonó como un lugar aburrido—nada de compras, nada de museos. Quedarse en la playa todo el día no le parecía bien.

Afortunadamente, nosotros encontramos un lugar que nos pareció bien a ambos: España. Es un país lleno de playas y sol, pero también con museos y ciudades antiguas. En resumen, nuestra visita a España fue excelente. Carolina y yo disfrutamos nuestras vacaciones de verdad.

Exercise 6: How Best to Describe It

1. helado (delicioso)
2. fotos (impresionantes)
3. jardín (grande)
4. madre (indulgente)
5. coches (nuevos)
6. canción (bella)
7. ciudad (pequeña)
8. idiomas (difíciles)
9. calles (anchas)
10. libros (interesantes)

Exercise 7: In Color

1. Las manzanas son **rojas, verdes** y **amarillas**.
2. El cielo es **azul**.
3. Los gorriones son **marrones**.
4. El papel es comúnmente **blanco**.
5. El agua del mar es **azul**.
6. Las berenjenas son **moradas**.
7. En el otoño, las hojas de los árboles se vuelven **anaranjadas**, **rojas** y **amarillas**.
8. La noche es **negra**.

Exercise 8: Not Naming Names

1. **Ellos** eran los mejores jugadores de fútbol en nuestro vecindario.
2. Es **su** dinero.
3. Estas noticias no **les** interesan.
4. **Nos** manda la carta.
5. Patricio es **nuestro** hermano.
6. **Ésas** son las más interesantes.
7. Pónte**lo**, hace frío.
8. Son **tus** problemas.

Exercise 9: Pronoun Mastery

1. **Nos** casaremos en **su** casa. We will get married in your/their house.
2. Luego **ustedes** estarán comprándo**selas**. Then you will be buying them for him/her/them/you.
3. **Quién** sabe cómo **ella** logró escapar de aquí. Who knows how she managed to escape from here.
4. No **te** duermas sin cepillar**te** los dientes y lavar**te** la cara. Don't go to sleep without brushing your teeth and washing your face.
5. **Nadie lo** hace como **tú**. No one does it like you.
6. ¡Levánta**te** a pie! Get up on your feet!
7. No sé a **quién se lo** digo. I don't know whom I am telling it.
8. **Mi** mamá **me las** regaló cuando **yo** tenía doce años. My mom gave them to me when I was twelve years old.

Exercise 10: Proper Adverb Manners

1. Los músicos cantan en voz alta. Cantan **altamente**.
2. Nosotros somos buenos estudiantes. Estudiamos **bien**.
3. Ustedes trabajan con mucha fuerza. Trabajan **fuertemente**.
4. Yo estoy llorando, llena de tristeza. Lloro **tristemente**.
5. Tú trabajas sin cuidado. Trabajas **descuidadamente**.
6. Ella se viste con ropa bonita. Se viste **bonitamente**.
7. Para vosotros, es fácil aprender idiomas. Los aprendéis **fácilmente**.
8. Usted habla con duda. Usted habla **dudosamente**.

Exercise 11: In the Right Place

1. Ahora vamos **abajo**. Now let's go downstairs.
2. El ruido se oye desde muy **lejos**. The noise is heard from very far away.
3. No podemos quedarnos **cerca**. We can't stay nearby.
4. Creo que no están delante de la casa, sino **detrás**. I think that they aren't in front of the house, but behind it.
5. Mira qué está pasando **allí**. Look what's happening over there.
6. Vamos **adentro**. Let's go inside.
7. Es posible que puedas encontrarlos **arriba**. It's possible that you can find them upstairs.
8. Nadie está **aquí**. No one is here.

Exercise 12: Questions of Quantity

1. La nieve está tan sucia, está **casi** negra.
2. La explicación no es clara. Es **poco** precisa.
3. No entiendo este libro, es **demasiado** difícil para mí.
4. No es nada rara. Es **algo** típica.
5. Prefiero el café. El té me gusta **menos**.
6. Es más que bonita. Es **muy** bella.
7. No creo que ella sea estúpida. Parece que es **bastante** inteligente.
8. Pedro es **tan** elegante como Paco.
9. El precio de veinte dólares no es **mucho** mejor que el de dieciocho dólares.
10. Mi tía tiene cuarenta años y su marido tiene cuarenta y dos; él es **más** viejo que ella.

Exercise 13: Prep Work

1. No quiero salir **sin** ella. (a, de, sin)
2. Esta carta es **para** ustedes. (por, para, con)
3. No lo he visto a él **desde** ayer. (de, en, desde)
4. Las semillas son sembradas **debajo de** la tierra. (cerca de, al lado de, debajo de)
5. Puedes encontrar la información **en** la Red. (en, sobre, entre)
6. Van a estar ocupados **hasta** las tres de la tarde. (hasta, a, con)
7. Es la opinión **de** la mayoría de la gente. (delante de, de, en)

8. No te inclines **contra** el vidrio. (contra, entre, con)
9. La montaña está muy **lejos** de la ciudad. (después de, lejos de, entre)
10. Las revistas están **sobre** la mesa. (hasta, por, sobre)

Exercise 14: And, Or, What?

1. Él va a esperar, **a pesar de** que ya es muy tarde. (por, a pesar de, cuando)
2. Fui invitada a su casa, **pero** no puedo visitarlos porque tengo mucho que hacer. (sino, excepto, pero)
3. Está enojada **porque** tiene que lavar los platos sucios que sus compañeras de cuarto han dejado en el fregadero. (porque, salvo, aunque)
4. No estamos cansados, **aunque** hemos pasado toda la noche bailando. (porque, sino, aunque)
5. El mejor amigo es alguien simpático **y** sincero. (o, y, e)
6. Estoy gritando **para que** te fijes en mí. (para que, y, excepto)
7. Este restaurante es tan bueno **como** el que está cerca de nuestra oficina. (que, como, pero)
8. Ellos están aburridos **cuando** no pasa nada. (cuando, para que, salvo)
9. No llegas temprano, **sino** tarde. (pero, sino, o)
10. Puedo comer cualquier carne, **salvo** el tocino. (sino, salvo, porque)

Exercise 15: Conjugation Frustration

For correct answers, refer to the first three verbs listed in Appendix A.

Exercise 16: Know Your Tenses

(more than one pronoun may be correct)

1. we begin/we began
2. they would put
3. I walked
4. you will return
5. you leave/let
6. make/do
7. they look (subjunctive)
8. I suffered
9. we will see
10. we couldn't (subjunctive)

Exercise 17: Basic Tenses

1. You are very tired.
2. Let's wait. Mauricio will arrive soon.
3. It rained all day.
4. I like to wake up early.
5. She would have money if she could work.
6. You graduated from college in 1994.
7. If you were lucky, you could have won a prize.
8. Please don't be offended.

9. We will review those problems.
10. It's possible that they aren't responsible.

Exercise 18: Perfect Tenses in Review

(more than one pronoun may be correct)
1. you have understood (subjunctive)
2. they have produced
3. I had tried
4. we have won
5. I (may) have done (subjunctive)
6. he had been
7. you have sold (subjunctive)
8. we (may) have said (subjunctive)
9. they will have managed
10. you would have seen

Exercise 19: Traveling in Time

Present Indicative Tense
1. Yo no **entiendo** nada de esto. (entender)
2. Nosotros **emprendemos** un futuro mejor. (emprender)
3. Ustedes **felicitan** a su nuevo compañero por su buen trabajo. (felicitar)

Preterite Tense
1. La persona que te **llamó** por teléfono no **fue** ella. (llamar, ser)
2. Tú **cometiste** tantos errores. (cometer)
3. Las chicas **se probaron** muchas cosas antes de comprar algo. (probarse)

Imperfect Tense
1. Aunque Dora **era** inteligente, **se comportaba** como una tonta. (ser, comportarse)
2. Nosotros **teníamos** que hacer algo muy importante. (tener)
3. Vosotros **parecíais** enojados todo el día. (parecer)

Future Tense
1. Yo **responderé** a todas tus preguntas. (responder)
2. Tú no **dejarás** que yo sea engañada. (dejar)
3. Ellos **aplaudirán** cuando oigan tu voz. (aplaudir)

Conditional Tense
1. Si ella pudiera, lo **señalaría** a él con el dedo. (señalar)
2. Me **gustaría** tomar el desayuno ahora. (gustar)
3. Los nietos **visitarían** a sus abuelos si eso fuera posible. (visitar)

Present Perfect Tense
1. Yo ya **he tomado** las pastillas. (tomar)
2. Tú **has regresado** a casa muy tarde. (regresar)
3. Nosotros **hemos platicado** por un rato. (platicar)

Pluperfect Tense
1. Él **había descubierto** su secreto. (descubrir)
2. Vosotros **habíais vuelto** aquí demasiado tarde. (volver)
3. Ellos **se habían mudado** a otra casa. (mudarse)

Preterite Perfect Tense
1. Yo **hube demarcardo** el borde. (demarcar)
2. Tú **hubiste hecho** algo terrible. (hacer)
3. Vosotros no **hubisteis visto** nada. (ver)

Future Perfect Tense
1. Tú **habrás caído** en la trampa. (caer)
2. Usted **habrá intentado** muchos esfuerzos. (intentar)
3. Nosotros **habremos escrito** un guión. (escribir)

Conditional Perfect
1. Usted **habría impuesto** una multa. (imponer)
2. Nosotros **nos habríamos ido** de aquí. (irse)
3. Ellos nos **habrían traído** algo para comer. (traer)

Exercise 20: What Mood?
1. indicative
2. imperative
3. subjunctive
4. subjunctive
5. imperative
6. indicative
7. indicative
8. imperative
9. subjunctive
10. subjunctive

Exercise 21: A Wish or a Command
1. Sea lo que sea. What may be, may be. (subjunctive)
2. Descansemos por un rato. Let's rest a while. (imperative)
3. Es cierto que nada se ha cambiado. It's certain that nothing has changed. (indicative)
4. Lamento que ellos no me estimen. I feel that they don't esteem me. (subjunctive)
5. Dame la mano. Give me your hand. (imperative)

Exercise 22: More Moodiness
(Answers may vary)
1. Tú vas a visitarlos mañana.
2. Van a la fiesta aunque no tengan mucho tiempo.
3. No es cierto que no tengamos problemas con él.
4. Sabemos que ella ha hecho algo importante.
5. Ellos llegarán a tiempo.

Exercise 23: Traveling in Time
Present Subjunctive
1. Que te **caiga** algo en la cabeza. (caer)
2. Yo deseo ganar, por supuesto, pero que **sea** lo mejor. (ser)
3. Son estúpidos los que **piensen** ser exitosos sin hacer ningún esfuerzo. (pensar)

Present Perfect Subjunctive
1. Es importante que tú **hayas obtenido** esta información. (obtener)
2. Él duda que vosotros **hayáis leído** este libro. (leer)
3. No estamos seguros que ellos **hayan visto** lo que pasó. (ver)

Past Perfect Subjunctive
1. Ojalá que ustedes **hubieran tenido** la felicidad que tenía yo cuando vivía allá. (tener)
2. Si la gente **hubiera percibido** que se les manipulaba, él **hubiera terminado** sus manipulaciones. (percibir, terminar)
3. Cualquier persona **hubiera hecho** lo mismo. (hacer)

Imperfect Subjunctive
1. Mis padres llegaron al acuerdo que yo **pudiera/pudiese** viajar a Canadá con mis amigos. (poder)
2. Es como si usted no **confiara/confiase** en nosotros. (confiar)
3. Sentí la música como si **corriera/corriese** por mis venas. (correr)

Exercise 24: One Thing Wrong
1. No es **necesario** repetir lo que digo.
2. Hace **cuatro** años que vivimos en este pueblo.
3. Nadie **tiene** que estar solo.
4. Las obras de van Gogh son muy **impresionantes**.
5. Probablemente, no tendremos **ningún** problema con eso.
6. ¡No **seas** tan caprichoso! o ¡No **sean** tan caprichosos!
7. Las canciones de Paco de Lucía son **bellas** y tristes.
8. No quiero que **pierdas** el trabajo por mi culpa.
9. Es **precisamente** lo que quería decir.
10. Teresa y yo **no somos** amigos ya.

Exercise 25: Final Corrections
(Answers may vary)
1. Mis hermanas jóvenes se llaman Astrid y Elena.
2. Cuando era una niña, me gustaba jugar con muñecas.
3. Lo estudio para mejorar la gramática.
4. Eres mi amigo, jamás te haría daño. (no is wrong here)
5. Cuando me ponga la ropa, estaré listo para salir.
6. Las tortas fueron hechas por la mamá.
7. Me siento muy avergonzada que no te reconocí.

8. El viernes pasado hacía mucho viento.
9. Ojalá que haga sol todo el día.
10. Se la daré mañana.
11. No tenía nada para comer./Tenía algo para comer.
12. Ponga usted el libro en la mesa.
13. Ya limpié la casa. (no reflexive pronoun needed here)
14. Estoy poniéndolos en la maleta.
15. Ella claramente tiene toda la razón.

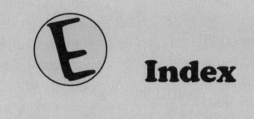 **Index**

Software License Agreement

YOU SHOULD CAREFULLY READ THE FOLLOWING TERMS AND CONDITIONS BEFORE USING THIS SOFTWARE PRODUCT. INSTALLING AND USING THIS PRODUCT INDICATES YOUR ACCEPTANCE OF THESE CONDITIONS. IF YOU DO NOT AGREE WITH THESE TERMS AND CONDITIONS, DO NOT INSTALL THE SOFTWARE AND RETURN THIS PACKAGE PROMPTLY FOR A FULL REFUND.

1. Grant of License
This software package is protected under United States copyright law and international treaty. You are hereby entitled to one copy of the enclosed software and are allowed by law to make one backup copy or to copy the contents of the disks onto a single hard disk and keep the originals as your backup or archival copy. United States copyright law prohibits you from making a copy of this software for use on any computer other than your own computer. United States copyright law also prohibits you from copying any written material included in this software package without first obtaining the permission of F+W Publications, Inc.

2. Restrictions
You, the end-user, are hereby prohibited from the following: You may not rent or lease the Software or make copies to rent or lease for profit or for any other purpose. You may not disassemble or reverse compile for the purposes of reverse engineering the Software. You may not modify or adapt the Software or documentation in whole or in part, including, but not limited to, translating or creating derivative works.

3. Transfer
You may transfer the Software to another person, provided that (a) you transfer all of the Software and documentation to the same transferee; (b) you do not retain any copies; and (c) the transferee is informed of and agrees to the terms and conditions of this Agreement.

4. Termination
This Agreement and your license to use the Software can be terminated without notice if you fail to comply with any of the provisions set forth in this Agreement. Upon termination of this Agreement, you promise to destroy all copies of the software including backup or archival copies as well as any documentation associated with the Software. All disclaimers of warranties and limitation of liability set forth in this Agreement shall survive any termination of this Agreement.

5. Limited Warranty
F+W Publications, Inc. warrants that the Software will perform according to the manual and other written materials accompanying the Software for a period of 30 days from the date of receipt. F+W Publications, Inc. does not accept responsibility for any malfunctioning computer hardware or any incompatibilities with existing or new computer hardware technology.

6. Customer Remedies
F+W Publications, Inc.'s entire liability and your exclusive remedy shall be, at the option of F+W Publications, Inc., either refund of your purchase price or repair and/or replacement of Software that does not meet this Limited Warranty. Proof of purchase shall be required. This Limited Warranty will be voided if Software failure was caused by abuse, neglect, accident or misapplication. All replacement Software will be warranted based on the remainder of the warranty or the full 30 days, whichever is shorter and will be subject to the terms of the Agreement.

7. No Other Warranties
F+W PUBLICATIONS, INC., TO THE FULLEST EXTENT OF THE LAW, DISCLAIMS ALL OTHER WARRANTIES, OTHER THAN THE LIMITED WARRANTY IN PARAGRAPH 5, EITHER EXPRESS OR IMPLIED, ASSOCIATED WITH ITS SOFTWARE, INCLUDING BUT NOT LIMITED TO IMPLIED WARRANTIES OF MERCHANTABILITY AND FITNESS FOR A PARTICULAR PURPOSE, WITH REGARD TO THE SOFTWARE AND ITS ACCOMPANYING WRITTEN MATERIALS. THIS LIMITED WARRANTY GIVES YOU SPECIFIC LEGAL RIGHTS. DEPENDING UPON WHERE THIS SOFTWARE WAS PURCHASED, YOU MAY HAVE OTHER RIGHTS.

8. Limitations on Remedies
TO THE MAXIMUM EXTENT PERMITTED BY LAW, F+W PUBLICATIONS, INC. SHALL NOT BE HELD LIABLE FOR ANY DAMAGES WHATSOEVER, INCLUDING WITHOUT LIMITATION, ANY LOSS FROM PERSONAL INJURY, LOSS OF BUSINESS PROFITS, BUSINESS INTERRUPTION, BUSINESS INFORMATION OR ANY OTHER PECUNIARY LOSS ARISING OUT OF THE USE OF THIS SOFTWARE. This applies even if F+W Publications, Inc. has been advised of the possibility of such damages. F+W Publications, Inc.'s entire liability under any provision of this agreement shall be limited to the amount actually paid by you for the Software. Because some states may not allow for this type of limitation of liability, the above limitation may not apply to you. THE WARRANTY AND REMEDIES SET FORTH ABOVE ARE EXCLUSIVE AND IN LIEU OF ALL OTHERS, ORAL OR WRITTEN, EXPRESS OR IMPLIED. No F+W Publications, Inc. dealer, distributor, agent, or employee is authorized to make any modification or addition to the warranty.

9. General
This Agreement shall be governed by the laws of the United States of America and the Commonwealth of Massachusetts. If you have any questions concerning this Agreement, contact F+W Publications, Inc., via Adams Media at 508-427-7100. Or write to us at: Adams Media, an F+W Publications Company, 57 Littlefield Street, Avon, MA 02322.

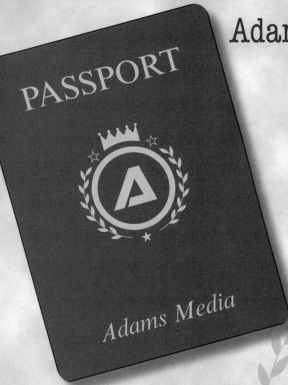